The Heritage of the Conquistadors

THE HERITAGE OF THE
Conquistadors

Ruling Classes in Central America
from the Conquest to the Sandinistas

SAMUEL Z. STONE

FOREWORD BY RICHARD E. GREENLEAF

UNIVERSITY OF NEBRASKA PRESS
LINCOLN AND LONDON

Acknowledgments for the use of previously published material appear on page xiv.

First paperback printing: 1992
Most recent printing indicated by the last digit below:
10   9   8   7   6   5   4   3   2   1

Library of Congress Cataloging-in-Publication Data
Stone, Samuel Z.
The heritage of the conquistadors: ruling classes in Central
America from the Conquest to the Sandinistas / Samuel Z. Stone;
foreword by Richard E. Greenleaf.
p.   cm.
Includes bibliographical references.
ISBN 0-8032-4207-7
ISBN 0-8032-9214-7 (pbk.)
1. Elite (Social sciences)—Central America—History—Case
studies.   2. Elite (Social sciences)—Costa Rica—History.   3. Power
(Social sciences)—Case studies.   4. Central America—Genealogy.
5. Costa Rica—Genealogy.   I. Title.
HN125.2.E4S755   1990
305.5'2'097286—dc20   89-27160
                                                         CIP

∞

To my wife, Haydée, *for tolerating my shortcomings and encouraging the fulfillment of my ideals.*

Contents

Appendixes

Foreword

Samuel Stone, a Costa Rican citizen with a state doctorate in political sociology from the Sorbonne, is one of Central America's best-known scholars. This book is the culmination of decades of research on the nature of political power in the Central American Isthmus and builds on his prize-winning work in Spanish that, when translated, is titled *The Dynasty of the Conquerors: The Crisis of Power in Contemporary Costa Rica.* In examining the context of the current turmoil in Central America, Dr. Stone laments the marked propensity in all five Central American nations to look toward foreign experts to explain problems of the region and to propose solutions based on North American or Western European concepts. He insists that the individual countries must confront problems with their own solutions, "understanding them in their own context," rather than relying on imported models and interpretations.

With meticulous genealogical research Professor Stone has proved that the ruling classes in Central America have a common familial ancestry, and he traces the current political leaders to the original dynasty of conquerors in the sixteenth century. The Spanish Conquest of Central America resulted in pronounced regional patterns making each of the modern republics different in political economy and culture. Because of their geographical isolation and the attendant fragmented political control, conquering families often developed an arrogant autonomy. The small urban centers became introverted enclaves. By the end of the sixteenth century privileged oligarchies who manipulated the political systems to their own advantage were firmly entrenched. The dynasty of conquerors persisted through family alliances within circumscribed regions and across national boundaries into the nineteenth century, and are evident in contemporary political organization. Dr. Stone has demonstrated that the nuclear family and its extended clan provide a useful tool for understanding Central American political reality. He provides fascinating insights into the contemporary social structure and political organization of Nicaragua, where both Somocistas and Sandinistas have a common family background. His projection of a Nicaraguan family quarrel into the international arena will enlighten many readers.

Dr. Stone's genealogical researches are interwined with another aspect of this work in which he seeks to explain why the five Central American countries are so distinctly different. He concludes that the distribution of economic resources throughout the region has preconditioned ways of organizing production, the governmental structures of the five nations, and the shaping of their values. He finds that "political change throughout has been the result of adaptation of social strata to economic interests of groups within the same ruling classes." The ample supply of land and labor tended to produce authoritarian and often repressive political systems toward the north, Dr. Stone argues, whereas their scarcity led to more paternalistic and democratic forms in Costa Rica. He shows how these factors conditioned behavior of élites in politics and suggests why in some countries, e.g. Guatemala and El Salvador, they relied on the military to run the political apparatus.

From a methodological and conceptual standpoint, Stone synthesizes his genealogical data with modern and contemporary social theory on political behavior in Central America. He applies ideas from, and enters into the debates of, major exponents such as William Durham, Guillermo O'Donnell, David Collier, Mark Ruhl, and Jeffrey Paige. He has taken their ideas into account but at the same time argues persuasively his own viewpoints.

Obviously this book is written from the perspective of a scholar resident in Central America, where the current crises are literally next door. Trenchant observations on why domestic policies have succeeded or failed in each country are coupled with explanations of foreign policies. Stone's views on North American and European responses to Central American conflicts are interesting reading and will challenge fundamental assumptions held by many observers of the scene.

RICHARD E. GREENLEAF
Director
Center for Latin American Studies
Tulane University

Preface

The most intriguing finding of initial research on the coffee planters in Costa Rica was that, as a social group, they emerged from Spanish colonial nobility, principally from the conquistadors. Their forefathers had monopolized power since the Conquest and have continued doing so until the mid-twentieth century. They were only one group (albeit the most important politically and economically) that had descended from the conquerors, for among others were cattle ranchers, sugarcane planters, and professional groups such as medical doctors, lawyers, and engineers. All were closely related by bonds of kinship and were tied to national power centers through political parties. In this sense they formed a ruling class.

The foregoing raised the main question leading to the preparation of this book: How does the Costa Rican ruling class compare with its counterparts throughout Central America? The query concerns the ways in which members of those classes in each country have organized production, taking into account the resources of land for export crops, labor, and capital available in their respective territories. Varying conditions have led to the development of different systems of government and religious expressions, as well as of national values and character.

Costa Rica is presented as a case study to show how a ruling class has related kinship to production and to government. It reveals the common social origin of members of the class, as well as the advantages derived from power and privilege. The conditions under which they organized production came to affect values; these, in turn, influenced their perception of themselves as a class, although in a negative fashion. In Central America, resources have been abundant in the north and scarce in the south. In Costa Rica, limited assets for production attracted less capital than in the north and hindered its accumulation. In addition, the absence of extremes of wealth and poverty made for greater rapprochement of ruling class members, both among themselves and with other social strata, and the resulting egalitarianism led to confusion of aristocratic and plebeian values within society. In spite of this, members of the ruling class never lost sight of their political prerogatives and, in their quest for power, became accustomed to confronting competition with their own kin. That sense of superiority, however, failed to offset weak cohesion among them engendered by the colonial experience. The fragility of their class structure can be sensed in the confused reaction toward value changes in national society.

Initial sources for this study came from research leading to the preparation of *La dinastía de los conquistadores*.[1] In Costa Rica they included national, congressional, and private archives (decrees and other documents), the bureau of property registrations, interviews, newspapers, and seminars. For this work I have consulted books, magazines, newspapers, and archives in and concerning Guatemala, Honduras, El Salvador, and Nicaragua; interviews were conducted as well.

Much of the research for the foregoing is based on genealogical studies. Genealogy has long been used by social scientists and is a most effective tool for unraveling notions of class, groups, parties, and other agglomerations of people. My personal experience over eighteen years in the School of Political Science of the University of Costa Rica allowed me to apply fresh field research by students dedicated to genealogical studies in rural communities, to understanding the nature of social, political, and economic structures. The method is as valid for comprehending lower and middle social strata as it is for determining successions in monarchies. It is, however, far more difficult to apply in the former cases. In Third World countries, where attention is increasingly focused on middle and lower classes, concepts of these categories might be clarified through the use of genealogy.

In genealogical studies, particularly of recent generations, I have relied heavily on interviews with knowledgeable people who are considered experts in the field. I have not selected families whom I consider important in the different Central American Republics, but have depended instead on publications by Central American specialists who have chosen the families they deem worthy of study. My own research has consisted largely in expanding their works into political and economic domains. There seems to be a propensity to study family trees of conquistadors in the southern part of the Isthmus, while in northern publications, noble figures of other European origins appear with frequency. Where important discrepancies in many of these genealogies occur, I have had to rely on my own judgment.

The people to whom I owe my gratitude are many. I carried out the research for and writing of this work as a member of the Centro de Investigación y Adiestramiento Político-Administrativo (CIAPA), a center for research and training in politics and administration. CIAPA is an independent, small Costa Rican "think tank," affiliated with Tulane University and devoted to studying and analyzing the nature of Central American economic, political, and social problems and their relationship with the outside world. I extend my gratitude to my colleagues on the staff of that institution for the benefit of their criticism: Rodolfo Cerdas Cruz, Jaime Daremblum Rosenstein, Constantino Urcuyo Fournier, and Rafael Villegas Antillón. Richard E. Greenleaf, professor of history as well as director of the Center for Latin American Studies of Tulane University, in addition to preparing a fitting and discreet prologue, read and criticized several drafts and was instrumental in helping me see this publication through. Richard N. Adams, professor of anthropology and director of the Center for Latin American Studies at the University of Texas (Austin), offered observations and criticisms as fine as any I have received. Munro Edmonson, professor of anthropology at Tulane University, read my manuscript and produced a lengthy and useful written account of his comments, and Douglas W. Schwartz, professor of anthropology and director of the School of American Research at Santa Fe, New Mexico, also made appreciated comments. Enrique Valverde Runnebaum, Mario Fernández Piza, and Enrique Robert Luján, all of the Costa Rican Academy of Genealogical Sciences, as well as Joaquín Alberto Fernández Alfaro, were of great assistance in orienting the many and detailed studies of Central American families presented in the appendixes. Luis Guillermo Solís Rivera and Joaquín Jiménez Rodríguez assisted me for many years in gathering and evaluating information. Their efforts produced enough data for a future book on the Central American industrial movement as well as another on Isthmian legislatures. Equally valuable were written comments by José Reina Valenzuela on aspects of traditional Honduran ruling families. Narciso Carmona Binayán of *La Nación* newspaper in Buenos Aires and a genealogist as well, provided excellent written criticisms, as did professor of anthropology Dwight B. Heath, of Brown University, much earlier, on one of the first articles leading to this publication. François Bourricaud, who directed my graduate research in Paris between 1964 and 1973, made important observations in his prologue for the publication of *La dinastía*. These were taken into consideration whenever possible.

My daughter Stephanie, along with Narciso Lacayo Pallais and Aminta

Lacayo de Quirce, helped me establish many kinship ties between the Sandinista hierarchy and traditional ruling families in Nicaragua. In this respect, mention must again be made of Joaquín Alberto Fernández Alfaro for his valuable contributions. Stephanie also assisted in research on the industrial sector in Costa Rica. I am deeply indebted to Patricia Andrews for making this book easier to read and far more comprehensible than it was when I presented it to her. The same applies to my son-in-law, Alberto Golcher, a Ph.D. candidate at the Center for Latin American Studies at Tulane University, who volunteered useful criticism of my text. I also wish to express my gratitude to Patricia Salazar Soto, who had the patience to plow through my manuscripts and endlessly type drafts while making prudent remarks, as well as to Maurico Terán González and to Victoria Salgado Gómez de Vargas, all of CIAPA, for their assistance.

I have previously published portions of chapters 3 and 4 in "Las convulsiones del Istmo Centroamericano: Raíces de un conflicto entre élites" and "El surgimiento de los que mandan: Tierra, capital, y trabajo en la forja de las sociedades Centroamericanas" in *Estudios,* published by CIAPA.

I have also previously published the four tales that begin chapter 7 in "Costa Rica: Sobre la clase dirigente y la sociedad nacional" and are used by permission of Dr. Daniel Camacho, director of the *Revista de Ciencias Sociales.* The same applies to portions of chapter 7, previously published in "Algunos aspectos de la distribución del poder político en Costa Rica," and the family tree of Vázquez in appendix 6, is based on material in a supplement to this article and "Los cafetaleros." Copyrighted material from these articles is used by permission of Dr. Jorge E. Romero Pérez, director of the *Revista de Ciencias Jurídicas.*

Lastly, as for my preceding works, the constant prodding and encouragement provided by my wife, Haydée, and my mother, Doris, made this work possible.

The Concept of Ruling Classes in Central America

*Plus ça change, plus ç'est
la même chose.*

Alphonse Karr, *Les Guêpes*

The Central American Isthmus is diverse, and to the outside world it has long evoked images of banana republics and revolutions. From north to south, the five small nations that compose the area are Guatemala, El Salvador, Honduras, Nicaragua, and Costa Rica. Panama is not considered by Central Americans to be part of the region for having belonged to Colombia until its independence in 1903. For that reason it has had closer cultural ties with northern South America. Nor is Belize felt by Central Americans to be part of the region, due to its historic ties with Great Britain, although Guatemala claims that territory.

Contrary to popular belief, these countries do not form a homogeneous group of societies in an ethnic, political, social, economic, or even linguistic sense. For example, about half the population of Guatemala is Indian and does not speak Spanish as a native language; it uses some twenty dialects and must often communicate through translators. Nearly half is mestizo, and there are small numbers of whites and negroes. About forty-five percent of the citizenry is illiterate.[1] Costa Rica, on the other hand, has no significant number of aborigenes, and roughly ninety percent of its people can read and write. For reasons such as these, few regional solutions respond to common problems. Agrarian issues in tiny El Salvador, where the population is dense, for instance, require different approaches than in the other countries, all of which are larger and more sparsely populated. Densities per square mile for 1987 were as follows: Guatemala 201, El Salvador 612, Honduras 108, Nicaragua 76, and Costa Rica 133.[2] In modern times, due to the tendency to consider those republics predominantly in the light of their relationship with the United States or the Soviet Union, such variances are often overlooked. In their external affairs, they must deal with nations other than the superpowers, due to pressing needs such as petroleum. Mexico and Venezuela have been the sole suppliers of that commodity to much of the Caribbean area since 1981 and this gives them strong political leverage with those small clients, who are keenly aware that Mexico, in particular, has never had any misgivings about using that type of advantage to satisfy its own interests.

The topic of Central America has become fashionable during the 1980s, primarily because of the advent of the Sandinistas in Nicaragua. It is usually discussed, however, from political positions or in the heat of ideological and religious arguments. In truth, the Isthmus has come to the attention of the outside world on only a few occasions. The possibility of building a trans-Isthmian waterway caught the fancy of Philip II of Spain shortly after the Conquest.[3] During the nineteenth century, interest in digging a canal through the narrow strip of land from the Caribbean Sea to the Pacific Ocean led to rivalries between the United States, England, and France. In the present century the region has been noticed on several occasions. One was the 1948 civil war in Costa Rica that brought José Figueres to power. Another was in 1954, when the United States government helped overthrow Marxist Guatemalan President Jacobo Arbenz. A third took place in 1969 during the so-called Soccer War between El Salvador and Honduras. The most recent event was when the Sandinistas ousted the third and last dictator of the Somoza family in Nicaragua in 1979.

The quest of ruling groups for leadership has led to regional conflicts, and differences in economic resources have given some of them advantages over others. This in part explains current political and social upheaval. Land and labor in Guatemala, for example, are cheaper than in Costa Rica. Capital in El Salvador has been more abundant than elsewhere. Such circumstances have led to armed clashes like the aforementioned Soccer War (over uneven distribution of land and labor); to disorder in the Central American Common Market (over price competition); to violence and terrorism (for ideological reasons but also poor wealth distribution); as well as to problems between the Somoza family and the Sandinistas. All these conflicts involve resources and the ways they are used by ruling classes in each country.

Contemporary problems of Central America can be approached through an analysis of the birth and development of the territories that formed the five Isthmian nations at Independence in 1821. Conquistadors and Spanish nobles, who came to constitute regional ruling classes at the beginning of the colonial period, were bestowed by the crown with power by virtue of their nobility. That prerogative gave them exclusive access to lucrative economic activities. In the remote New World, however, the monarchy was unable to exercise influence over the new Hispanic-American aristocracy, and notwithstanding royal attempts to control its development, indigenous sociopolitical fashions evolved in each territory. The king eventually recognized as members of the nobility those settlers with untarnished pasts who could prove even distant family ties with conquistadors. These personages, then, came to play a key role in the formation of the new societies. Those who oriented their lives around them eventually became divided regionally, as territorial jurisdictions of the conquerors were established and extended. Hence the origin of the five modern Central American ruling classes.

Before Independence those classes enjoyed undisputed privileges and prerogatives of power within their respective societies merely by virtue of their nobility. In 1812, however, the Constitution of Cádiz gave a legal basis to their position,[4] and they have generally been able to make that advantage work in their favor to the present. Power became the object of disputes among them and has remained the bone of contention among their descendants to this day. Their progeny still form bastions of social orders in all the republics and, in their quest for hegemony, are prone to taking arms and becoming champions of causes—genuine or fictitious—against their own kin. The Sandinista uprising against Somoza is a recent case in point, as shall be seen in chapter 2. "The more things change, the more they remain the same."

Ruling Classes Link Economic and Political Systems

This book deals with two topics linked by a third: a social class. The first topic concerns the original colonial Isthmian ruling class, which became divided with the establishment of the five separate territories. Hence the common ancestry of contemporary ruling classes. Many of the region's presidents, even today, are descended directly from noble colonial families.

For this same reason, many rulers from Central American nations have been and continue to be related to their counterparts in others.[5] For example, during the early nineteenth century, two sons of the Guatemalan family of Bernardo José Arce León and Dominga Fagoaga Aguiar (Manuel José and Pedro José Arce Fagoaga) were presidents of the United Provinces of Central America and of El Salvador, respectively. Their uncle, José Matías Delgado, had been one of the fathers of Independence. Two brothers from another Guatemalan family, Simón and Doroteo Vasconcelos, became presidents of Guatemala and El Salvador. Joaquín Eufracio Guzmán Ugalde, from Cartago (Costa Rica), married Salvadoran Ana María Martorell and became president of El Salvador. Their daughter married Gerardo Barrios Espinoza, also president of that country. Costa Rican Pedro Zeledón was secretary of state of Nicaragua, and Guatemalan Lorenzo Montúfar was congressman and presidential candidate in his own country and a diplomat for El Salvador and Costa Rica, as well as judge on the latter country's supreme court. During the twentieth century, Daniel Oduber Quirós and Rodrigo Carazo Odio, former presidents of Costa Rica, and Anastasio Somoza Debayle, late president of Nicaragua, were distant cousins as well as enemies. Evaristo Carazo Aranda and Policarpo Bonilla Vázquez (both of Costa Rican origin and presidents of Nicaragua and Honduras, respectively), Rodrigo Carazo Odio and Aniceto Esquivel Sáenz (presidents of Costa Rica), and Domingo Vázquez (president of Honduras) were all related. Further examples could be cited, but these suffice to show the existence of the great ruling class or Central American "family."

The foregoing raises the second theme of this study, namely, that of why the countries of the region are so different from each other in spite of family ties among founding members of their ruling classes. The availability of resources in each territory and the ways they have been used have led to diversity among contemporary societies. Politically, scarcity appears to have bred democracy, while abundance seems to have produced authoritarian systems of government. Economics has been reflected in politics through the saga of the ruling classes. These very classes, then, constitute the third topic as well as the factor that links the first two. Conditions under which production has been organized have forged different class values in each territory, and those values have made members of ruling classes in some countries more aware of their position than their counterparts in others. Class consciousness makes for greater cohesion and explains much about past and present attitudes of their members. It also provides indications of their possible reactions to future events.

Certain obvious concepts constitute leitmotifs throughout this work. One of these is political power, which is a relationship between those who govern and those who are governed. It is seen from the time of its birth during the Conquest and as it has changed form over the course of time. Two practical thoughts are relevant. It has been observed that in any issue that eventually reaches the desk of the president of a republic, the person with power is the one who "has the last cut." This means that as memoranda and opinions concerning a problem work their way from lower echelons of government toward the office of the chief executive, they are constantly edited and subjected to different interpretations. The individual who prepares the final version of the report—the one on which the president bases his decision—is said to be the person with power.[6] This interpretation assumes that at the end of the information process, a president can make a decision that will be carried out, yet this is not always the case. When confronted with a query over the nature of power, a recent Costa Rican president quipped, "When the president of Mexico says, 'Let there be light,' there is light; when the president of Venezuela gives the same order, it will, in all probability, be carried out; but when the president of Costa Rica gives that command, he hasn't the vaguest idea what the outcome will be."[7] The comments imply that the power vested in the chief executive varies from one country to another, and suggest that such differences could be reflected institutionally. In Costa Rica, more than in the rest of Central America, politicians and ordinary citizens constantly express their opinions through the media, explaining problems that should rarely involve the general public. The frequency with which these advertisements appear gives the impression that they respond to a lack of institutional power. Although public opinion knows and cares little about problems presented to it in this fashion, those who publish paid advertisements seem to feel that in the last instance public opinion will have the power to help them. This is seldom the case. Power is exercised in different ways and to varying degrees, and the question of how is a principal concept of this book.

A second idea dealt with is élitism.[8] In Central America this has been an offshoot of the dominance of interrelated groups. Elitist doctrine holds that in any society, a minority makes the principal decisions. It attains power through ordinary election, military victory, conquest, or monopoly over crucial resources (such as water in Oriental societies).[9] The élite cannot be controlled by the majority even through democratic means, due to the power, organization, political skill, and personal ability of its members. Its strength derives from its capacity to establish the terms of admission to its ranks, such as conformity with criteria of interests (wealth) and ideology (social origin, education, religion). The size of the élite depends on where the line is drawn between those who have greater or less political influence. From here stem the concepts of "political class," "inner and outer core," "ruling group," and others. Gaetano Mosca illustrates the problem: if all the generals in an army were to be lost, they could be replaced with members from the officers corps. If, however, the officers corps were lost, the army would disintegrate. The élite depends on its lower strata, who ensure future leadership resources as well as linkages with other classes. The problem in classical élitist analysis is where to draw the line between upper and lower strata.

The need of a society to produce is another notion dealt with in this work and is viewed as a neglected aspect of development as well as a factor taken for granted by political sectors throughout the Isthmus, although to a greater extent in the south than in the north. Today it tends to become less relevant for politicians as the Nicaraguan crisis drags on and as capital is consequently injected into regional economies by foreign governments to "buy friendship" and to bolster floundering currencies.

Finally, propensities—or lack of them—toward the development of welfare states is a notion that receives attention. Since the midtwentieth century the growing welfare systems have found support from people whose ideologies vary widely. Members of ruling classes, in spite of different family and work experiences, have found common interests by virtue of being on public payrolls, although the institutions that feed them become increasingly a target of productive sectors that must pay for their existence. Although public sectors throughout Central America have experienced relative growth, Costa Rica has the largest. In Guatemala, since the advent of the Christian Democratic administration of Vinicio Cerezo Arévalo, the state has grown by leaps and bounds, and the same can be said of Honduras. This suggests that political parties have found an expedient (though harmful) way to satisfy demands for employment and patronage, through offering jobs in government.

Kinship and Divisions within Ruling Classes

A Costa Rican social class formed by conquistadors and their descendants has provided most of the important office holders there since the Conquest.[10] One conquistador, Cristóbal de Alfaro, is forefather of all the presidents (with a single exception) since Independence, although judging the number of presidents is difficult due to coups d'état, revolutions, and vice presidents serving temporarily as chiefs of state. His family tree frequently crosses with that of another conquistador, Juan Vázquez de Coronado, who has generated over half the presidents[11] and over a quarter of the members of congress,[12] and was married to a cousin of Pedro Arias de Avila (Pedrarias Dávila), conquistador and governor of Panama.

Vázquez's family tree crosses with that of Jorge de Alvarado, conquistador of El Salvador and Guatemala, who is forefather of a tenth of the members of congress (some one hundred forty) in Costa Rica and was a brother of Pedro de Alvarado, conquistador of Guatemala.

The seemingly insignificant facts concerning kinship among conquistadors have allowed me to establish relationships among ruling classes throughout the Isthmus. As the following pages show, these ties of kinship open new horizons in the study of power in Central America, particularly within the perspective of political systems and their connections with production.

The relationship between ruling classes and kinship must be presented in precise concepts. Lineage is a foremost consideration in the configuration of those classes. Endogamy has limited access, but some outsiders have married descendants of the colonial nobility. Wealth has not been a determinant of class, although material considerations at times play an important role in determining positions held by members as well as admission of outsiders to its ranks. While economic differentiation has made for variations in levels of living within a given family, common background gives all members an accepted recognition in their class.

The concept of family is also important. Some individuals who have been influential politically and economically have been closely related, as in the case of the nineteenth-century Costa Rican President Juan Rafael Mora Porras and his brother-in-law, President José María Montealegre Fernández, or the Honduran Presidents Miguel Paz Barahona and his first cousins Luis and Francisco Bográn Barahona. Usually, however, the relationship is more distant and those involved are frequently unaware of kinship ties that unite them.

Even distant relationships often carry meaning. In Costa Rica, several large groups of people congregate periodically to celebrate their blood ties with important forefathers. One, with about four hundred members, meets each year to commemorate the fact that they all descend from Vicente Herrera Zeledón, president of Costa Rica during the nineteenth century and descendant of Juan Vázquez de Coronado. Such bonds can open doors of political and economic opportunity. Similar ties need not imply friendship, as with former presidents of Costa Rica Daniel Oduber Quirós and Rodrigo Carazo Odio, tenth cousins once removed, who have taken aggressive stances against each other. The important aspect of family, as considered in this work, is that those who compose ruling classes have had significant access to political posts (or influence over them) and this has often endowed them with fruitful participation in their economies, at least to a far greater extent than for those who are not related by ties of kinship.

Independence offered opportunities to ruling class members in each country to undertake economic activities that had been monopolized by both Guatemala (the seat of Isthmian colonial government) and Spain since the Conquest. This freedom led to the formation, within their classes, of groups dedicated to new activities, and the divergent demands of those groups came to be voiced through political parties. During the century and a half of independent life, opposing ruling groups have been in power at different times in each nation. Notwithstanding competition and even conflict among them, however, they have generally reacted when they have sensed that "outsiders" were encroaching on grounds that they considered their traditional prerogatives (as has occurred with the Communist Party or with Arab and Jewish minorities that have emerged economically and politically in many parts of the Isthmus).

As groups expanded and parties acquired greater permanency, some members sought active participation in political processes while others contributed only moral and economic support. This division has taken place in most organizations, and the "activists" have come to constitute the body from which a winning candidate selects individuals (usually, but not always, from his own followers) to run his administration. These activists can be said to make up political classes, and those who are chosen from their ranks to hold office within the winning party become the political élite.

Conservative and liberal administrations, which seem to have represented changes in ruling classes, have in reality involved mainly the descendants of traditional ruling classes. Even revolutions have rarely (if ever) meant significant alterations of existing social orders. The advent to power of José Figueres in Costa Rica in 1948, which has been widely viewed as a displacement of the traditional ruling class by new social elements, was in fact the replacement of one group (largely coffee planters) from the old national ruling order by another (generally of professionals and industrialists) from the same class. A similar interpretation has been given to the Sandinista movement that ousted Anastasio Somoza Debayle in Nicaragua in 1979. Many ranking members of the Sandinista junta that assumed power after the revolution, as well as the political administration that it came to preside over, are descended from colonial aristocracy. Somoza, along with many of the "Contras," also came from that class.

The division of ruling classes into competing groups responds largely to the emergence of new economic situations and interests. The classes from which those groups come reveal greater cohesion in the north than in the south. This is due to value differences that reflect the varying ways the dominant members organize production, using the resources available in their respective territories.

Production and Ruling Class Values

The evolution of Central American ruling classes has been conditioned by the divergent use their members have made of the combinations of land for export crops, labor, and capital available within their countries. This has made for class values peculiar to each country. Land suitable for that purpose has been plentiful (and as a result cheaper) in the northern part of the Isthmus, and this has usually been enhanced by the presence of large labor forces. Production has been easier to organize and profitability has been high, although property concentration among ruling class members has caused friction between them and other population sectors. By contrast, in the south, where those resources have been scarce, land has been more equitably distributed and interclass relations have been less abrasive. That has led to the formation of different values, with varying degrees of class consciousness in each country.

Today each Central American nation confronts what appear to be quite similar economic, social, and political difficulties, but the ruling classes react to them in different ways. In the north, their members are more conscious of status than in the south and, when threatened, are prone to close ranks and fight for what have traditionally been their prerogatives. Their southern counterparts are not as aware of their position and are consequently less cohesive and more vulnerable to social groups from other categories.

In Guatemala, colonial society was highly stratified due to the coexistence of a relatively small Spanish colony and large indigenous populations. The forefathers of the contemporary ruling class held positions of command that were never questioned by other social groups. This was one of the factors that have enabled its members to assume the relationship between power and wealth to the present. In El Salvador, the plight of ruling class members has been similar to that of their Guatemalan counterparts. The colonial experiences of both were similar because of the large native populations available. In El Salvador, however, during the nineteenth and twentieth centuries, their descendents acquired sufficient wealth to extend their spheres of activity beyond national borders. When social upheaval occurred, many were prone to leave and settle elsewhere, for foreign economic ties gave them a degree of freedom and mobility not enjoyed by their Guatemalan counterparts. As a result, their awareness of themselves as members of a national ruling class was diluted.

The traditional Honduran ruling class was overshadowed early in the twentieth century by the emergence of foreign banana interests, which provided more foreign exchange and taxes than did the sale of cattle raised by Hondurans. Today the army rules, although with significant traditional ruling class participation, for it recognizes the need to increase the role of civilians in government.

The rivalry in Nicaragua has been within the ruling class itself, yet a number of prominent families, to avoid losing their properties, remained in the country and even took jobs in the revolutionary Sandinista government after the fall of Somoza. Cohesion among its members is significantly less pronounced than among its neighbors to the north.

The evolution of the Costa Rican ruling class since the Conquest suggests that egalitarian values (stemming from the misery of the colonial period) clashed with authoritarian ideals inherited from Spanish aristocracy. The notion of its prerogatives was not clearly defined, for political privilege brought few commensurate material advantages. Exercising power in this situation did not endow its members with a sense of identity as a ruling class, for their status conferred little authority. The coffee planters who emerged from their ranks after Independence did find material rewards in holding power, but their notion of rule was lacking, as was their cohesion, and they began to disintegrate when rival social forces appeared. Today they are easily absorbed by the contemporary state bureaucracy.

The starting point in this work is the Conquest and settlement. Under the Spanish colonial empire, administration came to be conducted by the Council of the Indies, through viceroys and other provincial officials. The Isthmus (except for Panama) was organized politically as part of the Viceroyalty of New Spain (Mexico) under the Captaincy General of Guatemala. After independence from Spain in 1821, dissension among the five provinces arose over tendencies to annex themselves to the newly established and shortlived empire of Agustín de Iturbide in Mexico, and amid much discord, delegates from all the states (representing mostly upper classes) assembled in Guatemala to form the United Provinces of Central America. The federation ended in 1840, however.[13] The rest of the nineteenth century was characterized by unsuccessful attempts to reestablish union, with Guatemala bent on maintaining hegemony by force. The twentieth has seen contentions between conservatives and liberals, with alternate civilian and military governments in some countries and a prevalence of rightist military dictatorships in others (excepting Nicaragua since the advent of the Sandinistas). During both centuries, although at different times, production has been based on indigo, cochineal, cacao, mining, cattle raising, coffee, bananas, and more recently rice, cotton, cardamom, assembly of imported manufactured goods, and tourism. The protagonists of this evolution are discussed in the pages that follow, beginning with an account of how their forefathers acquired dominant positions at the time of conquest.

PART I

Patterns of Production and Politics

CHAPTER 1

Ruling Classes, Production, and Government

On 18 February 1519, Hernando Cortés left Cuba at the head of an armada of ten vessels with one hundred sailors, five hundred eight soldiers, sixteen horses, thirty-two crossbows, ten bronze cannons, and small caliber weapons. He was accompanied by Pedro de Alvarado, Francisco de Montejo, Bernal Díaz del Castillo, and other future conquistadors who are protagonists in the pages that follow. On the island of Cozumel he was joined by Jerónimo de Aguilar, a Spaniard who had been shipwrecked there eight years earlier and had learned Maya. Shortly thereafter he had his first armed encounter with Indians and, once peace was made, was offered twenty women as slaves. One of these was La Malinche, who spoke both Maya and Nahuat and was to play an important role in Cortés's life.

Spanish and Indian chroniclers tell of gifts sent by Montezuma to persuade Cortés to leave the territory. By August, however, the conquistador had won the friendship of the Maya and headed inland toward Tenochtitlán with four hundred peons, fifteen horsemen, six pieces of artillery, several hundred soldiers, and uncountable indigenous carriers. Indian texts tell of the cunning of the Tlaxcaltecas in using their subjects (the Otomí) to test Spanish military might. In this manner they became convinced of the superiority of the white man's weapons. This led to an alliance with them, with the secret hope of trying to defeat their ancient enemies, the Aztecs. The Ocotelolcos joined them.

Conquistadors and Indians differ with regard to the slaughter ordered by Cortés in Cholula, a city under Aztec domination. On 8 November, Cortés entered Tenochtitlán. Indian texts are emotional on the subject of his encounter with Montezuma. Cortés's permanence there came to a tragic end due to a treacherous attack, and indigenous texts tell of this episode in an epic poem similar to the Iliad. When Cortés and the Spaniards attempted to flee they lost over half their men in what came to be known as the Noche Triste (Sad Night), in June 1520.

A year later, Cortés launched thirteen vessels on the lake surrounding the Aztec capital, and the Spaniards besieged Tenochtitlán with reinforcements from Veracruz and eighty thousand Tlaxcalteca allies. Indian chronicles describe the Spaniards as men who had been initially taken for gods but who subsequently came to be regarded as barbarians. They also mention the choice of Cuauhtémoc as chief, following the deaths of Montezuma and Cuitláhuac (from smallpox). When Tenochtitlán finally succumbed, they related the episode in Cantos Tristes (Sad Songs).[1]

This brief preamble brings the conquistadors to the threshold of a new world, where they would found societies and establish patterns of power that, on the Isthmus at least, would persist into our times. Those structures were molded by the way they instilled notions of command in their off-spring, frequently with a slight sense of noblesse oblige, and these usually matured with a keen awareness of their inherited advantages in competing for power and wealth. This system has endured. What has changed has been the nature of the competition, limited until the twentieth century to descendants of conquistadors but increasingly open to other social classes in modern times, as political systems widen their bases of popular support. The conquerors forged their economies and governments with aristocratic colonists who followed them, and the ways in which they handled available resources in the different regions they settled had a bearing on the types of rule that emerged after Independence.

Colonial Aristocracy and Production

The noble and plebeian Spaniards who settled in the New World came from such culturally diverse regions as Andalusia and Catalonia, and mixed with peoples from a variety of native civilizations. In Central America, these indigenous populations differed widely from each other in aspects such as political organization. Certain tribes were ruled by chieftains, for instance, while in others authority was vested in councils of elders. The mixtures of cultures led to the development of five societies with notably distinct configurations, and in that synthesizing process conquistadors and noble classes played predominant roles.

It is often believed that the Spaniards who went to America in search of wealth did so in relative poverty. Capital was indispensable for expeditions to the new world, however, for those who undertook these adventures had to provide ships, arms, horses, and remuneration for soldiers and companions. That meant heavy expenses over long periods of time, and the crown did not normally underwrite such ventures. By the same token, many nobles who followed were also people of means.[2]

Economic preponderance of the noblility was not lasting, basically because the Isthmus depended on the captaincy general of Guatemala (the political organization for the entire region), which was in turn responsible to the crown. Both Guatemala and Spain abused their power at the expense of the other provinces. Due to the position of the former as seat of Central American government, as well as to its mineral wealth and the abundance of Indian labor in its territory, nobles of higher social standing settled there. They enjoyed better connections at the royal court in Spain than those of lower rank who went south, particularly to Costa Rica. When cacao became important, Guatemala interfered with production throughout the Isthmus for its own benefit. This had unfavorable repercussions on provincial economies, especially on Costa Rica's, due to the relative poverty of that territory. Church tithes and piracy by the British, the Dutch, and above all the Zambo-Mosquito (a mixture of Indians and blacks from the region of the Mosquitia on the Caribbean coast of Nicaragua) also contributed to economic decline. By the midcolonial period, lifestyles of the ruling classes had deteriorated throughout, although in Guatemala their members lived in more gracious fashion than their counterparts elsewhere. In isolated Costa Rica, the level of living of nobles sank to that of the populace. In 1719, the governor of that territory wrote to the crown complaining about the miserable situation, alleging that even he had to undergo the humility of tilling the land to feed his family. Egalitarianism developed in a material sense, but in terms of power a clear division persisted between the ruling class and the rest of the population.

Endogamy was an important characteristic of ruling classes throughout Central America and appears to have been more intense in societies with larger indigenous populations. In Costa Rica, for example, where native inhabitants have always been relatively few, marriage between first cousins within the ruling class appears to be less frequent than in neighboring Nicaragua, which has had a larger indigenous population. The genealogies of Costa Rican families in this book reveal only a handful of marriages between first cousins in modern times. In Nicaragua, however, I know of one family in which first cousins have married during five consecutive generations. Under such circumstances, permission must be obtained from the Vatican, and on the most recent occasion it was denied. Genealogies of aristocratic Guatemalan and Salvadoran families indicate situations similar to that of Nicaragua.[3]

Early in the colonial period, offspring of conquistadors and nobles undertook activities for export: agriculture, gold and silver mining, and cattle raising. Since then, those engaged in such enterprises have been significantly linked to power structures. Resources for such undertakings were more abundant in the north and diminished progressively toward the south.[4] Fertile lands for cochineal and indigo (two major export items) were located principally in Guatemala and El Salvador. Initially, Indian civilizations (also concentrated in the north) formed the basic labor supply. However, the decimation of native populations by disease and slave exports raises questions as to how the exploitation of human resources was able to continue, particularly because of the importance of labor for the survival of the *repartimiento* and the *encomienda*. Both were systems established by the crown for land and Indian distribution among deserving Spaniards.

Encomiendas originated during the Middle Ages as a means of obtaining an adequate and cheap labor supply, based on the practice of taxing Muslims and Jews during the Reconquest of Muslim Spain. With the discovery of the New World, the problem of an inexpensive and sufficient supply of workers arose once again, and the initial solution provided by the crown (as early as 1499) was to apportion Indians among conquerors and Spaniards "of merit" for use as forced labor. This system was known as the repartimiento. In the beginning, it did not include land, although the two resources (land and labor) eventually became intertwined. To reduce abuses of the Indians under the repartimiento, the crown introduced the encomienda in Hispanic America. This consisted of a grant to conquistadors and other colonists of a specified number of Indians living in a given area, in return for protecting them and instucting them in the Christian faith. While legally the encomienda did not include land, in practice it eventually did. The system provided the encomendero with tribute and, until 1549 (as a result of the enactment of the New Laws of 1542 to protect Indians), free labor. With the catastrophic decline of the indigenous population and the replacement of mining by agriculture, the encomienda lost its effectiveness and was abolished late in the eighteenth century. As native populations diminished, black slaves were imported from the Caribbean and elsewhere to augment them, and by midsixteenth century large parts of the Honduran and Salvadoran labor forces had been reconstituted. In spite of the awesome reduction of indigenous populations, the northern part of the Isthmus continued to enjoy more plentiful labor supplies than the south.[5]

The relative abundance of capital in the north as compared with the south is more difficult to establish but can be judged in terms of elements that attracted it. During the Conquest and the colonial period, mineral wealth (gold and silver) was always more plentiful in the north. Settlers of means first came in search of those metals and subsequently organized expeditions to "hunt" Indians for use as slaves. Profits made in this activity eventually went into mining and farming.[6] (The most abundant capital is still concentrated in Guatemala and El Salvador, although much current wealth is landed and liquidity has been a problem for development.)

By the end of the colonial period, aristocracy linked to production for export had become differentiated economically, particularly in the northern provinces. Everywhere except in Costa Rica (due to that territory's scarce resources), members of ruling classes had monopolized activities such as cattle raising, mining, indigo, and cochineal production, leaving little opportunity for people in other classes (and many of their own kin) to work in those fields.[7] Those denied a part in such activities came to feel that their only chance lay in the creation of a unified Central American market, for the individual Central American markets were too small to attract ships on a regular basis. In a sense they were right, for during the sixteen-year period between 1734 and 1749, an average of only slightly over four vessels went to the Isthmus each year. They generally sailed between the Central American ports of El Realejo (Nicaragua), Acajutla and Sonsonate (El Salvador), Caldera (Costa Rica), and certain Honduran ports, on the one hand, and El Callao (Peru), Panama, Guayaquil (Ecuador), Acapulco (Mexico), and occasionally Cádiz (Spain), on the other.[8] For this reason, a larger market could be created through a federation of the five provinces, and in general terms, this economic dichotomy within the ruling classes paved the way for political divisions between conservatives and liberals in their ranks after Independence.

Production and Government after Independence

In the north, as a result of better possibilities for making money, after Independence the descendants of conquistadors and nobles remained in production, delegating political matters to other sectors of the populations. These were generally military personnel who maintained order and thus created optimum conditions for economic undertakings. In making suitable arrangements for governing, the producers took care to place ranking army officials of trust in top government positions, particularly the presidency. They also reserved the tacit right to name certain members of their own class to important posts (frequently in the ministries of foreign affairs and the treasury). Through these cabinet members, they gained access to international markets and maintained direct control over currency. This can be seen in the family trees of several prominent Guatemalan and Salvadoran families. For example, from or closely related to the Arzú family came three ministers (two of foreign affairs and one of economy); from the Cabarrús family came one (of foreign affairs); from the Durán family came eight, five of whom were either of foreign affairs or the treasury; and from the Maestre family came four, three of whom held similar posts.[9] An interesting example is Pedro de Aycinena y Piñol, whose family was of noble Guatemalan extraction and in whose genealogy are many lower-ranking public officials such as mayors and municipal councilmen, during and after the colonial period, and even an early chief of state. He was minister of foreign affairs for two decades during the presidencies of Gen. Rafael Carrera Turcios (1851–65) and Gen. Vicente Cerna (1865–71).[10] Throughout those years he exercised the presidency as temporary circumstances demanded (notably upon Carrera's death) but always returned to his post as minister of foreign affairs. The southern part of the Isthmus (particularly Costa Rica), lived in extreme poverty throughout the colonial period, until the introduction of coffee to that country during the first half of the nineteenth century. After Independence members of its ruling class cultivated coffee and raised cattle, but increasingly tended to seek public jobs and to run the government themselves.

With Independence, economic divisions that had appeared within ruling classes during the colonial period acquired political overtones; out of them grew the liberal and conservative movements. Since then, struggles between the two have been given ideological interpretations. During the nineteenth century these concerned the church, control of traditional production, the ill-fated Federation of Central American States, and other issues. The liberal Francisco Morazán (a Honduran) served as president of the short-lived federation, and Justo Rufino Barrios (another liberal and president of Guatemala) dreamed of—and died for—Isthmian union. Conservatives like Guatemalan President Rafael Carrera Turcios (a significant Isthmian figure for forty-two years) fought liberals in every field. Pythagoras stated that power lives close to necessity, and this can be seen through the rise and fall of export crops, on the one hand, and the waxing and waning of political doctrines on the other.[11]

Liberal reforms of late nineteenth century illustrate the idea. They were introduced by groups from ruling classes for the purpose of modernizing economic structures to facilitate the export of raw materials. When Carrera and Cerna defended conservative causes in Guatemala, for instance, the principal exports were cochineal and indigo dyes, and both presidents sought support from (and backed) producers of those items. With the appearance of artificial dyes on world markets, Guatemalan producers of natural tints began to lose their predominant economic positions. Subsequently both Carrera and Cerna, following the example of Costa Rica half a century earlier, sought to convince agriculturalists to introduce coffee as a substitute. However, neither could promote that reform without undermining existing power structures based on cochineal and indigo production. It took the "liberal" revolution of 1871, led first by Miguel García Granados and shortly after by Justo Rufino Barrios, to enact legislation that introduced and stimulated coffee cultivation. Toward the end of the presidency of Cerna, commercial groups (generally conservative) attempted to establish alliances with the more liberal coffee planters. The latter, however, feared that the agreement would hamper them. In this manner, a conservative and anti-Central American Federation political movement, based on support from commerce as well as indigo and cochineal producers, lost hegemony to new coffee-producing groups who backed the liberal and pro-Federation position of Barrios.[12]

A similar situation occurred with coffee in El Salvador. Land suitable for that crop was in populated areas, which limited its supply, and as in Guatemala, only "liberal" reforms (as envisioned by potential producers) could open doors of opportunity. Those reforms took place under Rafael Zaldívar (1876–85), influenced by Barrios in Guatemala. It was in this manner that a powerful Salvadoran coffee oligarchy consolidated its political position. In Honduras, liberal reformers sought to diversify a cattle economy that had remained isolated from world markets, through government concessions to foreign mining enterprises under the presidencies of Marco Aurelio Soto (1876–83) and Gen. Luis Bográn Barahona (1883–91). (Both became important shareholders in companies engaged in the new activity.) Nicaragua experienced no economic transformation at that time for mining has been a principal venture in that country, and coffee did not displace traditional cattle raising until recently.[13]

Costa Rica presents different patterns from the others. Due to its poverty during the colonial period, it did not "inherit" any economic activity other than subsistence agriculture. For that reason its first public figures searched for undertakings that could alleviate economic stagnation. Coffee was introduced early (around 1830), and many families from the old colonial nobility became planters.[14] Economic activities in Central America can best be related to political parties in more recent times, particularly with the establishment of industry under the Central American Common Market in 1960. This, however, merits more detailed attention and is dealt with in the next chapter.

Ruling Classes in Modern Times

The nature of ruling classes throughout Central America and the ways in which they have set up governments have been determined by the possibilities of organizing production. These, in turn, have depended on the availability of land for export crops, labor, and capital in each country. In general terms, significant portions of Guatemala's one hundred nine thousand square kilometers and practically all of El Salvador's twenty thousand have been suited for export crops. El Salvador, in spite of being the smallest country on the Isthmus, has had a relative abundance of land for that purpose. Mountainous areas in Honduras make much of its one hundred twelve thousand square kilometers poor for farming. While the largest country is Nicaragua (one hundred forty-eight thousand square kilometers), the eastern half of its territory has generally been inadequate for agriculture. In Costa Rica (fifty-one thousand square kilometers), only the central plateau and certain coastal regions have been used for export production, although volcanic activity in that country has been advantageous for agriculture.

Changes in export crops notwithstanding, land (even those extensions good for nontraditional crops, such as flowers and cardamom), capital, and labor continue to be more abundant in the north than in the south. The greatest extensions of fertile lands in cold climates appropriate for agriculture are found in Guatemala. Temperate zones suitable for certain types of farming are found in the same country and in parts of Costa Rica and Nicaragua, although on a smaller scale. Good agricultural areas on the Caribbean coast are located principally between Lake Isabal (in Guatemala) and Trujillo (in Honduras).

Contemporary Central American exports have included coffee, bananas, cacao, cotton, rice, sorghum, flowers, cardamom, and beef. While these

TABLE I.
Coffee Exported from Central America
(metric tons)

	1950	1959	1970	1980
Guatemala	54,900	84,270	108,000	116,100
El Salvador	66,400	80,700	114,000	150,700
Honduras	6,400	15,300	33,000	50,100
Nicaragua	13,750	16,360	36,000	43,000
Costa Rica	18,730	42,740	78,000	72,000

SOURCES: René Coste, *Les caféiers et les cafés dans le monde*, vol. 2, 1961; PanAmerican Coffee Bureau, *Annual Coffee Statistics*; *Progreso* magazine, September 1971, p. 67; Organización Internacional del Café, Doc. EB 2497/84, 23 October 1984, p. 16.

products require different climatic conditions, all demand top-quality land, which has been more concentrated in the northern countries than in the southern ones. Land for high-grade coffee (one of the most important crops common to all Isthmian countries) is relatively more abundant in the north. Tonnages exported before the conflicts of the 1980s appear on table 1, which shows that greater quantities were produced in the north than in the south. Maps locating the lands for principal export crops during the colonial period also reveal that the greatest concentrations then were also in the northern provinces. The large production of the coffee bean in tiny El Salvador in 1970 contrasts with the far smaller area of cultivation in Costa Rica (which is more than twice the size of El Salvador).[15]

Economically active populations give an idea of the relative size of contemporary labor forces (see table 10) and clearly indicate the advantage of northern countries in this respect. (The small size of Costa Rica's supply of workers is somewhat offset by its high literacy rate.) Capital, along with land and labor, continues to be more abundant in the north. With the establishment of the Central American Common Market in 1960, the value added by the new industrial sectors in northern countries was greater than in the south, and three decades later the trend is much the same. More industry was established in the north because of lower labor costs, and while foreign investors participated heavily, national capitalists contributed an important share. By 1985, the effects on production of the political and social convulsions can be appreciated. Data corresponding to 1960, 1970, 1980, and 1985, in millions of U.S. dollars, are shown in table 2.

Possibilities of organizing production throughout Central America,

TABLE 2.
Value Added by Central American Industrial Sectors
(millions of U.S. dollars)

	1960	1970	1980	1985
Guatemala	449	937	1,713	1,531
El Salvador	254	555	742	657
Honduras	139	273	481	441
Nicaragua	204	532	676	701
Costa Rica	195	455	930	948

SOURCE: Interamerican Development Bank 1986:418.

then, have determined the nature of ruling classes and the ways in which they have set up governments. Where money has been scarce, they have gone directly into politics (as in Nicaragua but particularly in Costa Rica) and have regarded the state as an expedient vehicle for solving problems of employment both for themselves and for other sectors of the population. Table 10 compares the portions of populations working for governments. In the north, where money has been easier to make, ruling classes have remained in private sectors, have governed indirectly through armies, and have made the state serve the needs of their productive activities. Ranking members of those classes rarely occupy administrative posts, and the top public office is generally designated by the military from its own ranks. People chosen for secondary posts are also selected by them, but they come from all population sectors. Army presidents cannot usually speak for themselves, for they depend on decisions of producers. That has been an obstacle to treaties since Independence and a fundamental problem of the Central American Common Market. Under indirect systems, high-ranking officials who belong to the ruling groups are targets for guerrillas in today's convulsive Central America. Three recent cases come to mind: Mauricio Borgonovo Pohl, Alberto Fuentes Mohr (both in the 1970s), and Adolfo Molina Orantes (1980). The first was minister of foreign affairs of El Salvador and the other two of Guatemala. Some believe that the Guatemalan army did away with Fuentes Mohr and with Molina Orantes, while others feel that guerrillas were responsible.[16]

Producers have exercised control over their societies through generous compensation to top military officials in their governments. Thus toward midnineteenth century, the president of Guatemala received an annual salary of one hundred twenty thousand French francs, while in Costa Rica

TABLE 3.
Central American Dictatorships

	Number of Dictators	Combined Rule
Guatemala	5	74 years
El Salvador	6	44 years
Honduras	2	24 years
Nicaragua	6	68 years
Costa Rica	2	19 years

The dictators were the following: In Guatemala, Rafael Carrera Turcios (1844–65); Justo Rufino Barrios (1873–85); José María Reina Barrios and Manuel Estrada Cabrera (1892–1920); and Jorge Ubico Castañeda (1931–44). In El Salvador, Francisco Dueñas (1863–71); Carlos Ezeta (1890–94); Tomás Regalado (1898–1903), Carlos Meléndez, Jorge Meléndez, and Alfonso Quiñones Molina (1913–27); and Maximiliano Hernández Martínez (1931–44). In Honduras, Tiburcio Carías Andino (1933–49) and Oswaldo López Orellano (1963–71). In Nicaragua, Tomás Martínez (1857–67); José Santos Zelaya (1893–1909); and three Somozas (1937–79). In Costa Rica, Tomás Guardia Guriérrez (1870–82) and Federico Tinoco Granados (1917–19).

and Nicaragua, his counterparts were paid only half that amount.[17] When Gen. Dwight Eisenhower was president of the United States, with an annual salary of approximately $175,000, Gen. Miguel Ydígoras Fuentes received one million dollars as president of Guatemala.[18]

Ruling classes seek to organize production under optimum conditions of political stability, and under the social and political conditions prevailing in Central America, this has been accomplished more efficiently through dictatorships. Where there are greater possibilities for making money, there are greater commensurate efforts to achieve that stability. That is one reason why indirect rule has made for more authoritarianism than direct government, as is shown in table 3. Dictators in the north, with few exceptions (Jorge Ubico in Guatemala was one of them) have come from other social classes as *caudillos* (discussed in chapter 5); in the south (Nicaragua and Costa Rica) autocrats have usually been members of ruling classes and have emerged largely in response to situations of crisis.

Political stability has been sought in different ways in the north and in the south, but Costa Rica stands in contrast with the other nations. That country has had lengthy periods of stability, due not to dictators, but to groups from the traditional ruling class who have shared power over long periods of time. For example, from the end of the nineteenth century to the Great Depression, the country was governed for thirty-four years by close to a dozen respected neo-liberal politicians nicknamed the "Olympus" (El

Olimpo). During twenty-two of those years, Guatemala and Nicaragua had only one ruler each, Manuel Estrada Cabrera and José Santos Zelaya. During the 1940s and 1950s, Costa Rica was governed by several collectivist parties whose ranking members also came from the traditional ruling class. The most important were the Partido Republicano, under Rafael Angel Calderón Guardia, and subsequently the Partido Liberación Nacional under José Figueres Ferrer. Guatemala, El Salvador, Honduras, and Nicaragua, on the other hand, were ruled during those decades by dictators: Jorge Ubico Castañeda, Maximiliano Hernández Martínez, Tiburcio Carías Andino, and Anastasio Somoza García. The preponderance of aristocratic families in government in the south can be appreciated in table 4.

Family trees of conquistadors reveal that many of their descendants in Costa Rica and Nicaragua have held appointed and elected public office well into the twentieth century. Conquistador Cristóbal de Alfaro is forefather of forty-eight Isthmian presidents: thirty-seven in Costa Rica (where he is also ancestor of probably well over three hundred congressmen), seven in Nicaragua, one in Honduras, two in El Salvador, and one in Guatemala (see appendix 1). Conquistador Juan Vázquez de Coronado is forefather of thirty-four Central American presidents (twenty-three in Costa Rica and eleven in Nicaragua) and close to three hundred members of congress in Costa Rica (see appendixes 2 and 6) as well as a large number of other ranking public officials. A similar situation occurs with Conquistador Jorge de Alvarado, ancestor of twenty-two Isthmian presidents: eighteen in Costa Rica (where one hundred forty congressmen also are descended from him), one in Nicaragua, one in Honduras, and two in El Salvador (appendix 3).

Abundance of labor in the north has made for indifference between landowners and their peons. This is particularly noticeable in Guatemala and El Salvador. The absence of contact between labor and management (administrators constitute small buffer groups between upper and lower classes) is reflected in distant relationships between ruling classes and electorates.[19] As a result, in northern Central America, elections serve merely to justify political systems (which explains the historic lack of concern over suffrage and the general indifference toward electoral fraud). The paucity of laborers in Costa Rica, on the other hand, has resulted in more viable relationships with producers. Such a situation strengthens democratic values, for landowners have made more concessions to laborers than in countries where employers have never needed to be concerned over the welfare of the masses.[20] Elections are generally considered an honest process and have served to legitimate the system.

TABLE 4.
Presidents Descended from Principal Central American Families

Guatemala:	
from the Maestre family	1
from the Martín del Cerro family	1
from the Alfaro family	1
El Salvador:	
from the Buonafede family	1
from the Martín del Cerro family	6
from the Alvarado family	2
from the Alfaro family	2
Honduras:	
from the Bográn family	2
from the Alvarado family	1
from the Alfaro family	1
Nicaragua:	
from the Chamorro family	5
from the Cuadra family	8
from the Lacayo family	9
from the Alvarado family	1
from the Vázquez de Coronado family	11
from the Alfaro family	7
Costa Rica:	
from the González family	8
from the Acosta family	24
from the Alvarado family	18
from the Vázquez de Coronado family	23
from the Alfaro family	36

Details of family trees, with exceptions of Maestre, Martín del Cerro, Buonafede, and Bográn, are in appendixes 1–7. The president of Guatemala from Maestre is Jorge Ubico Castañeda; those from Martín del Cerro in El Salvador are Pedro José de Arce Fagoaga, León Avilés Escalón, Miguel Santín Castillo Barroeta, José María Cornejo Merino, Mariano Prado Baca, and Doroteo Vasconcelos Vides and in Guatemala, Simón Vasconcelos Vides; from Buonafede, Joaquín Eufracio Guzmán Ugalde and Gerardo Barrios in El Salvador; and from Bográn in Honduras, Luis and Francisco Bográn Barahona, whose first cousin, Miguel Paz Barahona, was also president. See Samuel Stone, "Las convulsiones del Istmo Centroamericano: Raíces de un conflicto entre elites," *Estudios* no. 1 (1979): 81–111.

A Recapitulation

Northern Central America, endowed with more economic resources than the southern part, attracted socially ranking settlers with greater investment capital and became the important area of the Isthmus both economically and politically. For these reasons the southern part was neither conquered nor colonized until half a century after the other territories. The north developed ruling classes of social importance even in Spain, a clergy of ranking noble extraction, and an officialdom. The south, on the other hand, became the land of nobles of lower status, a clergy of less social relevance, and of predominantly plebeian groups. Guatemala and Costa Rica represent social extremes, and the other countries vary according to their geographic position between those two. Dissimilarities between Central American countries have led to constant rivalries, despite attempts to consolidate them. Ricardo Jiménez Oreamuno, president of Costa Rica on three occasions beginning in 1909, is credited with stating that his country had three seasons: a wet season, a dry season, and a season of war with Nicaragua. This expression well describes the nature of relationships among the five nations since Independence. As late as 1885, the Isthmus lived in fear of Justo Rufino Barrios, dictator of Guatemala, who attempted to bring the region under his own control, and other antagonisms among these small republics have flared up frequently.

Value differences arise from the responses of ruling classes and other sectors of populations to the scarcity or abundance of resources. Where labor is abundant and there is little or no contact between peon and *patrón*, the two often scorn each other. Courage is another indicator of values, and an analysis of Central American literature shows that this has different overtones throughout the Isthmus. In Guatemala and El Salvador, to a greater extent than in the south, it constitutes an important ingredient of political leadership. In these countries, the prestige attached to leadership by the ruling class was low. In contrast, for the Costa Rican élite, the presidency has always been a highly coveted distinction. While value differences do not explain antagonisms between nations, they do indicate variations in national character traits associated with the conflict. This is discussed in chapter 5. The foregoing serves as background for attempting to approach some of the contemporary problems of Central America.

CHAPTER 2

Contemporary Conflicts

A Family We Already Know

In the city of Managua, there is a beautiful plaza with a magnificent statue of a horse. We supposed the rider was Bolívar or Morazán, but that was not the case. The monument was a noble family tribute dedicated to the memory of Anastasio Somoza I. He was seated on his arrogant imperial steed by the North Americans in 1932 and continued riding him until 1956, when he was assassinated by a young man named Rigoberto López.

In Nicaragua Rigoberto is remembered because his father died at the hands of Somoza and the lad swore vengeance. He was at the time a child and went on to study in El Salvador, where he practiced target shooting. He mastered the art, returned to his homeland and found a sweetheart. Together they attended a dance where they knew Somoza would be. Rigoberto entered unarmed. His sweetheart carried a revolver in her purse. While dancing they came very close to the general, and Rigoberto emptied the bullets in the weapon into his body. The first to die was Rigoberto himself. The news reached Washington, and President Eisenhower wasted no time in declaring the assassin a coward and in sending his own plane and surgeon, in a supreme but futile effort to save the life of the famous president who had been mounted on the bronze steed by another United States president.

Nicaragua today owes much of its progress to the Somoza family, although that family, through its wealth, has become a state within a state. Today Nicaragua has become too small for the Somozas and they are extending their domains into Costa Rica and Guatemala. They have their own port (Puerto Somoza), one of the largest Central American airlines with jet service, and a shipping line.

With the death of Somoza some raised a question: Who's boss in Nicaragua? Near the Presidential Palace is a fort of the National Guard: that of Anastasio Somoza II. As one approaches it, a triumphal march can be heard, but there are no loud and clear trumpets. It is the sound of the hooves of the tough horses of the old Somoza.[1]

Among the contemporary conflicts of Central America that have come to the attention of the outside world, the most important has been the one between the Somoza family and the Sandinistas. It developed as a result of the role played by Anastasio Somoza García and his sons (Luis and Anastasio Somoza Debayle) as regional champions of causes favorable to United States interests, in return for economic, political, and military support. The Sandinista success was a product both of his own greed and of popular resentment against the backing given to his regime by the United States. Other incidents publicized in the international media have concerned the Central American Common Market (CACM), continuous violence and terrorism in El Salvador and Guatemala, and the "Soccer War" between El Salvador and Honduras in 1969. These conflicts have involved economic resources and ruling classes. This chapter focuses on those events.

The Central American Common Market (CACM)

The CACM was started in 1960 by influential groups not engaged in traditional economic activities such as coffee, sugarcane, or cattle. Its purpose was to encourage production for a regional market by fostering the assembly of goods—using imported parts—through tax and customs duties exemptions designed to discourage imports of completed items. In a sense it was a revival of the old Central American Federation idea. From the outset it was plagued by economic and political problems. The first stumbling block was that all the countries started producing similar goods. The new activities (it is necessary to distinguish them from those established before 1960) have developed into the "spoiled children" of Central American economies, at the expense of agricultural sectors that must subsidize them. Furthermore, legislation has not channeled investments where they are most needed in developing agricultural societies. They have instead been concentrated in activities offering the fastest capital recuperation, which has meant excessive automation and minimal use of labor (in countries where unemployment is a serious problem). Development has been insignificant in such important areas as the assembly of farming equipment, for example. Protection granted for such investments has generally resulted in poor-quality products at high prices. A striking aspect of the CACM is that many of the largest investments have been made by foreigners, mainly North Americans and Japanese, who have sought to establish themselves principally in northern Central America, where labor is cheaper than in the south.

The manufacturing programs have affected both the political and economic positions of traditional ruling groups. Following the 1948 revolution in Costa Rica and the advent of President José Figueres, the coffee planters (the spinal cord of the economy as well as of the political system) experienced abrupt changes in their traditional hegemony. The National Liberation Party (PLN) headed by Figueres, which has won most of the elections since 1953, has represented groups not generally associated with coffee production. Land, labor, and capital have come to acquire different meanings for the followers of Figueres, on the one hand, and the coffee planters, on the other. The latter, who have always had to cope with scanty labor supplies (it has often been necessary to advance school vacations to allow children to help with harvesting), saw the new factories as rivals for workers, as did the banana companies. The new industrial groups developed a different concept of economic priorities. Land was no longer regarded solely in terms of traditional export products like coffee, but rather as a means of producing preservable products like tomatoes, chickpeas, and asparagus. Some coffee planters destroyed crops to plant other products, but generally failed. Liquid capital became a growing necessity and new sources of credit were opened for nascent assembly plants. Subsidies for such activities, ironically, came largely from taxes levied on coffee production, and the planters felt abused. Labor no longer implied traditional paternalistic relationships between peon and patron in the Costa Rican coffee complex, but developed characteristics of trade unions. Similar changes took place in the other Isthmian nations.

The new groups of nontraditional producers were able to establish their economic identity throughout the region by participating in local and national political systems, and in so doing they displaced important families engaged in traditional agricultural production. Such economic changes led to the rise of minority groups that would never have figured politically under the old order. In Costa Rica, for example, during the 1978 presidential campaign, Miguel Barzuna Sauma (a new industrialist of Lebanese origin) ran in the primary elections of one of the major parties (the Partido Unidad Social Cristiana—PUSC), with the backing of the generally conservative planter group. The planters preferred Barzuna over Rodrigo Carazo Odio, a maverick who severed relations with the PLN, the party of their old enemy José Figueres. Luis Alberto Monge Alvarez (married to an Ashkenazic Jew) ran in the primary elections of the PLN, and this national political rivalry was even interpreted in the Miami *Herald* and in several Costa Rican newspapers as a conflict between Arabs and Israelis in Central America. Barzuna lost to Carazo in the primary elections, and Carazo defeated Monge. Until the rise of these two foreign minority groups through the industrial movement created by the Central American Common Market, it would have been impossible for anyone with ties to them to run for such high public office, let alone as candidate of the conservative planter group. The CACM can be seen as an arena where ruling groups vie for leadership, and foreigners (today primarily North Americans, Japanese, and Mexicans) play an important role.

National ruling groups in the Central American countries confront each other through cumbersome governmental institutions where points of discord get bogged down in bureaucratic structures and little is accomplished. A good example of this is the failure of the payments system that has led both to occasional paralysis of the market and even to bilateral agreements to get around problems posed by its complicated rules and regulations. Other instances of international dysfunction have been the closing of borders to prevent trade (as Guatemala and Nicaragua have done in recent times), forcing the use of ocean transportation. A recent incident was the announcement of Costa Rica that it would withdraw from the Banco Centroamericano de Integración Económica (Central American Bank for Economic Integration) if Honduras continued to manipulate the nomination of the next president of that institution.[2] Armed forces are employed as a last resort, as in the "Soccer War" (to be discussed shortly).

The terms of trade of CACM nations with the outside world have been generally unfavorable for them, for while prices of their agricultural exports have fluctuated abruptly (and in many cases decreased), the manufactured goods they import have become more expensive. This means that to purchase a tractor in 1980, it was necessary for coffee-producing countries to sell more sacks of that product than in 1950. Because Central American economic activities require many imported items, the region is said to be dependent on industrialized countries that produce them. While the matter of dependency remains a moot question, it has often led to nationalistic stances and at times aggressive ideological political positions of ruling groups in their relations with the industrialized world. Reaction has been more pronounced in the smaller Central American countries than in the larger South American republics, and Isthmian groups that are often closely associated with foreign capital frequently develop strong antagonisms toward capitalist nations.

Feelings underlying these antagonisms have not been widely understood and are important, for what is really at stake for those developing nations is their competence to act alone, without constantly seeking economic assistance. In 1969, crises in productive systems throughout the continent prompted a visit to Central and South America by Nelson Rockefeller, representing the president of the United States. On the eve of his arrival, two declarations took the continent by surprise. One was an announcement by the Inter-American Development Bank that existing industrial programs, such as the one operating under the CACM, did not suit the needs of the area; the other was a declaration of the Special Commission for Latin American Coordination, motivated by the expropriation of a United States petroleum company in Peru, to the effect that Latin American and United States economic aims were not the same. It also expressed the need to create an economic image of self-respect. The statement of the Inter-American Development Bank made it clear that imitating other models of development was not a remedy for national problems, and that consequently the region should present its own solutions to obstacles instead of simply extending a hand for aid. The statement of the special commission was a protest against possible United States reprisals for the expropriation in Peru. Both declarations caused widespread reaction against the United States.

It is alarming that many expressions of this resentment over foreign participation in the CACM and elsewhere have passed unnoticed. Many outsiders continue to repeat that these countries need and want foreign investment, and the constant discord between the United Fruit Company or the Electric Bond and Share Company and most of the Central American governments passes almost unnoticed in the United States. These symptoms of discontent and mistrust are expressed in such novels as *El tiburón y la sardina* (The shark and the sardine) by Guatemalan President Juan José Arévalo and *Mamita Yunai*, by Costa Rican author Carlos Luis Fallas Sibaja, among others. In spite of a variety of expressions of such sentiments, United States (and Japanese) corporations in Central America, due to the small size of the Isthmian countries, still aspire to become the biggest employers. Although they provide foreign exchange and create jobs, it hurts the Central American to make him feel that he has not been capable of utilizing his own natural resources, and foreign interference in national politics adds insult to injury. Inequalities of opportunity for nationals in foreign corporations, frequently disguised with separate payrolls, has caused resentment. These and other aspects of industrialization under the CACM hurt national pride, and that was what the special commission meant when it said that the economic aims of Latin America and the United States were not the same. Foreign enterprises exact demands of balance sheets and profit-and-loss statements, but Central Americans often feel that this is at their expense, and that those companies do not understand that they do not go barefoot to invite being stepped on.[3]

In sum, the main purpose of the CACM was to make industry the driving force for the economic development of the region, but this had a negative impact on the traditional sectors and has led to the rise of new industrial and managerial élites who developed antagonistic attitudes toward foreign capital. At the same time the CACM has generated harmful side effects in terms of fiscal performance and the balance of payments of the member countries. Conflict between ruling groups—not harmonious development —has marked its evolution. This can be readily appreciated through the events leading to the Soccer War in 1969.

The Soccer War: Specter of the Agrarian Problem

The so-called Soccer War between El Salvador and Honduras in 1969 was another Central American conflict having to do with ruling groups, land for export crops, labor, and capital in a dramatic way. It involved four important issues: 1) both countries were unhappy with the negative effects of the Common Market on their economies; 2) they shared a common border that had been in dispute for over a century and a half; 3) over three hundred thousand Salvadoran immigrants were in Honduras (some 12 percent of the latter country's population) in search of jobs and land; and 4) both (but particularly El Salvador, where population growth appeared to have led agricultural expansion beyond the carrying capacity of the land) considered food a major priority.[4]

The events leading to open hostilities started with the introduction of coffee in El Salvador toward the end of the nineteenth century, and the consequent massive stripping of Indian communal lands by the army for members of the traditional ruling class. This created an abundant agrarian proletariat, leading to growing and explosive social unrest that has continued to undermine the position of that class. Expansion of coffee lands during the nineteenth century was rapid, displacing maize, rice, and beans.

Between 1866 and 1915, coffee exports increased from 10 percent to 85 percent of total exports; as with cotton, this produced a shortage of basic food crops. By 1933, coffee represented more than a third of the country's production.[5] Rapid population growth led to food and land shortages, and the resulting changes in land distribution provoked popular uprisings in areas of coffee expansion. The most serious one took place in 1932.[6] It is important to underscore the formation of this Salvadoran proletariat, for it was precisely due to its existence that the Soviet communist movement first attempted to penetrate Central America through that country during the 1920s.[7]

While this was occurring in El Salvador, territory was being acquired in neighboring Honduras by North American banana enterprises (United, Cuyamel, and Standard Fruit companies), and by the early twentieth century these had converted that country into the world's principal exporter of that fruit. Areas planted with coffee rose from forty-five thousand to ninety thousand hectares between 1945 and 1959. This expansion of commercial agriculture on large holdings took place precisely when land was becoming scarce for immigrants from El Salvador, as well as for small Honduran farmers.[8] At the same time, large Honduran landholders reacted to the growing strength of peasant organizations by forming a National Federation of Agriculturalists and Cattle Ranchers[9] By midcentury, aliens had become the principal force in the economy and, indirectly (though not disguised), in the political system as well (English capital controlled lumber, while other United States enterprises dominated mining).[10]

Coincident with the invasion of Honduran lands by Salvadorans, another explosive situation had been developing, for in Honduras, foreign interests could provide political administrations with foreign exchange more readily than could the cattle raisers from the traditional ruling class. When the Common Market was opened in 1960, many outsiders invested in El Salvador, fundamentally due to its large labor supply. Furthermore, given the impossibility for members of the Salvadoran ruling class to expand agricultural activities in their tiny country, many were eager to diversify their investments in partnerships with aliens. Industrial production in El Salvador started in this fashion, with strong participation of foreigners, for whose products Honduras soon became an important market. Further frustration for Honduras came when the land-hungry Salvadoran proletariat stepped up its invasion of uncultivated Honduran lands. Honduras has more than five times the land area of El Salvador, and the average farm is almost twice as large. The country is more mountainous (61 percent is on slopes), and the soil lacks benefits normally supplied by volcanoes.[11] Honduras' restriction of Salvadoran immigration brought El Salvador's land problem to a boiling point, endangering relations between the two countries and risking another closure of the Common Market. Pressure from large Honduran landowners resulted in the expulsion of immigrants and converted competition among groups within the two nations into rivalries between the countries themselves. The heat of a soccer game set off the war. Although the conflict lasted only four days, a peace treaty was not signed until a decade and a half after the first bullet was fired.

Events leading to the soccer war show the importance of the scarcity and abundance of land, labor, and capital, and reveal the different nature of the ruling classes in the two countries: aggressive and arrogant in El Salvador, condescending and more willing to compromise in Honduras. The episode highlights the tenacity of ruling groups (particularly in El Salvador) in quest of ways to protect their own interests. In El Salvador, the ruling class could not tolerate social unrest in its burgeoning population, and large landholders found a convenient solution in allowing it to overflow into neighboring Honduras, thus obstructing land reform in their own country. During the late nineteenth century, the Salvadoran government (acting in the interests of the ruling class) even attempted to abolish *ejidos* (land alloted to Indians for communal use) and to suppress peasant uprisings.

Precisely as this was occurring, Honduran authorities were enacting laws to justify expropriations of private lands for use as ejidos. In Honduras there has been a relationship between land tenure systems and the ability of that country's authorities to maintain political stability, although the ruling class has accepted reform more readily than its counterparts elsewhere. With the rise of coffee cultivation during the latter part of the nineteenth century, ownership of the land became concentrated in few hands. Coffee did not play as important a role here as in the economies of other countries, because of inadequate soil conditions, poor transportation facilities, and other problems. As a result, no strong and cohesive coffee planter oligarchy developed. Even as late as the 1950s, the largest Honduran landowners were technologically backward cattle ranchers and constituted the politically weakest oligarchy in Central America.[12] With the 1967 boom in sales of beef and cotton, they evicted tenants and took over thousands of hectares; conflicts with peasants became more frequent, and the latter organized themselves to resist the growth of latifundia.

The point to underscore is that agrarian reform in Honduras was stimulated by peasants who became the strongest in Central America because they were permitted to organize legally, whereas in El Salvador (as well as in Guatemala and Nicaragua) agrarian syndicates were outlawed and repressed. Flexibility and willingness to make concessions have been traits of ruling classes in both Honduras and Costa Rica, where they have had to confront multinational corporations in a struggle for scarce labor. Such qualities have not been generally charateristic of Central America, however, and one of the most relevant examples of rigidity was the ruling group headed by the Somoza family in Nicaragua.

The Somoza Family and the Sandinistas

The Central American conflict that has received the most publicity was the ousting of Anastasio Somoza Debayle (a son of Anastasio Somoza García) by the Sandinistas in 1979. During much of its modern history, Nicaragua has been a country with few land and labor resources. In recent times, coffee has been the principal export crop, although it is small by comparison with the rest of Central America, as can be seen in table 1. That product was followed in importance by gold and bananas until shortly before the second world war, when cotton production, encouraged by the Somoza family,[13] began to play a role in exports.[14] Ruling families from the colonial period, as well as their descendants, have not produced fortunes as large as those amassed in Guatemala or El Salvador. As in Costa Rica, politics has become one of the main occupations. Families such as the Somozas, the Lacayos, the Chamorros, the Cuadras, and many others fall into this category (see appendixes 4 and 5).

The rise to power and to permanence in politics of the Somoza family· were largely due to the backing of successive United States administrations, whose interventions in Nicaragua date from the discovery of gold in California, toward the midnineteenth century. The consequent massive migration of prospectors from the East to the West Coast made Nicaragua the key point on that route, because practically the entire journey could be made by water. Travelers went from New York by ship to Nicaragua, up the San Juan River, across Lake Nicaragua, and after a short stagecoach ride to the Pacific Ocean, on to California again by ship. To ensure control of any waterway that might eventually be built along that route, especially given the interest shown for such a venture by England and France since the midnineteenth century, about 1930 the United States converted Nicaragua into a protectorate under a national guard headed by Anastasio Somoza García,[15] a soldier from a noble colonial family who married into a yet older family from the same colonial aristocracy (see appendixes 1, 2, and 5). Somoza's first ancestor in the New World, Francisco Somoza y Gámez Ballesteros, settled in Guatemala toward the end of the seventeenth century.[16] A distinction has been made between "old" aristocratic families, who can trace their roots to the early colonial period (the Sacasas, the Chamorros, and the Cuadras), and "new" ones who arrived later (the Reyes, the Somozas, and the Ortegas, among others).[17] In the case of the Somozas, their family tree leads back to both "old" and "new" blood.

Anastasio Somoza García was above all a salesman and, with support from the United States government, soon came to be dictator. With continued backing, he and his family remained in power for almost half a century until the overthrow of his second son (Anastasio Somoza Debayle) by the Sandinistas in 1979. The Somoza family and friends became notoriously wealthy, and General Somoza maintained control of the political system through the army. At the prompting of the United States government he was able to take personal advantage of the second world war by confiscating properties of Nicaraguan citizens of German and Italian descent. That was the origin of his fortune.[18] Other nations like Guatemala and Costa Rica were encouraged to do likewise, and men were deported to concentration camps in the United States. Somoza's dictatorship generated resentment, bitterness, and controversy. For example, he allowed Spanish Republicans fleeing that country's civil war during the 1930s to enter Nicaragua and placed them in charge of public educational institutions. Members of the Communist Party and of the labor syndicates it often dominated took to the streets to cheer him.[19] During these same years Augusto César Sandino fought him (and the United States) in continued guerrilla warfare over the issue of national sovereignty.

The Somoza family had enemies both within and outside of Nicaragua, but United States support made it untouchable. One foreign opponent was former Costa Rican President José Figueres, who, after winning the 1948 civil war, gave asylum in Costa Rica to Nicaraguan dissidents plotting against their dictator. In revenge, Somoza backed invasions from Nicaragua against Costa Rica in 1948 and 1955. Fidel Castro was another staunch enemy of the family, for Anastasio Somoza Debayle (the third son, known as Tachito) had allowed Nicaraguan territory to be used for the preparation of the ill-fated Bay of Pigs invasion against Cuba in 1961. The most formidable foreign opponent turned out to be another Costa Rican president, Rodrigo Carazo Odio, who after his election in 1978, assisted Somoza's enemies (soon to form the Sandinista movement, comprising many from the traditional ruling class) in overthrowing the regime of Tachito, whose older brother Luis, had died of a heart attack after a three-year rule. Carazo allowed the use of Costa Rican territory for open warfare against Nicaragua. Raids were launched, guerrillas were trained there, and arms were supplied from Cuba and Venezuela through Panama to Costa Rica's border with Nicaragua. After Tachito's fall in 1979, Carazo was proclaimed a hero of the Sandinista Revolution.

The most numerous groups of enemies of the Somoza family, however, were his own compatriots living in Nicaragua. Many of the important ones also descend (by birth or by marriage) from colonial aristocracy and were related to him. They include Fernando Guzmán Cuadra (president of the National Development Bank and former minister of industry), Carlos Núñez Telles (one of the nine comandantes), Jaime Wheelock Román (one of the nine comandantes and minister of agrarian reform), his brother Ricardo (former ambassador to the Soviet Union), Ernesto Cardenal Martínez (minister of culture), his brother Fernando (minister of education), Luis Carrión Cruz (one of the nine comandantes), and Roberto Argüello Hurtado (president of the Supreme Court of Justice). These and many others can be seen in appendixes 4 and 5 as well as in the roster of leading Sandinistas who took control of the revolutionary government.[20]

The point to underscore is kinship among Sandinistas, the Somozas, and important former Sandinistas. The last include people such as Arturo Cruz, Alfonso Robelo Calleja, and Violeta Barrios Torres, widow of Pedro Joaquín Chamorro Cardenal, assassinated director of the opposition newspaper *La Prensa*. This paper has been censored, closed, and reopened on numerous occasions by the Sandinista regime. It was recently permitted to operate with no censorship, although the government refused to allow it to purchase newsprint. However, it did provide that commodity to the two official Sandinista newspapers, *Barricada* and *El Nuevo Diario*.[21]

Of particular interest are political and ideological divisions among members of these families, and the Chamorros serve as a case in point. Both Violeta Barrios and her late husband came from old aristocratic families. She was an original Sandinista leader but early abandoned their ranks. By contrast, a daughter Claudia and a son-in-law (Edmundo Jarquín) were Sandinista ambassadors to Costa Rica and Mexico, respectively. Her immediate family is most divided in the world of the press. For example, when her son Pedro Joaquín abandoned the directorship of the newspaper *La Prensa* and sought exile in Costa Rica, her daughter Cristiana took his place. One of her brothers-in-law (Jaime Chamorro Cardenal) works on the staff of the paper. Another son, Carlos Fernando, heads the official Sandinista newspaper *Barricada,* while another of her brothers-in-law,

Javier Chamorro Cardenal, heads the other official Sandinista newspaper, *El Nuevo Diario*. The assassination of Violeta's husband was a major incident that led to the downfall of the last Somoza, whom some blame for his death, while others censure the Sandinistas for attempting to embarrass the dictator with the horrendous act. With the fall of Somoza, a junta (initially of five members but later of three) that included Violeta assumed control of the nation in the name of the Sandinista movement. Relationships among members of this divided family can be seen in appendix 4 and are characteristic of other families involved in the Nicaraguan revolution, in the sense that while many oppose their Sandinista brothers and cousins, they seek ways of coping with them to avoid losing their properties.

Last but not least are the Ortega Saavedra brothers, Daniel (president of Nicaragua) and Humberto (minister of defense), whose kin are divided in a fashion similar to that of the Chamorro family. They do not appear in the genealogies of those colonial aristocrats presented in the appendixes, although they are members of the "new" colonial aristocracy.[22] They do not lack for social contacts with descendants of nobility, for they were schoolmates of, among others, the son (nicknamed El Chigüín) of Anastasio Somoza Debayle, and their grandfather was director of the prestigious Institute of Granada.[23] His illegitimate son was the father of the Ortega brothers, while a legitimate one, Eduardo Ortega Urbina, was minister of foreign affairs for the Somozas between 1972 and 1974.[24] Daniel and Humberto were educated by the Christian Brothers, and Daniel studied for the priesthood in the Salesian Seminary in El Salvador under Miguel Obando y Bravo, now a Cardinal and the principal mediator in Nicaragua's Civil War.[25] Due to a death in the family, the boys had to change from a private to a public school and this had negative social repercussions on them. Daniel eventually married (although not formally) Rosario Murillo, with whom he has five children.[26] Rosario is a grandniece of Rubén Darío, an intimate friend, from primary school to his deathbed, of Dr. Luis H. Debayle, father-in-law of Anastasio Somoza García.[27] Rosario, educated in England and Switzerland, eventually became the personal secretary of Pedro Joaquín Chamorro Cardenal,[28] director of the opposition newspaper *La Prensa* and archenemy of the Somozas. Today she is First Lady of Nicaragua. Such relationships do not happen by coincidence in Latin America, and they underscore the aristocratic social background of the Ortegas as well as the nature of political differentiation in Nicaraguan society.

Complications of the Nicaraguan Civil War

The Sandinistas could not have come to power without prolonged support from former Costa Rican President Carazo and last-minute backing from President Jimmy Carter of the United States, because of both material assistance and permission to use Costa Rican territory as a base against Somoza. Ironically, as soon as the Sandinista government established itself, Costa Rica again became a base, both for former Somoza supporters to start their long struggle for the recuperation of power and for the United States to attempt to contain the Managua regime within Nicaragua's borders.

When friction developed between Nicaragua on the one hand and the United States and neighboring Central American countries on the other, the Sandinistas accepted Cuban and Soviet help for their revolution. This provoked the resentment of the Nicaraguan Communist Party, which is vehemently anti-Sandinista,[29] for with the ousting of Somoza, its members felt that they had fallen into disgrace when they saw the young "clandestine groups" take command.[30] Generational professional jealousy," therefore, was the cause of their resentment. As a result of the Sandinista victory, Soviet policy for supporting foreign political movements changed significantly. Until then, aid usually went to a single communist party in each country. Beginning in 1980, however, the Soviets accepted the "focus" theories of Ernesto "Che" Guevara and Regis Debray, aimed at creating centers of guerrilla activity to promote popular uprisings. They revised their financing programs to support new Marxist groups that, like the Tupamaros in Uruguay, the Montoneros in Argentina, the M-19 in Colombia, the Cinchoneros in Honduras, and many others, had resorted to kidnapping officials of multinational corporations as well as politicians, demanding ransoms that soon became a source of funding far greater than what the Soviets had offered their traditional parties.[31]

Activity against the Sandinistas increased after 1982, and Costa Rican Social Democratic President Luis Alberto Monge Alvarez (Carazo's successor) was unable to control the use of his country's territory by the Contras. He had initially opted for neutrality to avoid involvement in the Nicaraguan issue, without losing United States economic aid for his bankrupt country. He also wanted protection against eventual Sandinista aggression, particularly because Costa Rica has no army. To underscore the importance attached to this aid, Oscar Arias Sánchez, an official Social Democratic presidential candidate during the 1986 campaign, told an interviewer that it was a shame that there were only nine comandantes. If there were ten, he quipped, Costa Rica might get more funds from the United States.[32] It was close to impossible to achieve neutrality, however, for Sandinista border aggressions (such as the assassination of civil guards in Las Crucitas and constant raids against coast guard and fishing vessels) outraged Costa Rican public opinion. Repeated incidents such as these —and boasting by Daniel Ortega to the effect that Nicaragua could conquer Costa Rica in fifteen minutes—eventually forced Monge to allow the United States to build a large military airstrip near the border separating the two countries. Translations of a few random newspaper headlines reveal the Costa Rican feeling of vulnerability: "Plan of Action against Costa Rica Reported in Managua"; "Monge Repudiates War Threat by Government of Nicaragua"; "Monge: Nicaragua Threatens Us with War."[33]

Fear in Costa Rica of a neighboring Marxist-Leninist state and constant war threats from the comandantes led to mass capital flight. Profits were not reinvested and the economy has been deteriorating at a time when the nation is deeply in debt. In addition, during these times of recession and unemployment, the steady flow of Nicaraguans fleeing from their war-torn homeland has brought in an estimated two hundred thousand refugees. The border between Costa Rica and Nicaragua is in great part the San Juan River, and it is impossible to know how many "wetbacks" have crossed it.[34] These Nicaraguan aliens represent close to a quarter of the economically active population of Costa Rica. Some thirty thousand Salvadorans have also entered the country, due to social unrest fomented largely by the Sandinista administration and Cuba. These exiles, who have brought diseases that must be controlled, are sheltered and fed by Costa Rican taxpayers, with help from the United Nations, at a time when the citizenry questions its own well-being. The Nicaraguan problem has also introduced repeated acts of terrorism, increased arms contraband, and drug trafficking on a large scale. Costa Rican public opinion, excluding the left, is strongly against the Sandinistas, and the thought of neutrality becomes meaningless and even offensive to many citizens.

Almost simultaneously with Costa Rica's involvement in the Nicaraguan conflict, Honduras became entangled as a result of swelling Contra ranks along that country's southern border. That nation was used increasingly by the United States to train its own troops as well as Honduran militia, and as a vantage point for flexing muscles in the Caribbean. As the Sandinistas continued to receive backing from the Soviet Union and Cuba, tensions increased and other nations were drawn into the conflict. With the victory of United States President Ronald Reagan in 1980, guerrillas fighting the government of El Salvador received aid from the Sandinistas, drawing that nation into the conflagration. In the early 1980s, the Palestine Liberation Organization (PLO) established several training camps in Nicaragua, and Israel became involved to counteract that measure. There were reports toward the same period that Israeli fighter bombers were shipped to Panama and sent on raiding missions against six PLO training bases in Nicaragua. Even today the PLO funds Nicaraguan, Salvadoran, Honduran, and Colombian guerrillas.[35] By the end of 1983, the Nicaraguan problem had come to include Cuba, the Soviet Union, East Germany, other Soviet bloc states, the PLO, Israel, the United States, El Salvador, Honduras, Costa Rica, and to an extent Guatemala. Many more were to follow, particularly after the organization of the Contadora and Lima groups by Mexico and more recently as a result of the Iran-Contra affair.

Border incidents between Sandinista troops on the one hand and Honduran and Costa Rican militia on the other increased in 1983. Central American nations that became involved in the conflict had different reasons for doing so, however. Regional tension kept foreign aid coming in from both the United States and the Soviet Union, among others, at levels never before reached in the area. In effect, foreign policy of Central American nations seemed programmed to maintain the situation as close as possible to open war, but without reaching that extreme. In this Central American brinkmanship,[36] there has been a lack of enthusiasm of the five presidents to put an end to the regional conflict, for all of them attach importance to economic aid given by the United States, the Soviet Union, and others as a result of the crisis. President Arias of Costa Rica, who was awarded a Nobel Prize in August 1987 for helping draft the peace project, recently complained that no one complied with the treaty. He blamed the Costa Rican Congress (where his own party has a majority) for his country's noncompliance; this reflects popular skepticism over the plan and particularly over the intentions of Managua.[37] Honduras, like Costa Rica, recognized the important material benefits obtained from the United States in exchange for use of its territory as a base and has permitted the Contras operating within her boundaries to continue receiving aid from the United States.[38] Guatemala's complications have been with Mexico (not Central America) over some forty-five thousand Guatemalans who have sought refuge in that country. For this reason Guatemala has remained aloof from the Central American problem. El Salvador is the only country that would like to see an end to the problem because of the guerrillas, supported by Cuba and Nicaragua, attempting to overthrow its government.

Mexico saw in the Isthmian imbroglio an opportunity to satisfy some of her own interests. That country has long vied with Venezuela for regional leadership and has wanted to have the United States use her auspices to solve crises in Latin America. She has had problems with Fidel Castro and fears that he will mobilize guerrillas to capitalize on her deteriorating social and economic conditions, which come out vividly in works such as *Los hijos de Sánchez*, by Oscar Lewis.[39] Along with Venezuela, Mexico has had vested interests and strong political leverage in the area, for since 1981 those two countries have supplied all Central America with petroleum at a very low cost.

Mexico was aware that other countries also had problems related to the Isthmian question. Panama feared that in an eventual outbreak of hostilities with Nicaragua, the military weakness of Costa Rica could lead to armed intervention by the United States, endangering Panamanian sovereignty over the canal obtained through the Carter-Torrijos treaties. Colombia faced problems with the M-19 guerrillas controlled by Fidel Castro in addition to disputes with Nicaragua over a number of small islands in the Caribbean.

In 1983, Mexico adroitly orchestrated these divergent interests of Panama, Colombia, and Venezuela with her own, with the justification of ending Nicaraguan border incidents with Costa Rica and Honduras, as well as of controlling Sandinista support for Salvadoran guerrillas. When a complaint against Nicaragua was taken by Costa Rica to the Organization of American States (OAS), Mexico asked Costa Rica not to acknowledge any OAS reply but to request instead direct intervention of Mexico in Central America. Mexico simultaneously called a meeting of foreign affairs ministers of Venezuela, Colombia, and Panama on the Island of Contadora (in Panama), and with no previous consultations with either the Central Americans or the OAS, the "Contadora" group officiously announced its intention of solving the Isthmian problem.[40] Latin America, the United States, and Europe applauded but were unaware of two considerations: 1) the four countries in the self-appointed group had different reasons and priorities to seek involvement, over and above the interests of the individual Central American nations, and 2) the Isthmian republics have always regarded Mexico with suspicion and mistrust.

Nicaragua accepted Contadora mediation immediately, but that was not the case with the other Central American countries, which felt that the group favored the comandantes because it proposed nonviable methods of inspecting and controlling levels of armament. Daniel Ortega and the Latin American left attacked the United States for hindering Contadora's efforts, and Mexico experienced frustration over not being able to impose its will on the Central American republics, particularly through the Costa Rican PLN, with which its official party, the Partido Revolucionario Institucional (PRI) maintained close relations. Mexico enlisted the assistance of both the Sandinista comandantes and the Socialist International (SI), an association of some fifty Socialist parties that has been playing a growing role in Latin American politics by taking aggressive stances against the United States. The SI has increasingly supported insurgent movements against El Salvador and has sought to legitimate the Sandinistas before the world.[41]

The result of this stalemate was that on the occasion of the inauguration of Alan García as president of Peru, the Contadora group met with him and with representatives of Argentina, Brazil, and Uruguay. They alleged that any prolongation of the Central American conflict risked military intervention by the United States, and the four new countries formed the Grupo de Apoyo or Grupo de Lima, for the purpose of backing Contadora. Critics attack the Oscar Arias 1987 peace plan for giving the Sandinistas time to consolidate their political and military positions and assert that Ortega has done nothing to comply with his obligations in the pact. They regard the prize as a political checkmate of United States foreign policy by the SI. The outcome that can be foreseen is a continuation of the diplomatic conflict between the United States, the Soviet Union and Cuba, the Central American republics, and the SI (now represented by Contadora and the Lima group).

The Central American conflict is a violent eruption of economic and political differentiation within the Nicaraguan ruling class, as well as an extension of that struggle, recently complicated by drug trafficking, into El Salvador, Honduras, and Costa Rica. These economic and political disparities explain the appearance of important parties, account for inequitable wealth distribution within and among families and classes, and clarify reasons for acceptance or rejection of some family lines by others of their own kin.

How the situation has developed in these small societies requires an analysis of problems involved after the Conquest for both Spanish colonial aristocracy and the crown in creating an American nobility. Few Spaniards were aware of the complications that would arise from mixing their own blood and values with those of a wide variety of native civilizations with different customs, languages, and religions. The mixing of so many cultures presented serious obstacles, not the least of which was prejudice. To this must be added the hate and envy felt by the conquered Indians, as well as rivalries among conquerors, priests, and others. From frictions and successes arose distinct national traits and value differences in the five territories. Values are reflected in institutions and in emotions and, given the enduring nature of conflict between Central American nations, it seems fitting to explore the ways they are expressed in regional literature, religion, education, and politics. The second part of this book is called "Power and Institutions: Shaping Isthmian Societies." The birth of power centers and the formation of societies through mixtures of Spanish, Indian, and other cultures, are dealt with in chapters 3 and 4. Chapter 5 dwells on value differences.

PART II

Power and Institutions:
Shaping Isthmian Societies

CHAPTER 3

Conquistadors and Nobility in the Making of Elites

A Proposition of Marriage

1530

Arias and Captain Morales and El Mancebo came close to the house on a hillside where the cousin waited, and seeing them tired in the heat of Castilla del Oro, the cousin did not know whether they were dead or alive. They embraced and continued past fences and walls of olden times and entered the house.

"Thou art in thy home; rest and then we shall talk," said the cousin.

Rested after the misery of the long voyage from Choluteca, they washed and ate. They rested for a full day, curing their wounds and those of the horses.

At night the cousin asked what tidings they brought. Arias raised the wine to his lips and said that he brought a message:

"Alvarado wishes to propose to you a matrimonial alliance." He looked not at the face of the cousin, for both knew of Alvarado's connivances. That was something they feared of his proposition.

They sipped their wine and looked at the cousin, Pedrarias, for they also knew of his misdoings. His daughter Isabel María first betrothed Balboa, whom he had beheaded after Balboa discovered the southern sea. He did the same to Hernández de Córdoba once Córdoba pacified Nicaragua. Isabel María then wed Contreras, who also suffered at the hands of the ruthless cousin.

The cousin was annoyed and said that Alvarado wanted to usurp his jurisdictions in Nicaragua and Costa Rica and control Central America, and that pacts of marriage for this purpose did not please him. He had more influence in court than Alvarado.[1]

This tale concerning a proposition of marriage is a starting point for understanding the birth, development, and expansion of power centers in Central and probably Latin America. None of these people or events are fictitious.[2] Arias (Gaspar Arias Dávila) was conquistador of Guatemala, and the cousin was a first cousin, Pedrarias Dávila, conquistador and governor of Panama. Conquistador Gaspar de Morales was also a cousin of Pedrarias, and Pedrarias el Mancebo was a nephew. Francisco Hernández de Córdoba was conquistador of Nicaragua; the discoverer of the Southern Sea, called La Mar del Sur (the Pacific Ocean), was Vasco Núñez de Balboa; and Rodrigo de Contreras was governor of Nicaragua. The daughter of Pedrarias who married Balboa and then Contreras was Isabel Arias de Peñalosa, although both men are said to have married a María, whose full name could well have been Isabel María, which is quite common. We do not know the name of the other daughter whom Alvarado (Pedro de Alvarado Contreras, conquistador, adelantado, and governor of Guatemala) wished to wed. Alvarado was first married to Francisca de la Cueva, who died from fever shortly after landing at Veracruz. He later returned to Spain and married her sister Beatriz. There is disagreement on his union with Luisa Xicoténcatl, with some calling it an informal arrangement instead of a true Christian marriage.

The story is significant for contemporary Latin American societies, and perhaps the most important aspect, besides the proposition of marriage, concerns the ties of kinship among conquistadors. Both Pedrarias Dávila and Pedro de Alvarado Contreras were members of Spanish nobility, and in those American territories that fell under their jurisdiction their descendants assumed positions of high status. That was accomplished through the institution of matrimony, which influenced many economic, social, and political aspects of modern Latin America. For this reason our story begins with an account of "How the conquistadors came to the newly discovered lands, with the valiant Hernando Cortés as captain who in due course of time became Marqués del Valle."[3]

Of Things Not Told in the Chronicles of Conquest

And if it had to be told and brought to memory, part by part, the heroic deeds of conquest by each of the valiant captains and strong soldiers who

were there from the beginning, it would be necessary to write a great book to
say things as they should be said, by a very famous chronicler with another
clearer eloquence and rhetoric than mine.[4]

These words of Bernal Díaz del Castillo indicate that in spite of all
that has been written on the bold deeds of conquistadors, not everything
has been said. The exploits of Hernando Cortés in Mexico and Francisco
Pizarro in Peru have been well covered in the pages of history, and the same
can be said of the conquest of Guatemala, El Salvador, and Honduras by
Pedro de Alvarado and his brothers, of Nicaragua by Francisco Hernández
de Córdoba, and of Costa Rica by Juan Vázquez de Coronado. Significant
achievements of the conquistadors, such as their establishment of zones
of influence (which eventually determined territorial limits of the modern nations), have generally been overlooked. Another consideration often
ignored is their role in the defense of strategic Spanish provinces such as
the Isthmian ones. Once they became encomenderos,[5] in exchange for certain concessions from the crown and in an effort to establish a traditional
society in which the arms profession would be the most prestigious, they
organized feudal armies that served military duty when needed.[6] Equally
important (yet unnoticed) were matrimonial ties among families of those
adventurers and their descendants (see appendix 7). In the following pages
the story of conquest is taken up once again, with the hope of casting new
light on the formation of power centers.

The conquest of Central America was carried out from three areas by
many heads of expeditions: from Panama north, from the Dominican Republic west, and from Mexico south. Thrusts into the Isthmus were led
led by rival conquistadors, in atmospheres of deceit, treason, hate, envy,
and, above all, greed.[7]

The first military incursions originated in Panama and were led by Pedro
Arias de Avila (Pedrarias Dávila), who in 1514, thanks to intrigues against
Vasco Núñez de Balboa, was named governor of the Darien territory. Such
an honor was due to his (and his wife's) high noble rank as well as to his
friendship with the bishop of Burgos, for these connections offset opposition from his enemies. His nicknames, "El Galán" (the Gallant) and "El
Justador" (the Jouster), underscore his military prowess. He was a brother
of the Count of Puñonrostro as well as grandson of Diego Arias de Avila
(Diegarias Dávila), chief auditor of the Kingdom of Castille. His wife,
Isabel de Bobadilla y Peñalosa, was a niece of the Marquise of Moya.[8] Upon
his designation by the crown as governor of the legendary New World
province, members of the Spanish nobility enthusiastically responded to
his call to volunteer for an expedition to Darien. In Seville some two thou-

sand offered their services.[9] The names of some are worth noting, for not a few would eventually go down in the annals of the Conquest: Gonzalo Fernández de Oviedo, Bernal Díaz del Castillo, and Gaspar de Espinoza. The wife of Pedrarias also went along.[10]

With the founding of the Province of Panama in 1518, Pedrarias appointed Gaspar de Espinoza as captain general of that territory. Through his subordinates, he gradually extended his zone of influence to the north, where he met with resistance. Opposition initially came from Gil González Dávila, who left Hispaniola (Santo Domingo) in 1522 to explore the Pacific coast from the Bay of Fonseca to Cabo Blanco (on the peninsula of Nicoya in Costa Rica). Hostility spread in 1524, when Pedro de Alvarado, a lieutenant of Cortés, penetrated Guatemala from Mexico. Pedrarias, jealous of these intruders, sent Francisco Hernández de Córdoba to conquer and settle Nicaragua. That same year Hernández de Córdoba founded the city of Granada. Pedrarias hastened to Nicaragua (in 1526), leaving Pedro de los Ríos as governor of La Castilla del Oro (Panama).[11]

The hegemony of Hernando Cortés expanded as his captains made their way south from Mexico. In 1522, Charles V created the Captaincy General of Guatemala because Cortés had been unable to govern the vast territory of Mexico and the Central American Isthmus.[12] Alvarado, who was to marry Francisca de la Cueva de Ubeda (daughter of a family with close ties to the court),[13] was named governor of this new political division, thanks to support from Cortés. That territory extended from Chiapas to the current border between Costa Rica and Panama.[14] This led to confusion: Alvarado was governor of Guatemala, which extended south to Panama; Pedrarias was governor of Darién (which ran north to Costa Rica) but had penetrated Guatemala's territory and conquered Nicaragua, where he had settled to live;[15] and in 1526, Diego López de Salcedo was named governor of Honduras.[16] The crown established boundaries for Panama, Nicaragua, and Honduras, to impede the governors of those provinces from usurping each other's territorial rights,[17] but in spite of that, López de Salcedo invaded Nicaragua after his term as governor of Honduras was extended. Upon his return to Honduras, his municipal councilmen imprisoned and replaced him with Vasco de Herrera as lieutenant governor. Given this situation, the crown designated Pedrarias as governor of Nicaragua, putting an end to his disputes with Alvarado over control of that territory. It is said that the lengthy conflict between conquistadors created unrest among the Indians, to the point that for two years men did not sleep with their women in order to avoid giving sons as slaves to the Spaniards.[18]

The conquest of Central America was characterized by confusion, for zones of influence contained contradictions.[19] After the death of Pedrarias in León, Nicaragua, in 1531, his son-in-law (Rodrigo de Contreras) was named governor of Nicaragua. In 1535, Francisco de Montejo, who had been ordered to conquer the land discovered by Hernández de Córdoba in Yucatán and Cozumel, asked the crown to unite Yucatán and Honduras under one governorship. To prevent this, Jorge de Alvarado Contreras (brother of Pedro) sent Cristóbal de la Cueva (a cousin of Pedro's wife) into Honduras. The crown then fixed more precise boundaries.[20] Further machinations in Honduras by Pedro de Alvarado, a constant source of friction among conquistadors and the clergy,[21] led Montejo (upon being named governor of that territory) to annul allotments of land and Indians made by Alvarado. Montejo conquered Yucatán and arranged for the appointment of his own son as adelantado (frontier governor) of that territory.[22] This stage of Isthmian history ended with a settlement. Chronicler Gonzalo Fernández de Oviedo speaks of "a certain trick of convenience" between Alvarado and Montejo: "There were discrepancies between both adelantados, who had agreed that Montejo would leave the governorship of Honduras to Alvarado, so that it could be joined with that of Guatemala. At the same time, Alvarado would cede Suchimilco [in New Spain] and Ciudad Real of Chiapas [which belonged to Guatemala] to Montejo."[23]

The conquest of the Isthmus was distinct from that of Mexico and Peru in several ways.

> *For [the] expedition [to Mexico] there were many debates, because certain noblemen wanted as captain Vasco Porcallo, a relative of the Count of Feria; others wanted Agustín Bermúdez or Antonio Velázquez Borrego, or Bernardino Velázquez, relatives of the governor of Cuba [Diego Velázquez]. Two important representatives of Diego Velázquez made a secret arrangement with a noble called Hernando Cortés, and it was in this manner that Cortés was given command. Cortés was of noble lineage from four sides: from Cortés, from Pizarro, from Monroy, and from Altamirano.*[24]

Bernal Díaz del Castillo makes it clear that in the conquest of Mexico there was but one leader, Cortés. The conquest of Central America, on the other hand, had many rival leaders.[25] Mexico and Peru had defined objectives, which were the kingdoms of Montezuma and Atahualpa.[26] Once Cortés destroyed Tenochtitlán (Mexico City), the conquest of central Mexico and the regions under Aztec control was practically over, although the territory as a whole was not completely pacified for a long time. Central America, with its welter of smaller aboriginal polities, had to be subdued piecemeal. The defeat of the Quiché, followed by that of the Cakchiquels and

Tzutuhils, was only the beginning for Alvarado. He still had to conquer the Tzendals and Tzotzils of Chiapas; the Mams, Pokomams, Ixils, and Kekchis of Guatemala; the Pipils and Lencas of the Pacific coast of El Salvador; and all this without counting Honduras and other territories with smaller tribes.[27] Conquistadors from Panama found similar situations in Nicaragua and Costa Rica.

Birth and Expansion of the Dynasty of Conquistadors

Kinship among conquistadors was strengthened after the Conquest by bonds of marriage among their families. Bernal Díaz del Castillo speaks of a relationship of noble blood between Hernando Cortés Pizarro and Francisco Pizarro, an illegitimate son.[28] Pedro de Alvarado was accompanied by five brothers in the conquest of Guatemala[29] and Pizarro by four in the Peruvian campaign.[30] Initial clashes among conquistadors—not a rational process of subdivision—established zones of influence of the first ruling classes in Central America. This may explain why El Salvador has no outlet to the Caribbean Sea and Honduras such a small coast on the Pacific Ocean.[31]

As conquistadors consolidated control over their territories, they continued trying to extend their hegemony. When Pedro de Alvarado was sent by Cortés to conquer Guatemala, he left his brother Gonzalo in charge as lieutenant governor. Gonzalo's greed, however, led to failure.[32] Pedro later attempted to seek a share of Pizarro's fortunes in Peru and appointed another brother, Jorge, as lieutenant governor.[33] Jorge's second wife was Luisa de Estrada, daughter of the governor of New Spain. Their son, Jorge de Alvarado Estrada, who settled in Mexico, married a daughter of Angel de Villafañe, conquistador of Florida, Mexico, and Guatemala.[34] A son of that marriage, Jorge de Alvarado Villafañe, became governor of Honduras; a grandson, Gil de Alvarado Benavides, settled in Costa Rica, where he was appointed lieutenant governor and founded the Alvarado family in that territory.[35] The Alvarados in Costa Rica, then, are of the same lineage as those in Guatemala, Nicaragua, and Mexico.[36] In 1658, a son of Gil, José de Alvarado y Vera Sotomayor, married Petronila de Retes y Vázquez de Coronado, great-grandniece of the conquistador.[37] When Pedro de Alvarado died, his brother-in-law, Francisco de la Cueva, was chosen as his successor.[38] When he refused the post, Pedro's widow, Beatriz, was made governor.[39] These relationships are also shown in appendix 7.

The importance of these unions for the ruling class can be seen through the marriage between José de Alvarado y Vera Sotomayor and Petronila de Retes y Vázquez de Coronado, which has generated ten presidents and forty-six congressmen in Costa Rica since Independence, to say nothing of many other public figures.[40] Something similar happened in the family of Vázquez de Coronado, who was the chief magistrate *(alcalde mayor)* in Honduras, Nicaragua, and Costa Rica, where he was appointed first adelantado (to be discussed shortly). Like the descendants of Jorge de Alvarado, Vázquez's kin settled throughout the Isthmus. Gonzalo (his son) and Diego (his grandson) were second and third adelantados of Costa Rica; other grandchildren (Juan and Isabel) went to Guatemala; and a daughter of Diego, to Nicaragua. Descendants of Vázquez spread over the Isthmus and, as can be seen in appendix 2, generated many presidents of Nicaragua and Costa Rica after Independence. Another example of a family of conquistadors that extended its power is that of Pedrarias. When he was governor of Nicaragua, his daughter María married Rodrigo de Contreras (a noble from Segovia), who succeeded Pedrarias as governor. Contreras was removed from office by a son-in-law, Pedro de los Ríos, who replaced him. Gonzalo Arias Dávila, a relative of Pedrarias, married another daughter of Contreras and was appointed chief magistrate of León, Nicaragua.[41] Other examples of intermarriage among conquerors abound. Alonso Calero, discoverer of the San Juan River between Costa Rica and Nicaragua and of Lake Nicaragua, was father-in-law of Hernán Sánchez de Badajoz, conquistador of Costa Rica.[42] Families like Alvarado, Arias, and Vázquez were closely related to each other and marital ties between their progeny have continued to this day.

Columbus, Alvarado, and Vázquez de Coronado, as well as his son and grandson, were given the title of adelantado, yet Cortés and Pizarro were not. Although adelantado has been considered as a title ranking between duke and marquis,[43] its meaning was quite broad. During the Middle Ages, an adelantado was named by the king to represent the crown as head administrator of a frontier province in civil and military matters. He was also a judge. With time, the position fell into disuse and became an honorary title bestowed on people of lesser status to bolster their prestige. Thus Ferrant Mateos, a mayor (alcalde) of Seville, was named adelantado, and the first Spanish governors sent to America held that title, as did Christopher Columbus. His discovery of America, however, came at the very end of the Reconquista when the title was obviously on the wane.[44] By the time of the feats of Cortés and Pizarro (well into the sixteenth century), the title had lost currency. Cortés and Pizarro received only the title of marqués (lower than adelantado). Much later during that century, it was revived in

America for other conquerors such as Juan Vázquez de Coronado and his descendants.

The nature of conquistadors, who have been called egotists, traitors, greedy, and cruel, also bears attention. Bernal Díaz del Castillo, who deemed himself to be one of them, averred that no men won more kingdoms and that they were very spirited. He was convinced that he had served his majesty like a good soldier and lamented that toward the end of his life poverty prevented him from going to Castille before his majesty to ask for help that he felt he well deserved.[45] The Peruvian historian Inca Garcilaso de la Vega, who like Díaz del Castillo personally knew many conquistadors, presented deeper insights into their personality. He described them as men with a thirst for gold, yet he qualified this by adding that they were not content to live in tranquility off the sweat of the Indians. They prided themselves in serving, and when they received money out of necessity, they considered it a loan, with an obligation to repay. Garcilaso de la Vega depicted conquistadors as a lineage of nobility who knew how to distinguish between money and idleness, and concluded (as a Castillian refrain goes) that the only thing that suited gentlemen like them was a life of struggle and effort.[46]

Others cast doubt on the nature of all early settlers, including conquistadors. The sixteenth-century historian Gonzalo Fernández de Oviedo commented that he had come across many men speaking different languages, and most were greedy yet restrained. There were more idiots than wise men, and more plebeians than nobles. In the beginning, he added, for every person of noble origin, ten humble people came to the New World. Fernando Columbus, son of Christopher, underscored that most Spaniards on Hispaniola were of low social status and feared punishment as delinquents, to which he added that laborers and vagabonds disembarked from the caravelles. Pedro Mártir de Anglería wrote that Columbus had said that the Spaniards he took with him were more given to being lazy and to sleeping than to working, more prone to sedition and having fun than to seeking peace and tranquility. For Columbus's first trip, "the monarchs ordered suspension of queries involving criminal doings and misdoings" of those who accompanied him, until after their return. The third trip was inaugurated with a pardon for all who had committed crimes, provided they remained on the island of Hispaniola, at their own expense and for a certain length of time, doing whatever the admiral asked.[47] One point of confusion concerning the nature of early Spanish settlers has to do with the number of criminals involved: what proportion were delinquents? Another has to do with the relationship between them and nobles who enjoyed immunity from degrading punishments.[48] Could a noble be a criminal? What was the meaning of "the moral value of the victims of justice"? Bishop Fray Bartolomé de Las Casas added to the dilemma when he stated that he knew some of those on the island of Hispaniola who did not have ears and always took them to be men of much good.[49]

Rivalry among chroniclers, which led them to mutual accusations of lying, makes it all the more difficult to judge the conquistadors. Many scholars who have pored through their lengthy manuscripts are prone to regard some with higher esteem than others. For reasons such as these, it seems necessary to attempt to evaluate the conquistadors and their achievements in the light of the fifteenth-century conflict between European monarchs and their nobilities. It is clear that conquistadors benefited highly from that contention and, thanks to it, became the backbone of the new societies in Hispanic America.

Conquistadors in the New Societies

The development of European societies was characterized by constant struggles between crown and aristocracy, where each sought rights at the expense of the others. One of the most noteworthy occurred in England in 1215, when the nobility, under force of arms, made the crown approve the Magna Carta, thus securing rights that set an important precedent for the future development of English government. For Spain, the issue was taken to the New World, where its most serious outbreaks took place in Central America, under the leadership of the sons of Rodrigo Contreras after he was deposed as governor of Nicaragua. They elaborated a plan to recuperate his lands and his rights by conquering Peru; had they succeeded, Hernando Contreras would have been proclaimed king. The conspiracy was organized in Granada, Nicaragua, but it failed.[50]

In Spain, in the late fifteenth century, after seven centuries of internal chaos and war against the Moors, three significant events occurred: one was the unification of a vast national territory in 1469 as a result of the marriage of Ferdinand of Aragon and Isabel of Castille (the Catholic Kings); another, as a consequence of that union, was the defeat and expulsion of the Moors in the battle of Granada in 1492; and finally, in the euphoria of that same year, came the discovery of the New World by the Admiral of the Ocean Sea. During those years the power of the nobility had been increasing, and in the eyes of the new monarchs, it was excessive. That rivalry, aggravated by the factious spirit of the aristocracy, led to general disorder in the new kingdom.[51] Initial efforts of the crown to gain control were aimed at undermining the nobility. Monarchs in other countries tried to imitate them, but nowhere was the effort more successful than in Spain. The Catholic Kings ceased summoning nobility to sessions of the *cortes* (parliament), where taxation was discussed.[52] Initially this seemed insignificant because the nobility was exempt from taxes and had never shown interest in that legislative body. By not attending those sessions, however, they unintentionally lost the right to voice opinions in matters pertaining to paying tribute. That contrasts with the firm attitude of English aristocracy in 1215. In addition, the Catholic Kings promoted men of humble background to the highest posts of government, not only to humiliate nobility[53] but also to recognize and use talent in Spanish society. The best example is Archbishop Francisco Ximénez de Cisneros, of humble social origins, who came to rule Spain temporarily. The aristocracy lost prestige when it was forced to accept people of inferior social standing as equals.[54] The discovery of America in the midst of this dispute between crown and nobility inadvertently provided the crown with an advantage over monarchs engaged in similar disputes throughout the rest of Europe. To encourage rapid colonization it bestowed members of the nobility who (under certain conditions) settled in the New World with exclusive access to positions of power.[55]

Spanish citizens who established their homes in America acquired the status of *hijosdalgo de solar conocido* (literally, sons of somebody of a known household). *Hidalguía de pobladuría* (nobility of settlement) was awarded to individuals who built a house, lived in it, and could prove their cleanliness of blood *(limpieza de sangre)*, which meant absence of blood of Moors, Jews, heretics, or people punished under laws of the Inquisition. Citizens who met these requirements could eventually enjoy honors and privileges of nobles in Spain.[56] *Hidalgos de pobladuría* in Spain had been plain citizens, but a caballero had been a noble. The foregoing in no way means that all Spaniards who settled in America were automatically made nobles. That status could be acquired only by members of a special class of settlers, carefully distinguished from laborers *(labradores)* and merchants *(mercaderes)*.[57] In Spain, only after three generations did *hidalguía de pobladuría* become "nobility by blood," but through it the second-born sons of noble families who ventured into the New World could attain a status that eventually allowed their families to become nobility.

Hidalgos de pobladuría were designated *beneméritos* (meritorious people). Their three fundamental obligations were to cultivate the land, to build homes, and to serve (with no excuses for refusing to do so) in public offices for which they might be named. Among their privileges were those of being favored with posts in the royal service, of having exclusive rights to receive land and Indian grants, of aspiring for encomiendas (see chapter 1, note 5), and of being given preference to hold the office of alcalde ordinario (mayor).[58] An early sign of the importance of conquistadors in the new social system occurred in 1584, when the Audiencia de los Confines, a court in Guatemala with jurisdiction over the Isthmus, ordered that in matters pertaining to encomiendas, conquistadores should receive preference over other settlers.[59]

Noble status could be acquired almost until Independence,[60] but in spite of rules governing admission to that class, a competent authority to approve candidates for nobility in the New World was lacking. Not even the crown, bent on implanting the Spanish social system in all of its colonies, could decide on contentious matters in the domain of the nobility.[61] It avoided the issue but did outline certain prerequisites for settlers to acquire noble status. The most significant one was that they prove blood ties with a woman descended from a conquistador.[62] Hispanic American nobility, then, established its own order, based on the lineage of conquistadors. The Conquest ended with the Isthmus firmly in the hands of a group of conquistadors, many of them wealthy, who exercised power in their respective domains. Once that episode was over, colonists came to settle, and many married women descended from conquistadors. Their offspring were entitled to enter the nobility.

Simultaneously, other types of blood ties began to develop. They involved *mestizaje,* or the mixing of Indian or later Negro and Spanish blood. Although the formation of ruling classes and mestizaje went into making up the new societies, this work is more concerned with the former process. Spanish author José María Pemán may have wished to express commoners' feelings towards nobility in a sonnet titled "The Spanish Noble." After describing his protagonist with scorn as a haughty, arrogant, and boastful person, he concludes that all he strove for throughout life was to have (if anything was left of his squanderings) a tomb that would read: "He was born to be much and was nothing."[63]

CHAPTER 4

The New American Nobility

"In matters pertaining to genealogical trees, it is safer to beat around the bush than to go to the roots of the matter."

These words could well express the ambiguous and disconcerting situation of Spanish citizens who followed in the footsteps of the conquistadors in search of wealth, encouraged in many instances by the promise of being admitted to the ranks of the new American nobility.[1] They were attracted to the New World for reasons that vary, but in general it was to "correct their bad peninsular luck."[2]

The conquistador, on the other hand, had come in search of an adventure for gentlemen, and this could bring him wealth or maybe a title. "He had surrounded himself with dark-skinned women who cooked for him, dressed him, cared for him, and shared his bed, and it was only the arrival of the white woman that drew him away from this paradise." From the beginning, the presence of the Spanish woman had a regulating effect, yet marriage to a white woman could bestow prestige upon the enterprising conqueror. Any encomendero who did not marry after a certain time lost his Indians. Furthermore, since no Spaniard married to an Indian could hold official posts or be member of the *cabildo* (municipal council),[3] the ambitious sought white wives. They eagerly pursued the daughters and sisters of their comrades, and these amorous episodes gave rise to the clans of conquistadors that came to form the backbone of ruling groups in colonial societies.[4]

Most of the first settlers held no social rank and had to incorporate themselves into a system that varied according to their background and behavior. Their conduct was affected by a number of factors: the hatred that male Indians felt toward them; the privileges that they, as white men, could offer Indian women;[5] the advantage of those born in Spain over those born in America; the stabilizing effect of white women on their own activities; and the distribution of Indians, mineral wealth, and good lands. Blacks soon followed and complicated the social order. Where there was an abundance of native women, the sons sired by Spaniards enjoyed fewer privileges than mestizos born in communities with small Indian populations. The offspring of these unions had to contend with prejudices, resentments, and conflicting values emanating from the Conquest.

Indian Attitudes towards the Spaniards

Indian attitudes towards the Spaniards ranged from hate, envy, and resentment to fear, scorn, and disrespect. They were, after all, the conquered people. One factor that contributed heavily toward the formation of their attitudes was the reduction of their populations during the first years of colonial rule, by disease as well as by lasting abuses committed by their conquerors. Reliable demographic information concerning indigenous civilizations from Conquest through much of the colonial period is difficult to find due to the tendency of chroniclers and conquistadors to exaggerate as well as to the practice of clergymen of counting only those Indians who accepted baptism. Members of the church were inclined to dramatize eloquently the cruelty of the first colonists, simply because it befitted the nature of their own mission, and all parties had a penchant for overstating the flourishing nature of newly conquered lands.[6] The decline in the indigenous colonial population of Central America was instrumental in the formation of the natives' attitudes towards their conquerors.

Estimates of population for the Isthmus from southern Mexico to northern Panama around the time of Conquest vary widely and run from two and a quarter million to five and even six million. Three-quarters of a century later, other assessments placed the Isthmian figure at slightly under one-half million, indicating a significant population depletion. Numbers seem to be more difficult to ascertain as one proceeds south from Guatemala, and while figures for each territory are subject to debate, they serve to indicate that initial populations were large but diminished dramatically in each case during the early years of the colonial period.[7] Thus the tax-paying Indians in Verapaz, Guatemala, dropped from twelve thousand in 1544 to less than two thousand in 1590. In Honduras (including the entire territory), the native population went from four hundred thousand in 1524 to less than five thousand in 1590. In Nicaragua it diminished from six hundred thousand tax-paying Indians in 1520 to around six thousand by 1570;[8] in Costa Rica, from an estimated one hundred thousand in 1564 to less than fifteen thousand by 1611.[9] Throughout the Isthmus, such decimations took place within roughly one-half a century, but they were not limited to Central America. To the north, in Mexico, the indigenous population fell from over twenty-five million in 1519 to a little over a million one century later in 1605; to the south, in Colombia (which at the time included Panama), it dropped from fifteen thousand tax-paying Quimbayas in 1539 to sixty-nine individuals in 1628.[10]

One reaction by the Indians to this dismaying situation can be sensed in their references to Spaniards as barbarians, savages, monkeys, and swine. Heinrich Heine's testimonial concerning Hernando Cortés first depicts him as a man with laurels on his head and then concludes that Cortés was nothing more than the caudillo of brigands.[11]

In Central America, nothing is more eloquent on Pedro de Alvarado than the Mayan book *El Popol Vuh* (The Book of Counsel), which extolls the virtues of Gucumatz and Cotuhá, two Quiché Kings endowed with the ability to foresee war, death, and famine. With the arrival of the Spaniards under Alvarado, they were hanged, thus putting an end to the Quiché.[12] The Chilean poet Pablo Neruda emphasizes the barbarity of the Conquest by depicting Conquistador Pedro de Alvarado as a despot who "on his hardened pace toward new captaincies" razed dwellings; pillaged; enslaved, ravaged, and killed Indian men, women, and children, and treated religions with abuse and contempt.[13]

The bitterness of the Indian toward the Conquest and colonization was pronounced and contributed strongly to the formation of his values. In fact his resentment is reflected by some Spaniards. An example is the will of Conquistador Sierra de Leguizamo (written in 1589 in Cuzco, Peru), in which he attempts to explain to the crown his feelings of guilt over the way his own people had treated the Incas.[14] He comments that at the time of the arrival of the white man, the Inca sovereigns governed their kingdoms in a way that commanded respect without conducing to "vice, laziness, or adultery" and remarks that the crown forcefully divested them of their power to obligate them to accept Christianity. In addition, it confiscated their lands, and the Europeans set evil examples through thievery and lascivious doings. Leguizmo begs God to forgive him for having been part of it all and urges his majesty to remedy the situation to "discharge his own conscience." Another Spaniard, Fray Bernardino de Sahagún, wrote that the Indians had been so maltreated that they were unrecognizable, adding that although they were considered to be barbarians of little worth, they were indeed law-abiding people who were far ahead of other nations that considered themselves adept at governing.[15]

Such observations and opinions vary depending on the pre-Columbian civilization, but they are largely the same throughout the continent. They reveal the sadness and desolation of the brutal Conquest for the Aztecs, the Mayas, the Incas, and other native American peoples. A consequence was the birth of new values. The sentiment of the Mexican Indian at the end of the deplorable event shows this:

Weep, my friends,
understand
   that with these happenings
   we have lost
   the mexicatl nation.

Neruda expresses the sadness of a conquest that razed everything in its path, and laments that from the remains only fragments can be collected, "like seashells, abandoned by the waves of time on the beaches of history."[16]

Colonists who followed the conquistadors had to deal with natives whose reactions had been forged by a variety of negative emotions, and the configuration of new societies began with the mixing of their populations. They entered into many types of relationships ranging from formal matrimony to concubinage[17] to affairs in which the conquistador treated his conquered subjects with arrogance. From the very outset, Spaniards were guided by a sense of superiority over Indians, whose services they considered an evident right, and had no scruples about taking advantage of Indian women. They would not treat them as equals.[18] The mestizo was a product of these unions, and he encountered contradictory values and emotions.

Race and Prejudice

Many have regarded the mixing of Spanish and Indian blood as an effect of a simple situation: the lack of white women. The problem is far more complex, for it led to the development of a peculiar class system and to racial discrimination. The whiteness of the Spaniard attracted Indian women because it entailed economic and political advantages for their

offspring. Children born of unions between the two enjoyed greater prestige and more privileges (exemption from taxation, for example) than the
progeny of two Indians.[19] The offspring of a noble Indian mother and an
important Spanish father sometimes achieved prominence. Furthermore,
he had certain advantages in Indian society and could even overcome social
barriers among whites.[20] Indian women who became concubines of Spaniards, however, faced serious problems with their own men,[21] worsening
an already strained relationship between the two races.

   Although it was difficult for a Spaniard to wed someone considered
socially inferior, from the beginning of the colonial period the crown
attempted to stimulate matrimony between Spaniards because it helped
them maintain their status.[22] In 1538, a royal decree in Guatemala ordered
that all holders of encomiendas marry within three years or surrender their
Indians to married settlers.[23] This, to an extent, satisfied the desires of the
crown, in spite of the tendency of white colonists to continue cohabita-
tion with Indian women.[24] An anecdote is told concerning the return from
Spain of Pedro de Alvarado with his new wife, Beatriz de la Cueva Villacreces, and twenty-one young damsels of "fine lineage" for the purpose
of marrying them to his lieutenants. He offered a reception and one of
his comrades overheard two of the women conversing behind a folding
screen: "Don Pedro makes us a bad gift with his old and run-down conquistadors, with scars on their faces, some without arms, some without
legs." "Do not worry about that," quipped the other. "They are wealthy
encomenderos, and even if they are old and decrepit, they will soon die
and leave us as rich widows, free to seek young and gallant husbands." The
conquistador promptly went home and returned with the Indian woman
with whom he lived, and when Don Pedro introduced everyone for the
occasion, the conquistador said: "May my chief keep his beautiful Spanish
ladies. I am happy with my Indian woman who has given me children who,
although mestizos, are my very own, and she cares for me without praying
for my death, but rather wishing me a long life." With these words he left
in search of a priest to legitimate his mestizo children.[25]

   Discrimination between races increased significantly, and toward the
end of the colonial period it became intense in Central America and elsewhere.[26] The best indication of its existence in Spanish colonies appears in
debates during the constituent assembly in Cádiz in 1810. Minutes of the
meetings reveal lengthy discussions on representation of overseas provinces as well as on social and racial discrimination, and the sticky question of biological equality arose. Another matter discussed was whether
Hispanic American blacks could be Spanish citizens.[27] These prejudices

suggest a class system in which color played a significant role, in which a political and economic barrier separated those who ruled from the others. The mixture of races is confusing and requires simplification. The following interpretation is a starting point: "These are not really classes [divided by their economic origin] but are rather races [divided by. . . geographic origins and by physical appearances]. . . . Race went hand in hand with certain modes of production and consumption . . . and came to determine the economic position [class] of settlers. In truth, race was more of a social concept than a blood or ethnic notion. It is not incongruent to say that blacks and Indians were classes, in addition to races."[28]

Prejudice, not only racial but above all social, was expressed in Mexico and Peru during the eighteenth century through the following formulas:

In Mexico:
*From Spaniard and Indian,
Mestizo
From Mestizo and Spaniard,
Castizo
From Castiza and Spaniard,
Spaniard
From Spaniard and Black,
Mulato
From Spaniard and Mulata,
Morisco
From Morisca and Spaniard,
Albino
From Spaniard and Albina,
look the other way
From Indian and look the
other way, Wolf
From Wolf and Indian,
Zambahiga
From Zambahigo and Indian,
Cambujo
From Cambujo and Mulata,
Albarazado
From Albarazado and Mulata,
Barcino
From Barcino and Mulata,
Coyote*

In Peru:
*From Spaniard and Indian,
Mestizo
From Spaniard and Mestiza,
Mestizo Quadroon
From Spaniard and Mestiza
Quadroon, Quinterón
From Spaniard and Black,
Mulato
From Spaniard and Mulata
Quadroon, Quinterón
From Spaniard and Mulata
Quinterona, Requinterona
From Spaniard and Mulata
Requinterona, White People
From Mestizo and Indian,
Cholo
From Mulato and Indian,
Chinese
From Spaniard and Chinese,
Chinese Quadroon
From Black and Indian,
Zambo
From Black and Mulata,
Zambo*

From Coyote and Indian,
  Chamiso
From Chamisa and Mestizo,
  Coyote
From Coyote Mestizo and
  Mulata, go no further.[29]

The foregoing indicates that at some level there was a color barrier separating those who ruled from the rest of the population. The problem with
such nuances is that perceptions of color become difficult if not impossible
to evaluate and are at best subjective.

It is necessary to simplify the concept of how settlers became incorporated into the new social order. The notion is based on the assumption that
a social barrier separated those who could perform certain economic and
political activities from those who could not. The initial relation between
conquistador and conquered was as follows:

Conquistador
Noble Indians
――――――――――――――――――*SOCIAL BARRIER*
Plebeians
Other Indians
Blacks (later)

Spanish aristocrats who married Indian nobility (even princesses) generally lost access to lucrative economic activities and political posts, except
when the crown sought to establish control over Indians and lands through
such bonds. For that reason, relations between a Spanish noble and an
Indian were usually limited to concubinage or to mere sexual intercourse.
Unlike nobles, Spaniards of low social standing (both military and civilian)
could improve their status by marrying an Indian princess.[30] Those in the
lower categories were limited to performing intermediary and subsistence
economic tasks and were excluded from political functions. It is difficult
to classify Indian chieftains. While these could hold some political posts,
they were restricted to their own areas.

Marriages between nobles and Indians (excepting princesses) were un-
usual because Spaniards lost their rights. Illegitimate sons of nobles and
Indian or mestizo women sometimes enjoyed the economic, social, and
political prerogatives of their fathers. In contrast, the illegitimate son of a
noble in Spain did not have the same rights as his counterpart in America.

Toward the end of the colonial period, the son of a noble and a black woman could also enter the scheme above the social barrier, but at the lowest ranks.[31] The most accessible activity for such people (called honest *pardos*, or honest browns) was the militia, where they could become officers. They were required to show a certain degree of "white blood," which underscores once again the importance of color.[32] At one time blacks felt an incentive to marry Indians because they alleged that their offspring could neither be slaves nor be forced to pay tribute. Spanish law did not see things this way, however.[33] Whiteness was perhaps the key to plebeians' success in establishing marital bonds with Indian nobility.

The Crown, the Clergy, and Class

It was not easy even for some noble children to penetrate the social system, for there were two obstacles. Royal decrees concerning matrimony between races were not insurmountable, but local priests could become a veritable impediment.

A few words should be said about the clergy. Guatemala City, as the Isthmian capital, was the most important religious center. In 1533, Lic. Francisco Marroquín became the first bishop, and that marked the beginning of an unfortunate ecclesiastical experience throughout the colonial period, characterized by constant discord between clergy and laymen, between high clergy and conquistadors, and within the clergy itself, to say nothing of corruption. Marroquín's first measure was to make attendance at mass obligatory, under penalty of three days in jail or a fine, which had the effect of widening the gap between clergy and laymen. He then demanded that tithes (which were generally paid in specie) be delivered to bishops in places often difficult to reach. Bishops were subsequently appointed in other territories, including Cristóbal de Pedraza in Honduras and Antonio de Valdivieso in Nicaragua. Bartolomé de Las Casas, although officially named in Chiapas (Mexico), made his presence felt over the entire Isthmus. Poor relations with the laity were aggravated by the dishonesty of most bishops and by rivalries among them. Pedraza was young, proud, ambitious, and greedy, and priests around him levied high charges for mass, confession, and funerals.[34]

Marroquín attempted to use his influence in Soconusco (Mexico), which fell under the jurisdiction of Las Casas. Intrigue among Franciscans (led by Toribio Motolinía) and Dominicans (by Las Casas) had unfavorable repercussions, particularly in Guatemala. In 1545, Las Casas, Valdivieso,

Marroquín, and Pedraza met in Gracias a Dios, Honduras, to discuss the liberation of Indians under the New Laws of 1542. The latter two, as encomenderos, refused to free their Indians, and Las Casas threatened to excommunicate those who would not. Marroquín, however, promised prompt absolution.[35]

The situation of the clergy underscores the confusion and disorder on the Isthmus during the formative stages of its societies. Costa Rica had no bishop, and the geographic isolation of the territory allowed for only eleven visits from the bishop of Nicaragua (with intervals of up to thirty-three years) during the entire colonial period.[36] This may very well have been a blessing, for the province could easily have suffered at the hands of immoral and unscrupulous church officials in the same ways its neighbors did.[37]

Although the crown discouraged marriages involving individuals of different races and classes, royal decrees could not make provisions for the wide variety of social situations that developed in the New World. For this reason the monarch allowed priests to interpret such problems as they saw fit. Ecclesiastic officials, then, were either a hindrance or a help for those who wished to enter the social system above the barrier. Their judgments were based on appraisals at the moment of baptism, when a child's race was entered into the books, based on empirical (although relatively accurate) criteria such as the appearance of children, and above all by what the priests knew of their families. In this sense they were expert genealogists. With time, distinguished families united with those of inferior social status, prompting members of the clergy to certify color of skin as they desired. This subjectivity helps explain why in the same branch of a given family some individuals appear to have "better blood" than their kin.[38] The terminology of "quadroon" and so forth was purely academic, and by the eighteenth century there was justifiable mistrust in parochial records.[39]

Social stratification in Central America until the midsixteenth century[40] can be understood in the light of distribution of economic resources and the establishment of political headquarters in Guatemala City. That attracted nobles of higher lineage who brought capital for their enterprises. In Costa Rica, because the scarcity of land for export crops and a limited native labor supply were of little appeal for high nobility, the territory was not conquered until half a century after the other provinces had been settled. Economic depressions in northern countries during the colonial period strongly affected the general populace but did not significantly harm ruling classes. There, antagonisms and jealous protection of the rights of each group converted state and church into scrupulous guardians of the upper strata of societies, and these came to be increasingly stratified and rigid. In Costa Rica, however, while such crises[41] did not erode the political status of the upper class, they did lower its economic level to that of the rest of the population. Because the church attached less importance to baptismal records, it was easier to cross the social barrier.

National value systems mirrored the diversity within Isthmian socioeconomic systems. The different nature of problems that affect the five nations today can best be seen through the formation of national values, particularly those concerning power and institutions. This is the subject of the next chapter.

CHAPTER 5

Political Cultures and Values

In the North:

The planter refilled the colonel's glass. From the residence, the meticulously kept lawn with luxuriant clusters of oriental trees, extended in all directions. This sumptuous cloister was a verdant island in the midst of thousands of acres of crops.

"How does everything look, Jacinto?"

"Sir?" asked the colonel, who had allowed his thoughts to drift. He had become lethargic with the drinks, the tranquility of the bucolic setting, and the occasional whiffs of a succulent meal being prepared in the nearby kitchen.

"Politics," repeated the planter. "How do things look?"

"Well, sir. The industrialists are gaining strength. They approached me the other day for help, but I played dumb."

"Jacinto, let's get serious. The crops this year are going to be the best ever and prices will stay up for a long time. There'll be lots of that; all you want," he added, making a familiar gesture with his thumb and index finger. "So we make the usual arrangements."

"Fine, sir. I was just trying to figure out who I'd get to help me organize this."

The two men ate in silence. After coffee and cognac, the future president stood up and said:

"Fine, sir. I'm leaving and thank you very much. I'll keep you posted."

In the South:

It was time for don Bartolo to talk. It was time for the president to se-

lect his candidate to run against General Chamorro. A decision had to be taken. Someone mentioned the name of don Carlos Solórzano.

"The son of don Federico?" he asked with interest.

"Yes, the son of don Federico."

When don Carlos walked into the president's office, a sign of surprise came over don Bartolo's face. That was not the son of don Federico he had in mind when he accepted him as his successor. However, by now the name of don Carlos was on everyone's lips.

"But didn't don Federico have another son?"

"Yes sir. He had several."

"Now I see. The one I had in mind was called El Gatillo."

And that is how don Federico, El Gatillo, with green eyes, blond hair, chubby and short, a son of don Federico and brother of don Carlos, did not become president of Nicaragua.

Patterns of Power

These tales (the second one is said to be true) illustrate fundamental differences in patterns of power in northern and southern Central America.[1] Indirect rule can be appreciated in the north (the planter through Jacinto) and direct rule in south (don Bartolo). The tales bring to light an important aspect that sets the five nations apart from each other. In the northern countries (Guatemala, El Salvador, and Honduras), the planter, taken symbolically as the one who organizes production, is the person who commands in national societies. At different periods in history, the planter has been a producer of indigo, cochineal, coffee, sugarcane, cotton, rice, and other products. More recently he has vied for power with traders and industrialists in all Central American nations. In spite of his ruling position, however, he does not hold political office. He allows the Jacintos to do that and he runs his society through them. Jacinto, the president-to-be, is usually from the military and is but a tool of the planter. He comes from another social class and is normally subservient to producers, who are generally of noble ancestry. In the southern countries (Nicaragua and Costa Rica), those who organize production are also descendants of the aristocracy, and they too command, although they do so because of their kinship ties and not because of wealth. In contrast to their northern counterparts, however, they rule directly. President Bartolomé Martínez (don Bartolo, president of Nicaragua from 1923 to 1924) came from the ruling class of Nicaragua, and in the tale he was selecting a member of his own social class as his successor. Jacinto treats the planter with subservience, whereas the name of don Carlos Solórzano, president of Nicaragua from 1925 to 1926, is immediately linked to that of his father by don Bartolo. This implies a friendship based on social class.

Forms of exercising power reflect values that are molded by the way economic resources are used to organize production. Differences throughout the Isthmus can be seen in acts related to courage and manliness, and excerpts from Central American tales illustrate varying manifestations of those notions. A starting point is the north, where caudillismo and machismo are components of leadership.

In Guatemala: An Epic

It was true. Experience had taught Juan Vargas how to handle those unruly and belligerent people from the coast. His harshness as foreman had brought rebellion to the surface, revealing, as he had always said, just who he was. The haughtiest ranch hands became humble when he disarmed them with blows from the flat side of his machete. They even came to admit that no one within twenty leagues could beat him at brandishing that weapon or a knife, or at putting a bullet where he wanted to put it. In the wake of fear came devotion of the rough and rowdy for the ill-tempered macho who knew how to make himself obeyed even by the most arrogant. Those loyal to him came to be imbued with that ingenuous and primitive love that country folk are so prone to feel for men who command. That's the stuff from which caudillos are made.[2]

In El Salvador: Macho

In El Salvador, courage is regarded much the same as in Guatemala. The following tale brings out an aspect of that trait that is common to all of Central America but more openly manifest in the north: machismo. The courage implicit in caudillismo does not necessarily go hand in hand with the bullying characteristics of machismo. In fact, the machismo displayed by don Rafael with regard to both his woman Juana and the slaying of the Indian is not compatible with the image of Juan Vargas because don Rafael lets himself be carried away by his emotions for Juana and by alcohol. He could never have won the "primitive love that country folk are so prone to feel for men who command," as Juan Vargas did.

When Don Rafael did not come to town to spend the night with her, he would send El Janiche to bring her to the farm. Juana had been very pretty and she still was. Their relations had come to an end one afternoon when he had come to her estanco *[bar] with the Chinchilla brothers. He had broken bottles and glasses, knocked over the only four stools, destroyed the table, and chased away with his pistol some half a dozen people. He had finally grabbed Juana by the hair and dragged her across the floor. After beating her brutally with no interference from the Chinchilla brothers, he had left to continue his spree in another estanco. And all of this simply because he wanted to do it. Because he was Rafael Abregos, owner and master of El Socorro.*

Now he had come seeking her again. In her room he and his companions heard the leather straps of her bed creak, and instants after she appeared there loomed a yawning Indian clad in nothing but an undershirt.

"Remember me, Don Rafael?" asked the Indian. Don Rafael looked away. It disgusted him that this woman, his woman, should now belong to that ugly and obnoxious Indian whose presence worried everyone. All of a sudden he lurched toward Don Rafael. El Janiche, sensing the danger, swiftly drew his pistol and fired. The Indian staggered and fell.[3]

In Honduras: Satire

Satire, as used in the following tale from Honduras, is to underscore with humor the author's concept of courage as having strong undertones of fear which are far from being epic or heroic. The noble and courageous image of the caudillo Juan Vargas in Guatemala stands in sharp contrast to both the candid fear of the Honduran soldier and the base ideals of his superiors. The following tale suggests that dramatic displays of courage do not play as important a role in the makeup of the national image of a leader as they do in Guatemala, for while the Honduran soldier does not openly show signs of fear he admits to himself that he is scared.

Guaro [a local liquor], bitter cold, ruthless Indians, peach trees; there's all that in my pueblo, and there's also me. I'm known in Santa Clara for being bravo. *Once they called me* gallo ronco *(hoarse rooster): I drew my .44, shot the man who said it, and laughed. Another time I slugged an Indian who wouldn't lend me his shotgun to shoot a man. I also laughed.*

I went to war. The general asked for volunteers to spy on the enemy and when no one stepped forward I said: "General, that's why I've come to war; to fight and to obey like a soldier. Not like a maricón *[literally, a homosexual; figuratively, a coward]."*

I climbed the hill called El Zapotal and from there I saw the enemy.

"Virgen Santísima: patas pa' qué te quiero!" (an expression of fear).

When I reported back to the general he told me to call Benítez and Juárez, a real coward, a chicken. They were talking and Benítez said he wanted to be minister of war. The other maricón wanted a customs house in a port to help him support his wife. Could you believe it?[4]

In Nicaragua: Courage and Affection

Courage and manliness in the following tale from Nicaragua are evident, but they are accompanied by manifest affection of Nicanor Villagra for his bull. Visible signs of affection are not compatible with courage in northern societies, and Villagra would be out of place in Guatemala or El Salvador.

Nicanor Villagra came to love Clarín, the tame, affectionate, and spoiled calf he had saved from the jaws of a jaguar. As the animal grew, so did the damage he did, for he lived in the house and, like a dog, chewed and soiled clothes, knocked over tables, and broke china, unaware of his growing size and strength.

One night he bleated like a full-grown bull, like the leader of a herd of cows, and opening his black nostrils he felt the weight and mightiness of his horns.

One day Villagra was branding calves when a steer, Cantaclaro, came limping in from the pasture, badly wounded. He looked on in silence as the nervous and bulky animal walked aimlessly around the corral.

"The tigre," said the foreman.

On the edge of the jungle Nicanor and his men found Clarín nervously rounding up his herd of cows. He had formed them into a circle, their horns bristling outwards, keeping the bleating and terrified calves in the center behind them.

In the twilight they spotted the crouching cat. The animal pressed against his own shadow. He dragged himself, preparing for a low attack, at the neck. The bull advanced.

"Now! Now! Charge!" Clarín attacked! He hooked him and felled him. "Drive! Push, boy, push! Sink those horns! Kill!"

The tiger stumbled, limped, lurched frantically toward a cow, killed.

"Kill the assassin! Kill, Clarín!"

Then came the blow. The fury, the shaking, pushing, rising head lifted the huge cat and drove him against a tree. The sound of the gutted howling body filled the jungle night. Again Clarín slammed the cat against the tree; more sounds of crushed bones and guts. Villagra jumped from the tree and ran toward the bull, throwing his shotgun to the ground.

"Villagra, no!" But Villagra didn't hear. Trembling in glory, he walked toward the bull.

"Villagra, the bull is in a fit of rage!" Villagra kept walking toward the animal, whose blood-filled eyes, fixed, stared at him.
"Villagra, loco." The bull lowered his head, stomping the bloody sod with his mighty hooves, and backed slowly away.
"Villagra! Stop!" But Villagra continued. Suddenly he yelled with euphoria. "This is my signature!" We saw his raised fist against the moon while the bull, docile as a puppy, lowered his head like a child and let himself be kissed on the forehead.[5]

In Costa Rica: Caricature

In the following tale from Costa Rica, caricature attaches even more ridicule than in Honduras to concepts of overt courage and manliness. It mockingly suggests that values surrounding the notion are absent; then again, that is the author's way of prodding or goading his own countrymen.

Five hundred Costa Ricans and one hundred Nicaraguans from the vanguard are sent to defend the nation's honor threatened by Guatemalan dictator General Barrios.
The general calls me with great composure, cold-blooded, and says, "Tomorrow at nine we attack. You will conquer or die."
"General, don't you believe we ought to wait for reinforcements?"
"Lieutenant González, discipline admits no arguments. Tomorrow you will plant the Costa Rican flag in enemy trenches."
"Yes, General. I will die like my uncle Chepe."
The next morning a message arrives from headquarters: "Salvadorans defeat Guatemalan army at Chalchuapa. Barrios dead. Guatemalan Congress repeals Central American Union. Long live Costa Rica. Long live Nicaragua. Long live El Salvador."
Signed: Felix Alfaro
Now I don't have to die like my uncle Chepe.[6]

Again in Costa Rica: Lampoonery

While the last tale from the south does not concern courage directly, it does contrast with notions about manliness in the north.

"Do you have a horse?"
"No, but I can rent one. What should I take?"
"Take a can of sardines, half a pound of sausage and half a dozen hard-boiled eggs. Don't forget something to drink."
We were going on a picnic by the river. I need not add that she was

going with her family in an oxcart and that if I failed to go I would lose her and would be ridiculed by my friends.

At six o'clock the next morning I was waiting at the door for my rented horse. I wore my best suit with my wide-brimmed fiber hat, red silk neckerchief, woolen shirt, and patent leather belt; and a saddle scabbard with a broken Smith and Wesson and with no shells; just to show off, to boast, like a man with hair on his chest.

When I saw them I dug my spurs into the horse, whipped him and loosened the reins. I wanted to conceal the nag's ridiculous aspect by coming to a screeching halt beside the oxcart. The horse raised his tail, straightened his good ear and took off like a bullet. When I was about five meters away he stumbled and fell on his nose. The saddle snapped off and I went sailing through the air and landed on my head on top of the oxcart. I sat there, stunned morally and hurt physically. They all left and when I decided to pick up my saddle and return to the city, I realized that my steed had gone back to his stable alone. I swore never again to accept an invitation to a picnic until I had my own horse and gear.[7]

Scope and Meaning of the Differences

The characters involved in the foregoing stories could not be interchanged. Juan Vargas, in the tale from Guatemala, could never have done anything the Costa Rican did without being completely miscast. He could never have gone on a picnic (let alone on a rented horse) and much less be thrown and lose his mount. Any such scenes would be somewhat akin to Lawrence Olivier acting the roles of Charlie Chaplin. Salvadoran macho don Rafael, in attempting to win back his woman from the Indian, could never have suffered being thrown from his horse before the eyes of his ranch hands. Furthermore, the way of life in El Salvador could never have permitted the display of nonfunctioning guns. In contrast, very few people in Costa Rica would be found carrying a weapon; until the recent Central American turmoil it was frowned upon as a sign of a bully. Again, Juan Vargas from Guatemala would never have suggested to his general to wait for reinforcements before attacking; nor would he have breathed a sigh of relief at not having to die as his uncle Chepe did. That uncourageous remark would have changed his caudillo image to one of a *pendejo*, or coward. Jacinto would never have been president in Costa Rica.

Differences in the ways of showing courage in the foregoing tales help explain the varying nature of leaders in the five nations. In Guatemala foreman Juan Vargas handled people with harshness and inspired fear, not emotions of compassion or pity in his role as leader of ranch hands. In El Salvador, the Chinchilla brothers and El Janiche stood by and watched don Rafael beat his woman in a macho fashion. The boss showed no emotion when El Janiche killed the Indian who had been sleeping with her. This is the manly way of doing things. In spite of such scenes, which are completely devoid of feeling and which his men are obviously accustomed to seeing, they treat their master with respect and are willing to follow him even on his drunken sprees. The Honduran has been a real macho in his home town, shooting men and slugging Indians. As a soldier who senses that war is his preferred element, he has the courage to be the only volunteer to spy on the enemy, and is probably in line for a promotion. Once he sees the adversary, however, he is struck with fear. In none of these scenes does he express that emotion, except to himself.

In Nicaragua, Nicanor Villagra reveals significantly different values related to courage. After seeing his beloved bull win in a struggle to death with a jaguar, and fully aware that the animal is in a fit of rage, he is emotionally compelled to jump from the tree where he has been watching the duel and risk his life to kiss the animal on the forehead. This manifestation of sentiment and courage has obviously earned him the respect of the ranch hands who witness the terrifying scene. Finally, in Costa Rica, Lieutenant González is to lead six hundred men into battle and is so frightened by the thought that he attempts to dissuade the general from going through with the attack. The commanding officer sees his subordinate's fear and reprimands him. González breathes a sigh of relief when the operation is called off, but the point here is that the general is not in the least upset by the display of fear of the man he has chosen to lead the army into battle.

Values surrounding the concept of courage vary in that the display of emotions in acts of bravery and manliness becomes less relevant as one proceeds from north to south. These traits are often noticeable in personalities of national leaders. For example, Justo Rufino Barrios (president of Guatemala toward the end of the nineteenth century and unquestionably an aggressive leader) died in battle leading his army against El Salvador. In Honduras, Gen. Tiburcio Carías (president toward the middle of the twentieth century) solved his problems with military opponents in a less glorious although very effective manner: by scattering nails from an airplane over roads leading to the capital. In Nicaragua, Gen. Anastasio Somoza García, in spite of his charm, was a tyrant yet had a visible soft spot for humble talented people, whom he helped. Many of them are members of the present Sandinista hierarchy.[8] As a last example, in Costa

Rica, when Otilio Ulate Blanco, a prominent politician before the 1948 civil war, learned that a military platoon had come to capture him at a friend's home, he jumped the fence in the back yard and fled. His friend was killed. Display of emotion (fear) had little or no bearing on his leadership, for Ulate went on to become president after the revolution. He was most admired for refusing to have bodyguards during an era when no other Central American president went anywhere without them. As chief executive, while walking alone in the crowded market area of San José, he was struck by a bicycle and suffered several broken ribs.

The excerpts from short stories also reflect some of the fundamental value and cultural differences between northern and southern Central America. Aside from marked variations in forms of exercising power, many other dissimilarities characterize the five nations. For example, inhabitants of northern countries speak differently from those in the south; large coffee planters in Guatemala and El Salvador do not know the names of their peons, while in Costa Rica their counterparts do. Salvadorans delegate responsibility to their administrators, while Costa Ricans have a propensity to remain on their plantations and make their own decisions; for this reason, they have little time for other economic activities. Honduras has had some ninety chiefs of state since 1824 while in the same lapse of time Costa Rica has had half that number. Costa Rica has the most expensive labor on the Isthmus while the cheapest is in Honduras, El Salvador, and Guatemala.[9]

Values expressed in the foregoing tales have their roots in the colonial period but carry over into both the independence era and the present. Under Spanish colonial rule, forms of government were similar throughout the provinces. By Independence, however, contrasts in economic systems had conditioned values, which became incorporated into the political systems of the young nations. Relationships that had developed between master and peon during the colonial period, for instance, were reflected in labor codes as well as in laws governing the new independent states.

Values related to social environments in northern countries (particularly Guatemala and El Salvador) have a bearing on tyranny, arbitrariness, arrogance, persecution, and cruelty. Those societies are characterized by a pronounced hierarchy and by a degree of contempt for life itself. They have been plagued with extremes of wealth and poverty and function as a result of a clear-cut division between those who command and those who obey. The southern part of the Isthmus, particularly Costa Rica, encourages such traits as simplicity, shyness, timidity, hesitation, plainness (even backwardness), sympathy, and compassion. The gap between rich and poor, while real, has been less significant than in the north.

The presence of the caudillo must be viewed within an economic, political, and social context. Historically, caudillismo has prospered when central
authority is weakened. When the wars for independence required more
troops, Charles III of Spain allowed aristocratic creoles and lower social
classes to be commissioned; this democratizing of the military gave the
ambitious an opportunity to aspire for positions of power. In a time of
weak central control, it is from the ranks of the lower strata that the caudillo emerges.[10] He predominates in northern societies, where wealth and
prestige are conferred by birth. Because the well-born seldom compete for
political posts, the potential caudillo has no influential rivalry in his quest
for power. He is in fact aided by upper class members, whose interests he
promises to protect.

Caudillismo prospers in those parts of Central America where the gross
national product *per capita* is lowest. In terms of GNP per capita Costa Rica
is far ahead of the others, despite its limited economic resources. The key
to understanding this is the more restricted distribution of wealth in the
north. Wealth is more widely spread out in the south, as a study of life
expectancy at birth will show. During the first half of the decade of the
1980s the advantages of Costa Rica (with a life expectancy of 73 years) over
the other nations (59 in Guatemala, 57 in El Salvador, 62 in Honduras, and
60 in Nicaragua)[11] is patent. Consumption of electricity, telephones, and
other factors also serve to measure distribution of wealth. In all these re-
spects, Costa Rica is far ahead of the rest of Central America, as is shown
in table 5.[12]

Machismo, another concept that appears in the tales from Guatemala
and El Salvador, is also a product of values formed in a particular setting.
Contrary to popular belief, this is not a general Latin American trait. In its
most widely accepted form it is characteristically Mexican and changes in
nature in Central America, particularly toward the south. In Mexico, land,
labor, and capital have been more abundant and have produced greater
wealth (although it is poorly distributed) than on the Isthmus. Extreme
poverty in that country contrasts with general prosperity in neighboring
United States and creates a sense of desperation. Thus his literature, music,
and particularly his jokes reveal frustrations in the form of aggression, fear,
weakness, and spiritual as well as material poverty.[13] He compensates for
these shortcomings in ostentation and frequently with sexual allusions, because sex is an easily exploitable subject.[14] Machismo or apparent manliness
is described in his music and in his humor: songs that say with disdain,
often mistaken for virility, that *la vida no vale nada* (life is worth nothing) and that tell of a daring, drunk, but *muy macho* Juan Charrasqueado.
Beneath this machismo, and not well hidden, is a feeling of depression,

TABLE 5.
Consumer Goods in Central America

	U.S.	Guate-mala	El Salvador	Hon-duras	Nica-ragua	Costa Rica
Electricity: (kw/hr/ person 1985)	10,781	220	305	282	381	1,086
People per auto-mobile (1985)	1.4	31	32	51	43	14
People per television set (1986)	1.7	27	14	50	20	5.4
People per telephone (1984)	1.3	62	42	92	63	7.9
People per physician*	438 (1985)	5,700 (1981)	3,002 (1984)	2,301 (1985)	1,456 (1984)	1,198 (1982)
Hospital beds per 10,000 people	53 (1986)	14 (1982)	14 (1984)	14 (1985)	16 (1985)	33 (1982)

SOURCE: *Encyclopaedia Britannica* Yearbook, 1988, pp. 803–23, 854–59.
*El Salvador includes only the public sector; Nicaragua taken from 1989 Yearbook.

of weakness, of something lacking. This makes for desperate attempts to manifest courage. In an ambience of frustrations resulting from striking injustices in the political system, machismo is a part of Mexican political culture that involves trust and confidence, political cliques *(camarillas)*, and bureaucratic families (where kinship is a "passport" to high political echelons.)[15]

Toward the south, desperation becomes attenuated and the importance of machismo changes. In Costa Rica, the figures in the tales of courage are anything but macho. In fact, the author of the stories has written in satirical fashion, precisely to criticize the low value placed on machismo.

Institutions

The distribution of economic endowments and its relationship with values has many implications. The offices of the presidency in El Salvador and in Costa Rica, for instance, do not have the same prestige for élites in those countries. Salvadorans are not interested in it as long as they can control it, while for their Costa Rican counterparts it is a highly coveted distinction.

Concern of ruling classes for their labor forces is also determined by values. Abundance of workers in the north gives employers less to worry about in terms of their cost, their availability, and their welfare. Management has tended to disregard minimum wages and labor codes, and workers have grudgingly accepted this, although the situation seems to be changing as they organize to defend their own interests. Employers tend not to take social security systems seriously because of the expense involved, and their indifference makes for a greater propensity toward violence in northern systems. One outcome is that labor ministries have played relatively insignificant roles, and disputes must often be resolved by the president of the republic. In Costa Rica (where mechanisms for solving problems without the intervention of the president are also deficient, but probably to a lesser extent than in the north),[16] employers compete for workers. As a result greater interdependence among social strata has developed, along with a powerful labor ministry and a vast (if costly) social security system. All have become mainstays in the nation's democratic way of life and contrast with similar institutions in the north.

Trade unions too function differently in north and south. Impersonal relations exist between labor and management in banana-producing coastal regions and in industrial sectors throughout the Isthmus. In Guatemala's coffee-growing areas of the interior, labor, by virtue of its numbers, has been treated in a largely collective fashion. In Costa Rica, on the other hand, closer personal relations are found between coffee planters and their workers, with the result that disputes are usually handled on an individual basis by the ministry.

The nature of relationships between labor and management is also relevant to the question of values and institutions. The ease with which management in El Salvador has been able to obtain and replace peons has made for little contact between the two groups, and administrators constitute a buffer group between them. The slaying of the Indian by El Janiche and the way the patron treats his workers throughout the story in the first tale from El Salvador illustrates the scorn felt for that race. Equally evident is the disdain the Indians have developed for landowners. These resentments have repercussions in the political system: apathy and distrust of the upper class by the population in general. In Costa Rica, on the other hand, competition among employers for scarce labor has yielded higher salaries and has brought labor and management into direct contact; as a result, the producer knows his workers and has special rapport with them.[17] Friction between classes is not as pronounced as in El Salvador, since the ruling groups must be responsible to the people. Power and values, as related to economic resources, help explain propensities toward dictatorial or democratic forms of government, welfare, and patron-client relationships in Central America.

The welfare state in Costa Rica both is conditioned by and conditions the national value system. The population demands increasing benefits, despite their negative effects on production, and has become accustomed to living beyond its means. In the overpopulated northern countries, ruling classes have had greater concern with controlling production and with restraining public expenditure. For this reason, in El Salvador, even with recent social and political upheaval, production has generally maintained growth superior to that of most Central American nations. As late as 1983 it ranked second, behind only Guatemala. In Costa Rica, on the other hand, in spite of the absence of popular uprisings, and due to public expenditure as well as to fear of Nicaragua, production decreased.[18] The propensity to control public expenditure can be seen by comparing Honduras and Costa Rica. The former country suffers from a noticeable deficiency in public services such as street lighting, telephones, sewage disposal, pavement, and water. Those services, poor as they may be, are however in great part paid for, while in Costa Rica payment for most of them is still outstanding. This accounts for Costa Rica's high per capita debt[19] and growing inflation, for loans are constantly renegotiated with foreign creditors and government bond issues to construct these utilities are purchased by the nationalized banking system with currency printed for that purpose.

Another aspect of patterns of power concerns the ease or difficulty with which new groups can emerge to challenge the hegemony of traditional ruling classes. This involves immigrants. In Costa Rica, where members of old élites were zealous guardians of their positions, little was done to attract long-term immigration.[20] Notwithstanding the economic success of the coffee planters during the nineteenth century, the ruling class failed to acquire the know-how (furnished in nations like Brazil and Argentina by immigrants) to transfer profits to other activities.[21] By keeping potential rivals out of the country they maintained their position until the midtwentieth century, when the Central American industrial movement gave new groups access to economic and then political power. Immigration during the nineteenth century was encouraged only for specific purposes and not as a long-term policy for settlement.[22] Blacks were brought in for railroad construction and banana cultivation, not by Costa Ricans but by the United Fruit Company. Italians and Chinese also came for railroads. After World War II, Jewish and Arab immigrants began to acquire importance, although not to the point of displacing the old order.

In the northern countries, where traditional families ruled their societies through the military, attention was not paid to the slow buildup of immigrants (particularly Syrians and Lebanese seeking refuge from political upheaval in their own lands). The indirect system of government enabled the ruling classes to remain ignorant of the influx of aliens until it had become a fait accompli. Thus in Honduras, toward the end of the nineteenth century, foreign banana interests had started to outproduce traditional families, and after the 1929 depression, Arabs became active in commerce and industry. In fact, Arabs have become eminent in everything but agriculture and cattle raising, which are still domains of the old ruling class. The foregoing explains the Middle East flavor of Honduran national society.

The abundance or scarcity of labor affects the formation of values among children and adolescents. A starting point could be the *Tío Conejo* (Brer Rabbit) stories. From south to north, as the disparity and disdain among classes become consequently more pronounced, Tío Conejo is treated with greater cruelty. In the north he not only is frequently killed but is in addition treated with increasing brutality.[23] In Costa Rica, on the other hand, he is rarely killed.

Short stories read in secondary schools also reveal contrasting values in northern and southern Central America. Value differences between north and south are reflected in three tales concerning venomous snakes in Guatemala, Honduras, and Costa Rica. The stories are quite similar, but in the two northern countries they have a macabre finale while in Costa Rica there is a "happy ending." In the one from Guatemala, a peon takes his young son to a sandy beach on the banks of a mountain stream. The man dozes off and is awakened by screams from his son, only to discover that the child has been bitten on the hand by a deadly serpent. He goes through some brief moments of mental anguish in deciding what to do and with little hesitation takes his machete, puts the boy's arm over a log, chops off his hand, and applies a makeshift tourniquet with his handkerchief. The story ends with the mortified father walking home with the unconscious boy draped over his shoulder. The outcome of the story is left to the imagination of the reader.[24] The tale from Honduras concerns an attractive unmarried Indian woman who lives on a plantation with a man she does not know well. When he goes to town to sell some eggs (which she fears will provide him with drinking money), she is propositioned by the plantation administrator. Together they plan to kill her companion so that she can live with her new lover. When the man returns, she gives him a bottle of liquor and as he starts drinking he comments that he almost killed a snake behind the hut but that the reptile escaped. That night, while she lies in bed with him, a pet cat finds the serpent and brings it to her side. Upon hearing the horse of her lover approach, she attempts to sit up and unwittingly braces herself on the snake's head, sinking its fangs into her hand. When her lover enters, he finds the man in a state of drunken oblivion and discovers that she is dead. He leaps on his horse and speeds away. The finale is as dismaying as a Verdi opera.[25] The tale from Costa Rica concerns a woman who takes her young child to the river to keep an eye on him while she launders clothes. She goes back to the house for something and leaves the child alone; upon her return, much to her horror, she finds the child playing with a colorful but deadly snake. She nervously approaches him, smiling, talking, praying, but trying to avoid startling the boy or the serpent. She touches the child's arm and reaches the back of the hand in which he is gently holding the reptile. She softly works her own fingers through the child's fingers and succeeds in grasping the serpent's head, whereupon she takes a stone, kills it, and faints. Her husband arrives a few seconds later and upon seeing the dead snake and blood on her hand, believes that his wife has been bitten, mounts his horse and gallops after a doctor. The story has a very happy ending by comparison with the others.[26]

Such endings are not as common in tales from the north. The one from El Salvador in the first part of this chapter, where the foreman kills the Indian courting don Rafael's woman, is another example of a gruesome ending in a northern story. The tale from Nicaragua, however, where the bull kills the jaguar, much to the rejoicing of Villagra, has a happy ending in spite of the brutal theme. In sum, grim and happy endings on the northern and southern extremes of the Isthmus, respectively, reflect value differences stemming from varying types of relationships among men, which in turn give way to varying concepts regarding fate.

The foregoing also has a bearing on religion, which is deeply ingrained in family and school. Religious values, as they are expressed in the north and south, respectively, evoke images similar to the grim and happy endings in short stories. The patron saint of Costa Rica is Our Lady of the Angels (Nuestra Señora de los Angeles), and once a year the devout make pilgrimages, often on foot from distant parts of the country, to the cathedral in Cartago to pay homage. The journey, which is their penitence, is in a sense an attractive adventure that in modern times has become more of a frivolous spree than a religious act (although this trend has been improving in recent years). In the north, however, penitence at times acquires aspects of a gruesome sacrifice. In Honduras, for example, during pilgrimages to the Virgen de Suyapa (the patron saint of that country) the devout can be seen crawling towards her basilica on their knees along dusty and stony roads, while tossing small bits of broken glass into the air in attempts to cut their own backs. In Guatemala, a French observer toward the midnineteenth century watched an almost savage cult in religious processions. He commented on seeing an individual with a cut in his head, bathed in his own blood.[27] Today, the religious spirit displayed in that country on January 15 for the Black Christ of Esquipulas as well as during Holy Week is far and away the most ardent and fanatical on the Isthmus. People from El Salvador and Honduras make pilgrimages to Esquipulas for the occasion, and the rite is even celebrated in distant Costa Rica.

Value differences can also be seen in political parties, for there is greater tolerance of party disloyalty in Costa Rica than in Guatemala, for example. In Costa Rica, it is not uncommon for politicians to change political and ideological affiliations to assure themselves a position in government. On the other hand, towards the north, political solidarity increases and affective ties to parties pass from one generation to another. For this reason, political divisions among ruling families often acquire characteristics of feuds. Examples are liberals and conservatives in Nicaragua (as symbolized by rivalries between the cities of Leon and Granada), *azules* and *colorados* (blues and reds) in Honduras, and so forth.

Only labor has been discussed as a factor of production that, depending on its abundance or scarcity, endows each Central American nation with special traits. The same applies to land and capital, however. A substantial part of Guatemala is suitable for cultivating high-quality coffee, for instance. In Costa Rica, on the other hand, land for the same purpose is found only in parts of the central plateau. This affects land values. Toward the midnineteenth century, the price of an acre of coffee land in Costa Rica was eighty-eight dollars. A quarter of a century later (in 1877), similar land in Guatemala cost only seventeen dollars. In 1857 a French traveler remarked that "around San José land is as expensive as in the suburbs of Paris,"[28] and the situation has remained much the same. Shortly after World War II, the United States government wanted to buy land for its embassy offices in San José. Its first choice was turned down by the State Department because, it complained, land could be acquired for less on the Island of Manhattan.[29]

Value differences are reflected in the personalities of leaders. In northern countries, political life has been largely characterized by the glorification of the role of the soldier, of martial arts, and of virile or macho traits. The lives of most presidents reflect this. Gen. Rafael (El Indio) Carrera led Guatemalan armies against liberals for decades, and the soldiers of Gen. Justo Rufino Barrios followed him to his death on the battlefield at Chalchuapa. In El Salvador, Gen. Maximiliano Hernández massacred thirty thousand Indians and Gen. Tomás Regalado was known for his attempts at adroitness in martial arts.[30] Honduran Gen. Francisco Morazán, who is said to have taken swigs of cognac before going into battle, was the outstanding military and political hero of Central America for fifteen years until his death at the hands of a firing squad organized by political opponents in Costa Rica. In Nicaragua, Gen. José Santos Zelaya's ambition and cunning in playing liberals against conservatives kept him in power for fifteen years, and the fame of Gen. Anastasio Somoza García stemmed in part from his expert marksmanship. In Costa Rica, on the other hand, political figures have been quite the opposite. President Otilio Ulate Blanco, mentioned earlier in this chapter as having jumped over a backyard fence rather than confront police, is a case in point. Another example is Manuel Mora Valverde, a founder of the Communist Party of Costa Rica, who although not a chief of state, controlled enough arms and men to keep the 1948 civil war going, but chose instead to lay them down to avoid more bloodshed. The goal of Gen. Tomás Guardia Gutiérrez's rule was to bring an end to half a century of rivalry between liberal and conservative families, and Gen. Bernardo Soto Alfaro avoided—through a keen sense of statesmanship— a civil war that he could easily have quelled through the use of arms.

In this chapter certain Central American values, as they make themselves manifest in literature, education, religion, politics, and other aspects of life, were discussed to provide a more meaningful setting against which to understand some of the ways that ruling classes have confronted problems in recent times. Values themselves also offer an insight into perspectives for political and economic development, which is the topic of the last part of this work. The following chapter is a brief analysis of the ways in which similar problems have developed in dissimilar Isthmian cultures.

PART III

Perspectives

CHAPTER 6

Similar Problems in Dissimilar Cultures

The way people do things in different countries reflects culture. Direct and indirect forms of exercising power and the values attached to leadership, to religion, to politics, and to other facets of Central American societies—all form part of culture. Classes have perceptions of each other, and these vary from one culture to another. A peon in El Salvador does not expect the planter to know his name. That is not the case in Costa Rica. A planter in Guatemala is not expected to be invited into the home of a laborer; his counterpart in Costa Rica is, and, furthermore, it is assumed that he will accept. In Guatemala the peon does not invite the planter to his daughter's wedding or to toast with him at the reception; in Costa Rica the planter is expected to accept such an invitation and to drink and dance at the reception. A peasant in Guatemala does not name the planter as the godfather of his child; his counterpart in Costa Rica does and, if relations between them are good, he expects the planter to accept. These varying cultural patterns raise queries regarding future orientations of Isthmian societies. Toward what end is their cultural heritage leading them? To what extent can it help or hinder their development? What is the role of their ruling groups in this process?

In the search for answers to these questions, one cannot overlook the dramatic change that has been taking place in Central America during the decade of the 1980s as a result of the regional conflict. For this reason changes during the last decade are extremely difficult to judge. The 1987 peace treaty has yet to produce results because it has been regarded as a Sandinista victory over the policies and presence of the United States in the area. Thus, when towards the end of that year Salvadoran insurgents launched two major military offensive operations against government bases, blocked transportation, and committed acts of sabotage, many concluded that they had taken advantage of the peace initiative to regain strength. By the same token, toward the beginning of 1988, when the president of Costa Rica expelled active Contras from his country, opponents of the Sandinistas developed doubts as to their capacity to conquer the Managua regime, and many even wondered where Costa Rica stood in the conflict. In March, when the United States sent thirty-two hundred troops to Honduras, it could be clearly seen that the United States still considered the Sandinistas as a threat to its security against the Soviet Union. Soon after, opposing forces in Nicaragua signed a cease-fire, but new divisions arose within the ranks of the Contras and spread more doubt on the meaning of that agreement. Further confusion developed when the Nicaraguan government declared the United States ambassador *persona non grata* and the United States retaliated with a similar move. Finally, in this same vein, it was not mere chance that the cessation of United States aid to the Contras coincided with the emergence of Fidel Castro as an important figure in the Isthmian problem.

The economies of all the nations are in critical condition. The main problem throughout is the impoverishment of salaried workers whose purchasing power has declined by at least fifty percent during the last seven years, with no apparent strategy to counteract that. A high rate of unemployment has caused the appearance of "informal" activities, such as street vending and contrabanding, that constitute an important part of gross domestic product although they usually generate minimal collective incomes. In this, Nicaragua has been the country most affected.[1]

Traditional ruling groups are being challenged, minorities are on the rise, and the region is a battleground, ideological and real, between Contras and Sandinistas for some, and between East and West for others. In general, political issues reflect the old colonial divisions within ruling classes, where some strove to maintain their positions through traditional economic activities and others sought their own hegemony in new fields. The latter were often symbolized by the contrabandists. This dichotomy led to the rise of conservatives and liberals after Independence and, in our times, to those who aspire for leadership through the private sector and those who seek the same goal through direct control over the state. Thus the conflict pits conservative groups who respect existing social, economic, and political institutions against collectivist organizations that seek comprehensive change of those same institutions through the state.

The foregoing reveals a conflict between the concepts of privatization and statism (in other words, private and public sectors, respectively), and that contradiction is one of the principal aspects of political and economic life of those countries in our times, in the Third World in general and in Central America in particular. For several decades, political regimes of Central America have relegated to the state responsibilities that could better be handled by private citizens. Examples in Central America are the Corporación Nacional de Inversiones (CONADI) in Honduras and the Corporación Costarricense de Desarrollo in Costa Rica. Both are public and are dedicated to many activities ranging from shrimp farming to making aluminum pots and pans.

Recent United States administrations, however, have felt that the excessive weight of public sectors retards development, and the United States Department of Commerce, along with the Agency for International Development (AID), now tie economic assistance to transfers of public enterprises to independent entrepreneurs. That has happened in Guatemala, for example, but the government in that country is interested in having private citizens operate only a portion of nationally owned corporations (a mobile telephone service, for example). Toward mid-1988, the government came under pressure from producers to lift price controls on beans, beef, pork, chicken, bread, milk, vegetable oil, and lard. The step caused significant price increases and threatened to put an end to government attempts to control inflation. Subsequently, entrepreneurial groups tried to increase exports to levels that would restore, by the year 2000, standards of living attained in 1980. In El Salvador, congress strengthened the private sector when it allowed importers and exporters to open dollar bank accounts for international transactions (this was a tacit admission of an overvalued currency—by 40 percent in 1987, according to the International Monetary Fund). In March 1988, in accordance with structural economic adjustments called for by AID, Honduras announced the sale of no less than seven state-owned enterprises belonging to CONADI. In Costa Rica, after a crisis of private banks in 1988 and again in accordance with structural economic adjustments called for by AID, congress approved reforms to partially privatize the nationalized banking system. In Nicaragua, as would be expected, the state (not the deteriorated private sector) has played the foremost role in orienting the economy. This can be seen in the recent government intervention in the San Antonio sugar mill (the largest in the country) and shows that Sandinista tolerance of a mixed economy has reached its saturation point.[2]

Many problems are common to all Central American countries but to varying degrees and in different settings. Indebtedness, for example, is common throughout but is less intense in Honduras than in Costa Rica or Nicaragua. The Costa Rican economy and society are to a large extent based on costly welfare, while those of Nicaragua are today geared to war. By the same token, illiteracy is not as serious in Costa Rica as in Guatemala, but solutions in a country with few Indians are in no way similar to those in one with a massive indigenous population. Cultural differences, then, explain the nature of problems and determine how ruling classes cope with them. In the following pages my purpose is to cast light on contemporary problems in the context of the development of each country.

Nature of the Problems

Debt

The regional debt burden grew during the 1980s and by 1987 surpassed eighteen billion dollars. Servicing this obligation has been particularly onerous for Costa Rica and Honduras.[3] Foreign public debt per capita in 1985 in comparison with 1987 appears in table 6.

Guatemala has faced problems in servicing her foreign debt; a decline in exports and a rise in the cost of maintaining a rapidly growing public sector. For a number of years there was optimism over what was dubbed the "reinitiation" of democracy under the civil Christian Democratic government of Vinicio Cerezo Arévalo, as well as over the start-up of a hydroelectric plant (which some felt would mean fuel savings) and over decreasing petroleum prices and interest rates. Between 1984 and 1985, foreign debt remained stable at about two and a half billion dollars, but servicing it in 1988 ($638 million) required the equivalent of one-fifth of the national budget, or more than what is allotted for health, defense, or education. Budgets continued to grow, and the one approved by the new civilian congress for 1989 was 3.6 billion *quetzales*, almost three times as great as the 1985 budget of the military government. All the while, the economy produced in a mediocre way (by comparison with neighboring El Salvador, whose economy in the 1980s was the most productive in the area in spite of civil strife), and that made for a lack of confidence of the private sector in the economic policies of the administration. Furthermore, the entrepreneurial sector feared new taxes and anticipated growth of the state bureaucracy.[4]

In El Salvador, in spite of political turmoil, the productive capacity of the country was maintained surprisingly well, and that is reflected in her relatively stable debt since 1982. The economic growth was due to a

TABLE 6.
Foreign Public Debt Per Capita of Central American Nations
(U.S. dollars)

	1977	1985
Guatemala	97	242
El Salvador	127	288
Honduras	200	457
Nicaragua	394	1,437
Costa Rica	605	1,397

SOURCES: *Progreso* magazine, December 1979, pp. 40–45; Banco Interamericano de Desarrollo, *Progreso económico y social en América Latina: Informe 1986* (Washington, D.C.), pp. 252, 276, 284, 308, 332.

great extent to foreign private and public capital. Private funds came basically from remittances made by Salvadorans living in exile, principally in the United States. By the end of the 1980s it was estimated that about one million Salvadorans lived there—20 percent of the population of that small nation. A stabilization program for 1986 included unification of the exchange rate, increased interest rates, restraints on credit for the public sector, readjustments in the tax system, restrictions on imports of luxury items, and higher minimum wages.[5]

In Honduras, improvements in the economy were offset by foreign debt servicing, a deterioration in the terms of trade, and reduced export earnings. Debt accounted for half the deficit in 1985, and scarcity of foreign exchange gave uneasy administrations constant worries over payments for interest and principal. The budgetary deficit in 1988 was equal to one-third of government expenses. Higher taxes, a reduction of subsidies for export, and new import taxes on luxury items have been decreed by international financial institutions. Social and political tensions related with the Nicaraguan problem have discouraged investments. They have also caused a reduction in savings and, as in the rest of the region, have undermined private sector confidence in the administrations. In this sense the country's future has been precarious.[6]

Nicaragua's foreign debt (per capita) has been the second highest in the world, due to military expenditures, social services, and a sharp drop in production. The first two items alone accounted for 80 percent of expenditures and have provided 85 percent of public jobs. Between 1984 and 1987, budgetary deficits of the central government increased over ten times (from eleven billion *córdobas* to one hundred twenty-one billion). The government consolidated several ministries in an effort to reduce the deficit, but most of this was financed internally by the central bank and contributed heavily to inflation.[7]

In Costa Rica, the welfare state has led to a more equitable distribution of wealth than elsewhere and has set standards of living not commensurate with production or income. This does not facilitate restoring order in a society ridden with debt, abuse of credit, and corruption. Social security, telephone networks, paved roads, electricity complexes, retirement programs, public housing, and, above all, the availability of jobs in the public sector have become ingrained in national values, with no productive basis to pay for them or to maintain them. Forty percent of the foreign debt is owed to private banks at high interest rates. Although successive administrations have paid lip service to belt-tightening and to reducing spending, the state continues to grow, and the citizenry buys increasingly on time over longer periods.[8] The budget has increased in the ministries of labor and social security, education, health, and public security. Despite a foreign debt the size of Costa Rica's, there is surprisingly little evidence of financial pressure to slow down the pace of life, and the continuing approval of more loans gives the impression that the country's growing external obligations represent no problem.[9]

A question has arisen as to the amount of Third World debt that will actually be paid off. Fidel Castro attempted to organize debtor nations to refuse to pay their obligations, but initially the idea found little following. Brazil, however, and more recently Peru and Argentina, set their own amortization schedules, and the reaction of the industrialized world is being carefully watched throughout Latin America. Past demands of international financial institutions on underdeveloped economies have created explosive social and political situations. Peru and Venezuela are good cases in point. Recently there has been talk of allowing debtor nations to apply portions of their obligations in their own currencies towards their own social and economic development (which in the long run is largely paid for with aid from foreign countries). This appears to satisfy the banks, the debtor nations, and even the United States government.

Domestic debt is not included in table 6. Between 1980 and 1986, that of Costa Rica increased three and a half times, from ten billion colones to thirty-four billion, with a jump of over eleven billion during the last two years.[10] Official reports indicate that it is expected to double by the end of the decade.[11] National budgetary deficits and funding for state institutions are often met through borrowing and government bond issues purchased by the central bank with money printed for that purpose.

Foreign public debt (table 6) shows striking increases as one proceeds south. Nicaragua's debt has surpassed Costa Rica's only in recent years as a result of the war. In a general sense, it reflects a tendency of southern countries to live farther beyond their means than in the north. Much of the debt crisis in Latin America can be understood in the light of bankrupt governments extending guarantees to insolvent public autonomous institutions. The capacity of those government agencies to meet their obligations is nonexistent, yet international monetary organizations have continued to extend loans. As international public financial institutions have become wary of offering loans to those nations, foreign private banks have taken their place, but with increased interest rates.

Taxes

All the countries in question are seeking ways to raise taxes to meet obligations, but their productive systems can hardly tolerate more increases. Nor can they pay for standards of living ostentatiously flaunted by the media before their impoverished populations. Political administrations do not want to accept past lessons that show that as taxes increase, people find ways to avoid them, traditionally through tax evasion and contraband. The Guatemalan government, in an attempt to reduce tax evasion, hired a Swiss company to control foreign trade. It soon became a target for the private sector, although the administration claimed that the measure was beginning to produce results. Opposition to it was so great that the government could not renew its contract, and came to use the firm merely as a consultant.[12] The Sandinistas more than tripled their revenues between 1985 and 1986 through a 260 percent increase in direct tax collections and a 240 percent improvement in the indirect ones.[13] Today, however, the national economy is virtually paralyzed. In 1988, the Social Democratic administration of Costa Rica approved a dramatic tax increase on luxury items to cover 36 percent of that year's budgetary deficit.[14] In spite of this, more taxes on goods and services such as petroleum products, telephones, and so forth, have been announced.[15]

As with indebtedness, taxation reflects values. In northern countries, when legislators establish tax policies, they are prone to giving greater consideration to encouraging production rather than to seeking added revenue for the treasury. They also seem to attribute greater importance to collections. In the south, taxes are levied with greater concern for the treasury than for production. In short, where abundance of land, labor, and capital have made entrepreneurial activities attractive, the thinking of legislators reflects a concern with production more than where there is scarcity of those factors.

Inflation

Inflation rates are difficult to calculate with rapid and continuous increases in the cost of living. More reliable indicators are exchange rates, although they too leave much to be desired because of their fictitious nature. Inflation is difficult to cope with when money is not backed by production. Given faltering production and increasing indebtedness, the only recourse of administrations to satisfy consumers is borrowing or printing money. Throughout the region the purchasing power of currencies has plummeted, salaries have grown very slowly, and inflation has steadily increased.[16] It is far more pronounced in Nicaragua because of the state of war. This creates black markets where dollars can be obtained at rates that vary depending on the supply. This is reflected in constant devaluations, shown in table 7. In recent times it has been significantly easier to obtain dollars in certain countries due to "laundering" from drug trafficking operations. For these reasons, exchange rates are largely academic.

Shortages of foreign exchange have made the plight of the Central American Common Market even worse, to the extent that Guatemala decided to operate independently of the regional clearing house, a mechanism created in 1981 to regulate payments among countries. (Costa Rica wasted no time in following suit.) Guatemala's trade with Honduras came to a standstill, and problems involved with a payments system have even led to bartering. The country with the greatest deterioration in trade is Nicaragua.[17] Costa Rican nationalized banks will not buy Central American foreign exchange at all, and will not even quote Nicaraguan córdoba exchange rates with other currencies.[18]

Inflation can be appreciated through purchasing practices. Foreign exchange in Central America is required largely for imports, travel, and debt servicing, and its use reflects national values. For example, all automobiles are imported, and as shown in table 5, Costa Rica has two or three times as many cars, in relation to its population, as other Isthmian countries. A tour of San José raises questions as to how so many vehicles can fit into such a small city. The Costa Rican is far more inclined to spend his money for imported luxury items than to invest in a savings account. As duties on luxury items increase, the credit system is adjusted to make purchases feasible. Monthly payments come to be considered by consumers as one

TABLE 7.
Exchange Rates with U.S. Dollar (Highest Points on Black Market)

	1970s	1984	1985	1986	1987	1988 June	July	Dec.
Guatemala	1.00	1.47	2.90	2.50	2.57	2.47	2.47	2.72
El Salvador	2.50	4.00	5.80	5.20	5.45	5.40	5.40	5.30
Honduras	2.00	2.70	2.70	2.30	2.30	2.40	2.40	2.70
Nicaragua	7.00	300	900	2,400	15,000	30,000	300[a]	2,800[b]
Costa Rica	8.60	53.00	57.50	59.25	68.00	69.00	76.80[c]	80.00

SOURCES: 1970s, *Progreso* magazine, October 1978, pp. 43–46; 1984, *Central America Report* 11(49):392; 1985, Ibid., 12(48):364; 1986, Ibid., 13(49):392; 1987, Ibid., 14(48):384; 1988, Ibid., 15(8):6.
[a] These are new córdobas, worth 300,000 old ones. On 14 February 1988, the Sandinista government issued new córdobas, each equivalent to one thousand old ones. See *Central America Report*, 26 February 1988, 15(8):57. That was followed in July by a 125 percent devaluation, thus leaving the rate of exchange on the black market (which reflects the availability of dollars) at three hundred. See *Central America Report*, 15 July 1988, 15(27):216. To follow rates of exchange in Nicaragua, therefore, it is necessary to convert old córdobas to new córdobas.
[b] See *Central America Report*, 2 December 1988, 15(47):369 for data concerning this entire column. For reasons presented in the foregoing note, this figure should be 2,800,000.
[c] "Minidevaluaciones" have occurred every two weeks.

more fixed expense (such as rent or electricity), and where increases in expenditures are involved, they do not have serious repercussions on styles of life. These variations from one country to another reflect value differences that, as shall be seen in chapter 8, make themselves manifest in distinct types of class consciousness.

Capital Flight

The presence of the Sandinistas has spread fear among investors throughout the Isthmus. Capital flight has been intense, and profits have been reinvested only to the extent deemed indispensable by producers.[19] Deteriorating political situations coupled with falling prices of principal export commodities on world markets become aggravated with alarming speed: "Earlier this year, buoyant world coffee prices were, along with low oil prices, one of two bright spots in the region's overcast economies. Now, with the world's major coffee producers selling off much of their reserves, the price has dropped more than 25 percent, forcing Central American countries to revise their spending plans."[20] Similar situations exist with other traditional earners of foreign exchange such as sugar and meat. Fear of Nicaragua, rising costs of living, and lack of confidence in the competence of regional political administrations have affected trust, caused loss of legitimacy, and led to the expatriation of national capital. It is frequently heard that under such circumstances the best investment is in capital markets outside the area, or even in certain central bank bonds, but not in productive activities. This panorama is made bleaker by inconsistencies in United States policy toward the Caribbean region, as in the case of sugar, which is mentioned further on. Central Americans view with dismay and perplexity the chain of events leading to the deterioration of their economies.

Before the installation of the Sandinistas in Nicaragua, the United States paid little attention to regional economic ills caused by price fluctuations of principal export items on world markets. Because the area was involved in the East-West conflict, however, the bipartisan commission headed by Henry Kissinger to study Central America made recommendations that culminated in the Caribbean Basin Initiative. This raised hopes and expectations throughout, but they are rapidly vanishing as the United States defends principles of free trade with Japan on the one hand, and on the other protects its own fifteen thousand sugar producers by curtailing imports of that commodity from the Caribbean area. The Soviet Union has been fast to move in as a client.[21]

Public Sectors

In northern countries, public sectors are proportionately smaller than in the south (see table 8). While figures concerning Nicaragua might be incomplete, clearly more job seekers find public employment in southern Central America than in the north. The size of public sectors becomes even more dramatic when presented as percentages of economically active populations, as is shown in table 9.

A principal means of political parties and organizations of rewarding faithful members is offering them jobs in government, and there are many ways of disguising this type of patronage or "spoils system." Recipients of contracts for large public projects, for example, use "floating labor forces" whose salaries, while charged to private payrolls, often depend on government funding. Thus while official Costa Rican statistics, for example, indicate that approximately 20 percent of the economically active population is on the public payroll, the correct estimate is closer to one-third.[22] The main problem is that the state inevitably grows under such circumstances, and in Costa Rica, where the system first became implanted on the Isthmus, the state is far and away the largest employer in the country.

The size of public sectors is a clear indicator of values within a society,

TABLE 8.
Public Sector Employment in Central America, 1984[a]

	Central Government	Decentralized Institutions	Total	Population	% Public Sector
Guatemala	123,367	38,034	161,401	7,963,000	2.0
El Salvador	73,146	37,071	110,217	4,857,000	2.3
Honduras	47,391	36,009	83,400	4,369,000	1.9
Nicaragua	66,000	—	66,000	3,272,000	2.0
Costa Rica	60,381	69,619	130,000	2,523,000	5.1

SOURCES: Rethelny Figueroa and Juan Francisco Pinto, in *Revista Centroamericana de Administración Pública* 8 (1985), Sección Estadística; taken from Inter-American Development Bank, *Annual report 1986*.
[a] Number of positions officially created.

TABLE 9.
Public Sectors as Percentages of Economically Active Populations, 1985

	Public Sector	Economically Act. Population	%
Guatemala	161,401	1,696,000	9.5
El Salvador	110,217	1,593,000	6.9
Honduras	83,400	763,000	10.9
Nicaragua	66,000	504,000	13.0
Costa Rica	130,000	770,000	16.8

SOURCES: James W. Wilkie and Adam Terkal (eds.), *Statistical Abstract of Latin America* 24 (1985); *Encyclopaedia Britannica* Yearbook, 1986.

for it shows the propensity of the citizenry to look to the state to solve problems. This pattern of collectivist political ideologies on the Isthmus has been most manifest in Costa Rica, yet as European doctrines like Christian socialism, Christian democracy, and social democracy have taken root in Latin America, tendencies to seek state intervention as a panacea have become more pronounced. Table 9 shows Guatemala with a greater number of people on the public payroll than would be predictable on a curve derived from the table. This responds to policies introduced by the Christian Democratic administration of Vinicio Cerezo. The growth of public sectors is accompanied by cumbersome problems. The point was made clear in May 1988, when some one hundred seventy-five thousand public employees walked off their jobs demanding salary raises. The government

TABLE 10.
Enlistment in Central American Armed Forces

	1980	1985
Guatemala	22,000	43,000
El Salvador	18,000	49,000
Honduras	18,000	22,000
Nicaragua	8,000	75,000
Costa Rica	8,000	13,828

SOURCES: *La Nación,* 19 January 1987, p. 9A (taken from U.S. Departments of State and Defense); *Central America Report,* 7 July 1987, 14(27):213.

claimed that increases would unbalance the budget and authorities called the strike illegal.[23] The points to watch in appraising public sectors are 1) the extent to which political parties find roots in them and 2) tendencies of populations to look toward them for jobs.

Armed Forces

The growth of armed forces as a result of turmoil can be seen in table 10. Central American armies are relatively large and consume significant shares of national production. The Nicaraguan army is the largest, although Honduras is supposed to have a more modern and powerful air force. Regional military forces have grown throughout in recent years as a result of the Sandinista regime, although efforts have been made in Guatemala and El Salvador to subordinate them to civilian governments. While Costa Rica has had no real army since 1949, it does have a sizeable and growing police force, armed and trained to offset (at least temporarily) any aggression from Nicaragua and to attempt to control growing public strife resulting from the deteriorating economy. The chaotic international situation and the deteriorating economy, however, have been forcing the conversion of that police force into a growing military organization. At the same time, paramilitary groups (numbering at least fifteen) are acquiring greater influence in government and civil affairs (in keeping with regional tradition). During the 1980s the Costa Rican budget for police and public security increased more than 400 percent. Regional military forces are looking for an active, unified role in containing the crisis, although it is clear that the United States does not count on the Central American Defense Council against the Sandinistas.[24]

In a region that is living through an economic depression without precedent, the military is the only area that shows real growth in spending. In both El Salvador and Nicaragua, more than half of the already strained government budgets are to pay for war. In Guatemala and Honduras, corresponding figures exceed 25 percent. All the Central American nations have been rapidly modernizing their armies, and while Honduras and El Salvador have increased their air power with sophisticated equipment, Nicaragua and Guatemala have significantly improved the efficiency of their troops.[25]

The size of the armed forces in general should be judged in terms of the roles they play in offsetting civilian influence in government. The predominance of civilians over the military can be a condition for obtaining credit from financial and political institutions like the World Bank, the International Development Bank, the United Nations, and UNESCO. This becomes all the more significant as ruling classes withdraw from productive activities and political administrations begin to feel a reduction in tax income.[26]

In Costa Rica, the military situation has been quite fortuitous. During the second half of the nineteenth century, the country had the most important army on the Isthmus, but it declined during the first half of the twentieth century. When José Figueres won the 1948 civil war, he feared that the coffee planters might object to his revolutionary measures (particularly high land taxes) and attempt to win support from the army to replace him. In fact, Figueres's own minister of security, Edgar Cardona Quirós, attempted to overthrow him, precisely due to the excessive taxes he proposed.[27] The planters feared that under the new revolutionary order, having both government and the army in the hands of Figueres could be dangerous. That is why both factions saw common grounds to abolish the army.[28]

Values play an important role in the configuration of outlooks of Central Americans toward the military. In Guatemala, where ruling class awareness is strong, as is that of the army itself, conflict between the two is almost inevitable. In El Salvador, although ruling class awareness is weaker, loyalties among members of classes graduated from the military academy are strong and conflict seems inevitable, particularly due to the economic support that the army receives from the United States. In Honduras, ruling class awareness is relatively weak and the army is the most powerful political factor. That is why it is often said that the country has two governments (military and civilian) but that the army rules. The ruling class has no choice but to remain in the good graces of the military. In Nicaragua, the hierarchy of both the Sandinista and Contra armed forces is made up of ruling class

members, a fact that underscores divisions within that class and compli-
cates speculation as long as there is no reconciliation between the two
factions. In Costa Rica, despite the half-century of nonmilitary tradition,
many realize that a more effective system of self-defense is becoming increasingly necessary, for there is a widespread feeling that national security
is at stake.

Agrarian reform

In Latin America, agrarian reform came into fashion half a century after the
Mexican Revolution of 1910. Central America's most acute problems have
appeared in El Salvador, due to the small size of that densely populated
country. The problem lies in converting productive properties capable of
competing on world markets into minifundia with proprietors who lack
both know-how and access to those markets and who will eventually have
to be bailed out by the state. Cooperatives have produced mediocre (if not
poor) results throughout.

Guatemala has no legal land reform program (undoubtedly to avoid
alarming capitalists) but political administrations have found ways to dis-
tribute farms to growing numbers of peasants who are now becoming
more demanding. This lack of definition has acquired explosive propor-
tions and raises questions as to how long political administrations can
appease both the "haves" and the "have-nots." The church is one of the
main supporters of the movement. In El Salvador, the government has announced the second phase of agrarian reform (although the first and third
have been completed) and both the press and landowners predict further
confrontations between proprietors and *campesinos* (peasants). "The move
is seen as an offer by President José Napoleón Duarte to compensate for
his waning popular support and faltering negotiations with guerrillas." In
Honduras, as elsewhere on the Isthmus, campesinos are demanding land
reform and claim that the government is dragging its feet. To avoid further
social tensions in rural areas, President José Azcona recently announced
changes in the laws governing land. The Sandinistas have been distributing land to individuals instead of to cooperatives, principally in areas of
Contra activity for propaganda purposes. Most of the other land thus far
distributed has gone to cooperatives.[29]

Land reform is fundamentally a political issue in class conflict staged
by the left, the church, and often by landowners themselves. Where the
left and the church take the initiative, political administrations, for fear
of alienating productive ruling classes, merely pay lip service to the concept. Landowners who seek expropriation of their farms under the aegis of

agrarian reform do so because they need liquid assets for other activities, and they use their friendship with administrators of that institution as a means of achieving their desires.

Human rights

Issues involving human rights have surfaced throughout Central America with the exception of Costa Rica. Guatemala is the most highly questioned nation in this context, for individual and institutional violations have not ended under the Christian Democratic government, and official rhetoric emphasizes this fact. During the first ten months of civilian rule, 224 people were put to death for political reasons. The number of murders, kidnappings, and disappearances is down considerably from previous years but is still disturbing. This decrease in violence appears to have more to do with past terrorism than with consolidation of the civilian regime. The OAS has painted an unrealistic picture of the country as a tribute to the "reinitiation" of democracy, and the persecution of Indians has received international attention. In El Salvador, the OAS claims that the human rights situation has improved but that violations attributed to the fratricidal nature of the war with the guerrillas continue. Honduras too has had a poor record for some years, although not as bad as Guatemala and El Salvador. Successive administrations have denied the existence of the problem, while paradoxically promising to correct the situation. In 1988, in what appears to set a precedent for Latin America, the Inter-American Court on Human Rights found the government guilty of the death of a student in 1981.[30]

Nicaraguans and Salvadorans fleeing political upheaval in their homelands have sought haven in the United States as well as in other Central American countries. On the Isthmus, those most affected have been Honduras and Costa Rica, where immigrants present health problems and compete illegally in labor markets by working for lower salaries than nationals. The number of refugees in Honduras is estimated at some one hundred thousand. Recently, about one thousand were repatriated by the United Nations High Command for Refugees, and more were expected to return to their homelands.[31] For those governments involved, these present other problems that include shelter, food, and disease. Recent immigration controls imposed by the United States are bound to have repercussions on El Salvador as exiles are forced to return from the United States. In addition to the jobs they will require, they will cease sending remittances (estimated at $400 to $600 million annually) to their families, which is more than El Salvador receives in aid from the United States.[32]

TABLE II.
U. S. Military and Economic Aid to Central America
(millions of U.S. dollars)

	1980	1981	1982	1983	1984	1985	1986
Guatemala							
Military	0.0	0.0	0.0	0.0	0.0	0.3	10.3
Economic	11.1	16.6	23.9	17.6	33.3	73.8	77.2
El Salvador							
Military	6.0	35.5	82.0	81.3	196.5	128.2	132.6
Economic	57.8	133.6	182.2	231.1	331.1	326.1	350.8
Honduras							
Military	4.0	8.9	31.3	37.3	77.5	62.5	88.2
Economic	51.0	33.9	78.0	101.2	209.0	138.9	157.9
Costa Rica							
Military	0.0	0.3	2.1	2.6	9.2	9.2	2.7
Economic	14.0	13.3	120.6	212.4	177.9	208.0	187.3
Totals	143.9	241.8	520.1	683.5	1,034.5	947.0	1,007.0

SOURCE: *Central America Report*, 3 October 1986, 13(38):303.

Foreign Aid, Development, and Values

Foreign aid from the United States, Germany, Canada, Japan, Israel, the European Economic Community, and the Interamerican Development Bank has flowed into all Central American countries (including Nicaragua, until 1985) in recent years. In 1988, the United Nations approved a regional aid package of $4.3 billion, much of which will go into servicing foreign debt.[33] At the present time, United States aid has tended to diminish throughout the Isthmus, but for varying motives in each case. Thus in Guatemala, aid in 1988 was down by 25 percent from 1987, when it reached almost $200 million (see table 11). Aid has kept El Salvador afloat and accounts for its success by comparison with Nicaragua, for example. It was reduced from $110 million to $85 million in 1988, however, because of that country's decision to grant amnesty to those involved in the 1985 assassination of United States marines. The impact of such capital injections is still great.[34]

In Nicaragua, during the half-century of Somoza rule, most regional economic assistance from the United States supported the anticommunist stances of the three members of the family who governed. Nicaragua became an axis from which United States power was wielded throughout the Isthmus and the Caribbean.[35] The advent of the Sandinistas, however, led to a significant change in United States criteria for extending aid to Central America. As the Managua regime increasingly leaned on the Soviet Union and Cuba for support, aid to that country decreased (although it was not suspended until 1985) and was channeled to other nations in the region, particularly Costa Rica and Honduras.[36] In Costa Rica, in spite of charges by AID of misuse (by wealthy and influential people) of a $95 million fund of accumulated donations, the nationalized banking system was reorganized in accordance with AID's conditions and assistance was assured through 1989.[37]

Foreign aid has had both positive and negative effects. In an era of rampant inflation, excessive public spending, decreasing production, and consequent devaluations in all Central American countries, the massive inflow of dollars has served to bolster faltering currencies. As the Nicaraguan problem has dragged on, this aid has been maintained. Continued economic assistance has to an extent had negative effects on production, for it has caused beneficiary nations to overlook their own problems, while depending on the United States to bail them out.

The trade embargo declared by the United States against Nicaragua has been somewhat offset by credits, donations, and even investments, fundamentally from socialist countries. Those nations have increased their aid for armaments but also for textile production, mining, port construction, and hydroelectric plants. Additional help has come from Sweden, Finland, Norway, Peru, India, China, and the Soviet Union, among others (see table 12). Even the Costa Rican state-owned electric company, the Instituto Costarricense de Electricidad, supplied over one million dollars monthly of electric energy to Nicaragua for a number of years, without requiring the Sandinista administration to pay for it. (Today Costa Rica imports power from Honduras.)

This aid was given in just ten weeks. Two months later the Sandinistas received from the European Economic Community further material assistance amounting to many millions of dollars (thirty tractors, fourteen trucks, three hundred transistor radios, and much more). Additional help came from Cuba, Hungary, Korea, the Soviet Union, India, Spain, Poland, Czechoslovakia, and Denmark for food staples, clothing, construction material, office supplies, and farm and irrigation equipment. Nicaragua has also received private donations from the Hungarian Solidarity Committee,

TABLE 12.
Economic Assistance to Nicaragua, 1 May–15 July 1986
(U.S. dollars)

Peru	21 million
Sweden	36 million
Norway	11 million
Finland	20 million
United Nations	50 million
Organization of American States	70 thousand
International Investigation Center of Canada	76 thousand

SOURCE: *Central America Report*, 25 July 1986, 13(28):223; 13 May 1988, 15(18):142.

the Friedrich Ebert Foundation (which helps fund the Socialist International), the Danish University Students' Association, the Hamburg Evangelical Church, the Ecumenical Council for Refugees, Tierra de Hombres (Switzerland), Belgium, and Holland, for food, clothing, medicine, sports equipment, tents, medical equipment, and video and photographic equipment.[38]

Significance of Some Dissimilarities

What do the foregoing pointers indicate? They show a general deterioration of regional economies that can be appreciated through a few eloquent headlines from the front-page index of the *Central America Report:* "Coffee prices falling"; "Continuing decline of the Central American Common Market"; "Foreign debt saps already anemic economies"; "Exchange measures provoke trade crisis"; "Building decline reflects crisis"; and "Industry in five-year slump."

National ruling classes in northern Central America have placed government at the service of production by 1) incurring relatively small public debts, 2) refusing to openly encourage agrarian reform, 3) being willing to engage large armed forces to keep order, 4) supporting the use of small public sectors (as percentages of economically active populations), 5) maintaining relatively stable currencies and minimal inflation to protect their business interests (Nicaragua and Costa Rica have had more violent exchange rate fluctuations than other countries), and 6) trying to restrain inflation to protect their businesses. Their southern counterparts, on the other hand, have created productive systems at the service of government by doing just the opposite. They have incurred large public debt by creating huge public sectors. In Costa Rica, the elimination of the army in 1948 released economic resources for more welfare, orienting populations down the path of affluent societies with no productive basis to support them.[39]

The response of the ruling classes under circumstances such as the presence of the Sandinistas is largely determined by values and the social environment in which they develop rather than by pressures from the United States or from other countries opposed to its policies. In the north, they are more aware of their status than in the south, and when threatened, their members are more prone to close ranks and to fight for what have traditionally been their prerogatives. In the south, their counterparts have less arrogance about their position and can be more easily displaced by others groups. How this functions can best be seen through a case study of Costa Rica. Chapter 7 deals with Costa Rica and the relationship between its ruling class and economic and political development. Chapter 8 clarifies the role of similar groups (also based on kinship) in the other countries and attempts to show how they have forged values that contrast with those of Costa Rica.

CHAPTER 7

The Costa Rican Ruling Class and Values

Four Tales

Hermenegildo lived on the coffee hacienda with his wife and eleven children, six of whom were blondish. He and his brothers had been born there, and all could see that today life was better than it had been in earlier years. In December, Hermenegildo had used his hard-earned Christmas bonus to make a down payment on a record player. The preceding year he had done the same with a set of aluminum furniture, and he still had a few payments to make. Furthermore, all his children had beautiful plastic toys such as he had never seen as a child, when his parents' furniture as well as his own toys had been made by his father. There was no doubt that one lived better today, and this made Hermenegildo feel good.

But all that glitters is not gold. One day one of his little blond children became ill. He became so weak that Hermenegildo and his wife had to take him to the hospital, where the doctor said that the child was suffering from malnutrition. "You can tell by just looking at the color of his hair," he added. "I'm afraid I have to keep him here."

Four months later, on a cold rainy Sunday, Hermenegildo and his wife prayed before a small tombstone. He begged her resignation. Crying, she asked, "Why?"

* *

Carlos Anchía lived beyond Jocotal de Río Segundo. He owned a small farm of about twelve acres next to the Jocotal River, where he grew beans. In October the heavy rains set in and for a full week it poured relentlessly. The river flooded and when on the sixth day Carlos surveyed his crops, he saw that the bridge had been washed away. It was his only link with the outside world. His first sensation was one of panic, for that was the bridge over which all the products of the district reached the market. He meditated and finally decided to talk with don Jacinto Benavides, a municipal councilman and a friend.

The next day he went to see don Jacinto and was told that he was in the municipality. He went there and was told that don Jacinto had gone to the capital with a group of congressmen. Depressed, Carlos returned to his humble shack. He went back several times but was unable to see don Jacinto because he was always busy with congressmen. He decided to request a hearing with the municipal council, where he explained his problem and returned home with some hope. Days, weeks, and even months went by, but the bridge was not rebuilt.

Carlos Anchía lost his crops.

*   *

"Mr. President," stammered Juan Carreras. Uneasily, he turned to his small group of followers in search of support, knowing that he would not get it. "Mr. President," he repeated. "As secretary general of the syndicate of state employees, it is my duty," he faltered, "to inform you that the group I represent is not willing to accept further delays in salary increases," Juan Carreras stared at his companions with a sense of insecurity, although this seemed to bolster his courage.

"Mr. Carreras," answered the president. "As chief of state, it is my duty to to inform you that my investiture does not allow me to surpass the limitations imposed on my administration by the national budget. I have given instructions to the effect that this be made clear to you. It is inconceivable that this type of problem should have to reach the desk of the president of the republic."

Under the stares of his colleagues, Juan Carreras stammered: "I inform you, Mr. President, that if by the fifteenth of this month our grievances have not been fully satisfied, you alone will bear the responsibility of a general strike." With apprehension he awaited the reaction of the president.

Very ill at ease, the president turned to the members of his cabinet in search of moral support, knowing that he would not get it. After a few words with them, he again addressed Mr. Carreras: "As president of the republic and in the presence of the members of my cabinet, I give you my solemn commitment to satisfy your grievances to the best of my ability and as expediently as my office allows."

*   *

The congressmen took the firm and irrevocable decision that Costa Rica urgently needed an agrarian reform. But it occurred to someone to ask whether any of them actually knew anything about problems related to land tenure and farming. Of the fifty-seven members, only one owned a small farm.

The congressmen then took another firm and irrevocable decision, ordering a three-week course for members of the legislature on general problems affecting agriculture. This would furnish the lawmakers with the necessary knowledge to enact a significant agrarian reform.[1]

In these tales are hidden many of the problems that affect modern Costa Rican society. The one concerning Hermenegildo has to do with inflation and serious problems of malnutrition that result in part from propaganda aimed at convincing the populace that it is preferable to own a record player than to feed one's family adequately. The tale about Carlos Anchía has to do with inadequacies of local government in regional development and suggests one reason why new institutions, like the communal development committees, have been emerging in competition with municipal government. Juan Carreras's experience with the president of the republic underscores the gravity of a public sector emerging as a power and brings to mind the sad image of Uruguay, until recently a prosperous and democratic country that was swallowed by an oversized state bureaucracy. Finally, the anecdote regarding the congressmen[2] reveals some of the implications for a developing society of the transfer of power to people who understand little about agriculture and the significance of production.

A clearly discernible link ties the problems of Hermenegildo to those of Juan Carreras and the president of the republic, of Carlos Anchía and councilman Jacinto Benavides, and of the fifty-seven congressmen. It is the Costa Rican ruling class with its detached attitude that, under the stress of change, has set the entire society adrift. To grasp the meaning of this, it is necessary to revert to the Conquest and to present these and other national problems within a comprehensible context. Members of this class, working with a marked scarcity of resources (by comparison with their Central American counterparts), have shaped the political system as well as their own perception of themselves as a class.

Power of Ruling Class Members

During and after the Conquest, two types of Spaniards—nobles and plebeians—came to Costa Rica and mixed with relatively small indigenous societies. The fundamental difference between them lay in the exclusive access of the former to positions of political privilege. Toward the middle of the colonial period, in the principal cities of Heredia, San José, Cartago, and Alajuela, nobles accounted for approximately 20 percent of the Spanish inhabitants, and some of them were relatively wealthy. Don Antonio de Acosta Arévalo, for instance, owned extensive cacao farms (the most lucrative crop during the seventeenth century) as well as a fleet of some fifteen sailing vessels that plied the Caribbean Sea along the Isthmus. Juan de Echavarría Navarro de Ocampo Golfín bestowed dowries amounting to more than twenty-six thousand pesos, in addition to cacao farms, upon his six daughters at the time of their marriages.[3] The money and power required for activities such as cacao cultivation (including the construction of roads, bridges, ports, and so forth) enabled people like these to lead comfortable lives. During the seventeenth and eighteenth centuries a mule cost only two pesos, a horse eight, and a mare three. A bushel and a half of corn or wheat cost only one peso. Indian labor was twelve pesos a year for a man and eight for a woman. A teacher earned twenty-five annually for each four students.[4] The low price of these goods and services, in contrast with the dowries Echavarría Navarro gave his daughters, underscores the affluent position of at least part of the Hispanic American colonial nobility in the territory.

Marriage of nobles was generally limited to their own class. Juan Vázquez de Coronado Anaya, conquistador of the southern part of the Isthmus, is an example (see appendixes 2 and 6). His lineage crosses with those of other nobles such as don Antonio de Acosta Arévalo and don Nicolás de González y Oviedo, who settled in Costa Rica later during the colonial period. Their descendants came to form a group that, thanks to their noble birth, had exclusive access to public office. Not all held those posts, but those who did had to come from that class. By Independence in 1821, patterns of kinship were consolidated in the political system, and in Costa Rica, where twenty-eight signers of the Declaration of Independence took control of the new republic, twenty-three were related either as brothers or cousins, or as fathers, sons, and grandsons. All descended from conquistadors and nobles. Similar patterns are found in legislatures during most of the nineteenth century and part of the twentieth.[5] The ruling class eventually divided into groups and many of them have opposed each other politically, due fundamentally to economic reasons. Political and electoral competition among descendants of conquistador Cristóbal de Alfaro (appendix 1), ancestor of thirty-six presidents in Costa Rica and eleven elsewhere in Central America, provides examples of such opposition. Since 1905, the following cousins descended from him have been rivals for the presidency:

1905 Cleto González Víquez and Bernardo Soto Alfaro
1909 Ricardo Jiménez Oreamuno and Rafael Yglesias Castro
1919 Julio Acosta García and José María Soto Alfaro
1923 Ricardo Jiménez Oreamuno and Alberto Echandi Montero
1928 Cleto González Víquez and Carlos María Jiménez Ortiz
1932 Ricardo Jiménez Oreamuno, Manuel Castro Quesada, Carlos
*   María Jiménez Ortiz, and Max Koberg Bolandi*
1936 León Cortés Castro and Octavio Beeche Argüello
1940 Rafael Angel Calderón Guardia
1944 Teodoro Picado Michalski and León Cortés Castro
1948 Otilio Ulate Blanco and Rafael Angel Calderón Guardia
1958 Mario Echandi Jiménez and Franciso J. Orlich Bolmarcich
1962 Francisco J. Orlich Bolmarcich, Rafael Angel Calderón Guardia,
*   and Otilio Ulate Blanco*
1966 José Joaquín Trejos Fernández and Daniel Oduber Quirós
1970 Mario Echandi Jiménez
1974 Daniel Oduber Quirós and Rodrigo Carazo Odio
1978 Rodrigo Carazo Odio and Luis Alberto Monge Alvarez
1982 Luis Alberto Monge Alvarez and Rafael Angel Calderón Fournier
1986 Oscar Arias Sánchez and Rafael Angel Calderón Fournier
1990 Rafael Angel Calderón Fournier

The foregoing presidents and candidates ran for office during the twentieth century. During the nineteenth century, candidates, almost without exception, descended from Alfaro. In 1940, 1970, and 1990, the name of only one person is given. This is because, to the best of my knowledge, the other contenders did not descend from Alfaro.

Other examples include Presidents Juan Rafael Mora Porras (1849–59) and José María Montealegre Fernández (1859–63), who were brothers-in-law and prominent members of the nineteenth-century coffee planter aristocracy. When Montealegre succeeded Mora in office, quarrels between them led to Mora's execution (along with another brother-in-law, General José María Cañas) by a firing squad at the order of Montealegre. Finally, President Alfredo González Flores (1914–17) was succeeded in a military coup by a distant cousin Federico Tinoco Granados (1917–19). Similar situations occurred between other presidents whose names can be found in the family trees in appendixes 2–3. In Costa Rica, some half-dozen presidents have been ousted by their own relatives, distant though the relationship may have been in some cases.

The Coffee Complex and the State

Coffee planters were able to produce the first real wealth known by the new republic. Their activity proved beneficial both for themselves and for small and middle size producers from other social categories. Initially, this resulted in the rapid expansion of business, for to satisfy demand on the English market and to ensure good quality of the final product, the planters bought crops from other producers and blended them with their own in industrial plants called *beneficios*. This created a mutual dependence among producers, for while the minor ones came to depend on the planters for the sale of their coffee, the latter needed the former to satisfy demand and to maintain quality. At the same time, the plantation owners' awareness of the scarcity of labor led them to strengthen economic, social, and even political ties (exceptional in Latin America) with their own labor forces. The planters produced and marketed their own crops, but the increased volume of business eventually created a need for exporters. These were generally of German and Spanish origin, and established bonds of friendship and kinship with the planter group.

Initially, production costs were defrayed by the planters, but when their capital became insufficient to cover expenses brought about by rising demand, they sought advances from their British clients. There were several periods of economic depression, but the second half of the nineteenth century was generally one of boom for coffee and led to the establishment of the first private banks. These financed the entire national crop, working through the planters, who continued assisting smaller producers. After the 1948 civil war, banks were nationalized to make credit available to larger sectors of the population. When they offered to provide capital directly to small producers, however, these refused because they were satisfied with the existing system.[6] The mechanism, then, has not varied for over a century, in spite of three changes in the source of financing.

Since the planters controlled the most lucrative economic enterprise in the country, the establishment of a relationship between the complex they created and the nation's political system was inevitable. As new groups from their own class undertook other activities—usually in export agriculture—similar ties developed between the economy and politics, but never involving as many people. Linkages between those engaged in the coffee complex and the political system came to exist at all social levels. A glance at several aspects of the political system can help understand this.

Costa Rica is divided into seven provinces with eighty-six subdivisions called cantons. These are in turn made up of districts, the number of which depends on population size. Cantons are governed by municipal councils composed of regidores. Political parties present tickets with their candidates for president, congressmen, and regidores, and the selection of the aspirants (in theory at least) starts with assemblies held in districts and subsequently at cantonal, provincial, and national levels. In rural areas, aspirants at district and cantonal levels are usually linked to export agriculture and often have close ties with (or work directly on) large plantations but come from classes of lower status than that of the planters. Cantons that do not produce for export (excepting those located in large urban centers) rarely if ever have a "native son" elected to the legislature.[7] At provincial and national levels, candidates have generally come from the national ruling class and, until recently, primarily from the planter group. In the congress of 1920 people first noted that congressmen elected from rural areas were beginning to emerge from other social backgrounds. Because a number of them were named Hermenegildo, which reflects peasant extraction, it was mockingly referred to as the "congress of the Hermenegildos."

The first planters, most of whom descended from conquistadors and held important political posts,[8] did not easily adapt to their new affluence, but generations that followed are responsible for the creation of good public schools, the emergence of professionals prepared in European universities, the construction of railways and roads, and refined tastes that can be appreciated in the national theater, a replica of the Paris opera. A change took place toward midtwentieth century when the planters began to lose the heritage of their forefathers, and the power vacuum they left soon began to be filled by collectivist political parties that converted the state into an institution to satisfy the needs of those parties. The result was a rapid growth of the number of state employees that went from 10 percent of the economically active population in 1950[9] to about 30 percent in 1988.[10] Much of this change took place through taxes levied on coffee production, and in this sense, the planters underwrote the cost of their own decline.

The political parties sought to consolidate their hegemony in other ways and obtained additional support from their clientele by establishing an obligatory Christmas bonus for employees. There were also changes in the public educational system, and both of these innovations made the planters lose interest in civic affairs. Export agriculture continues to form the backbone of the economy, although as industrial production, other nontraditional activities, and tourism grow and new forces emerge, it loses the position it once enjoyed. Change has been introduced fundamentally through the regulation of credit and through tax and exchange incentives, all subsidized by coffee and by agriculture in general. Many of the planters have diversified their investments and even expatriated capital. Power, then, has become the object of dispute among the planter group (in open decline), industrialists, merchants, the public sector, and others. Members of the ruling class have increasingly sought white collar jobs in the public sector, exposing themselves to and developing new values as their own varying ideologies converge with those of others employed by the state. The political decline of the traditional ruling class can be appreciated through the comparison of the descendants of conquistador Juan Vázquez de Coronado in the legislature and total number of Costa Rican legislators (figure 1). Congressmen descended from Vázquez were generally coffee planters who lived in important urban centers, while those who began to replace them in the twentieth century were usually municipal councilmen *(regidores)* from rural areas.

The Power Vacuum and Contenders to Fill It

Lester C. Thurow[11] has outlined a political-economic situation in which problems that apparently have no solution appear everywhere: inflation, unemployment, deterioration of the economy, environmental contamination, irreconcilable demands of pressure groups and an extraordinarily complex regulation of all phases of life. Do these problems have no solution, he asks, or are our leaders incompetent? Have we lost our working habits? Should we surrender our social advances in order to compete with others?

Thurow observes that economic deterioration has political impacts, for as levels of living decrease, discontent with government increases. A decadent economy means sacrifices in consumption habits, and in a democracy, that creates tensions that are more difficult to control than under dictatorships. Meaningful arrangements are never made and the politics of confrontation rapidly approaches. Programs which would improve national standards of living are vetoed by minorities, and no one has the ability to impose solutions, nor is any solution acceptable to all.

When policies are adapted to solve problems, Thurow warns, some people win and some lose. Some incomes increase and others decrease. It is a game which adds up to zero in the sense that losses are equal to gains. Sports add up to zero, because for every winner there has to be a loser. The crux of the matter in a society is to decide how losses are to be divided and

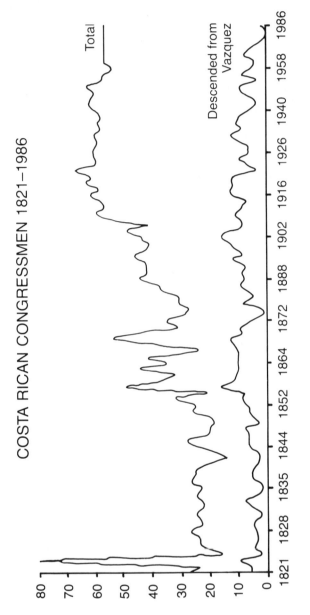

COSTA RICAN CONGRESSMEN 1821–1986

Total

Descended from
Vazquez

FIGURE 1. Number of Costa Rican ruling-class congressmen descended from the conquistador Juan Vazquez de Coronado (appendix 6), compared with total number of congressmen 1821–1986.

THE COSTA RICAN RULING CLASS AND VALUES · 117

that is precisely what the political system is least capable of doing. When there are gains, it can divide them, but when there are losses, it becomes paralyzed. With political paralysis comes economic paralysis.

While these thoughts describe the United States in the 1980s, similar assessments apply to contemporary Central America—particularly to Costa Rica—and raise issues concerning leadership, decision making, and how Isthmian ruling classes confront problems in their own societies. Political leaders throughout are influenced by their cultural heritage. In Costa Rica, an impasse has developed due to the withdrawal of the planters from the political arena and the consequent emergence of others. During the 1986 campaign, sixteen political parties registered at both local and national levels, which is excessive for a country with only two and a half million inhabitants and fewer than a million voters. A political party can register nationally with the signatures of only three thousand citizens, and on a local level (which is at times more difficult), with those of one percent of regional population.[12]

As in a zero-sum game, political paralysis comes from economic deterioration. In Costa Rica, the latter is a result of a loss of confidence in the ability of administrations to confront national and international problems, coupled with a feeling of insecurity caused by Sandinista Nicaragua. Some incomes increase and others decrease, but the afflictions remain the same. With the deterioration of the economy, losses must be shared, but that is precisely what the ruling class—through the political system—is incapable of doing.

Many problems that Costa Rica faces today can be attributed to a political party system that switched the basis of its support from a rural to an urban population, through growing dependence on patron-client relationships in the public sector. This has inadvertently created a welfare state that the economy cannot support. The problem can be better understood in the light of groups now contending for authority.

The planters, after more than a hundred years of economic and political hegemony, have lost their predominant position. Did their lack of diversification of profits contribute to their decline?[13] Why did they neglect the public education system (probably the key element in their relationship with the scanty national labor force)? Why did their "advantage of taken positions"[14] (suggesting that sons of politicians have the edge over those in families not involved in politics), inherited from their forefathers during the preceding century, cease to function after the midtwentieth century? Foreign exchange provided by their undertakings is needed increasingly each year, but few seem to worry about the problem of who is going to replace them.

The new industrial sector emerged around 1962 in Costa Rica (1960 in the rest of Central America) with the establishment of the Central American Common Market. Under its wing, new groups (some from the ruling class) began to import semimanufactured goods for assembly (much like a set of Lego toys) and to sell inferior goods at inflated prices within the region under quasi-monopolistic conditions (see chapter 2). They have emerged economically and politically through subsidies provided by agriculture (principally coffee) and thanks to a clientele that has no choice but to purchase their products. President Luis Alberto Monge Alvarez (1982–86) attempted to discontinue government subsidies to industry but was forced by pressure groups to desist.

Industrialization has been accompanied by one irregularity: contracts signed since 1962 between potential investors and the Ministry of Industries show *authorized* capital but not the amounts actually *paid in*.[15] Neither the ministry nor the Chamber of Industries follows through to determine how much capital was actually put into the business.[16] The system lends itself to questioning both the criteria used for granting subsidies and other benefits in that sector, as well as the very nature of ethics and legitimacy in public administration and business.[17]

Groups representing commerce, whose imports are heavily dependent on foreign exchange provided by coffee exports, have also participated in the race to fill the power vacuum. During the nineteenth century most important merchants emerged from the traditional ruling class, although during the twentieth many have come from other social origins. They have acquired an autonomy exceeded only by that of the planters, although that advantage has been eroded since the early 1980s by a stagnating economy and a mushrooming foreign debt,[18] which have led administrations to devote dwindling supplies of foreign exchange to meet government obligations. With fewer dollars for commerce to use for imports, its future is uncertain, although spokesmen have been successful in mustering public opinion by predicting dire changes in patterns of consumption if enough foreign exchange for imports is not available.

As with the industrial sector, activities of the business community have raised the question of legitimacy in the eyes of the public, adding to the national value crisis. For example, exporters at times understate the cost of goods on invoices presented to the Central Bank to obtain export permits and request importers of those goods in other countries to remit only the value declared and deposit the remainder directly in foreign bank accounts.

Overinvoicing, also a practice, consists in arranging to have exporters in foreign countries present buyers in Costa Rica with inflated invoices that are used at the Central Bank to buy dollars to pay for those imports. The difference between their real and declared values is pocketed by the importer, who thus avoids taxes and accumulates foreign exchange.

Parties of the left. The Communist Party was organized after the 1929 depression in the banana-producing areas where there were large concentrations of labor, much of it foreign.[19] It was originally called Partido Vanguardia Popular but became divided and later consolidated its position through a coalition called Pueblo Unido. With the advent of Fidel Castro in Cuba, other leftist organizations emerged (see chapter 2); due to lack of Soviet funding, one even sought financing from holding up banks. In spite of not having won over 6 percent of the votes in any campaign, the left has been successful in placing members (often strategically) in most administrations. A new branch (Alianza Popular) competes with Pueblo Unido in spite of their coalition. The former follows the Soviet line, and the presence of both Cuba and Nicaragua endows it with a vitality lacking in the old guard. It could be said that it represents an autochthonous version of Eurocommunism. There are even two Communist newspapers that use the same name. All leftist groups confront difficulties reconciling their nation's situation with communist doctrine, for they lack a necessary ingredient: a proletariat.[20] "Undermining the new coalition's interests is its waning popular support, embarrassingly patent during the February 1986 general elections when its two component parts received 2.3 percent and 2.7 percent, respectively, of total votes cast."[21]

Labor unions are relatively new in the Costa Rican political arena. They have had the least acceptance in the coffee complex (which employs the greatest number of workers), and this for two reasons. One has to do with its paternalistic labor-management relationships that make the peon feel sufficiently secure with the planter to avoid upsetting him by joining a union. The other is that many peons own small parcels of land and sell coffee to large producers. In this sense they are both proprietors and laborers and do not have the same goals as unions. Organized labor, on the other hand, has been accepted in banana-producing areas and subsequently in the industrial and public sectors. Banana companies maintained a rigid separation within their personnel between upper and intermediary hierarchies, on the one hand, and employees of lower status, on the other, and this facilitated the development and growth of unions. The principal one (United Brands, formerly United Fruit) was forced to cease much of its activity in the country during the Monge administration, and this has to an extent undermined the position of organized labor. Something similar, yet not as extreme, developed in the 1980s in the industrial sector, where management in some of the largest firms learned to cope with organized labor, while in others there have been constant clashes between the two. In both cases labor-management relations generally leave much to be desired.

Social Democrats and leftist parties that have participated in the political arena have sought support from and control of labor unions. The PLN has followed in the footsteps of the Mexican PRI by offering candidacies for congress to representatives of different interest groups, including "youth" (which in the Latin American political sense, has little to do with age, and implies being younger than the older political orders),[22] women, blacks, and labor unions.[23] The problem confronting labor organizations is to determine how to align themselves with political parties to best achieve their goals, because alone, their chances of acquiring power are limited (with the exception of syndicates of state employees, who could eventually establish an important position of national leadership).

The modern *welfare state* is another contender for power in the political arena. Its existence is due fundamentally to the use by political parties of economic resources to satisfy partisan electoral interests. Before the 1948 civil war, large and small parties could legally register, but those with access to capital had advantages over the others. Legislation was introduced to have the state finance campaigns, with the hope of concentrating funds in the hands of parties rather than private groups, but it actually made little difference because parties are controlled by private groups even today. The important role of capital in campaigns is now played in primary elections, which in 1986, for example, cost a candidate an estimated five hundred thousand dollars.[24] Funds for primaries, contrary to those for national elections, must be supplied by candidates and their friends.

Parties found in the welfare state an expedient vehicle for developing a spoils system where jobs are doled out to followers in payment for favors and services. Through these modern patron-client relationships, the state soon became the country's largest employer.[25] The public sector has organized syndicates in banking, utilities, transportation, teaching, communications, and other fields, and these have formed a National Association of Public Employees (Asociación Nacional de Empleados Públicos). This is the largest and most powerful trade union and when its demands (usually for salary increases) are not met, it has been able to paralyze government. Within the political arena, it is far and away the most powerful participant and grows under the sponsorship of all parties. The new political system incorporates people from classes that previously did not participate in government, although the traditional ruling class occupies much of the upper hierarchy.

With the extension of urbanism and growth of the welfare state, political parties have increasingly developed patronage by seeking government employees as their clientele, and the very concept of public servants has become distorted.[26] For example, a former president of the state housing institution recently revealed that members of the board of directors have the right to receive a cut in each housing project, equivalent to 2 percent of the value of the total number of houses to be constructed.[27] Change is visible in the attitude of public servants, who increasingly regard authority with scorn. For instance, since midcentury, it has become common for state employees to address the public in the familiar *vos* (usually reserved for close family members or intimate friends) instead of the respectful *usted*. This seems to express a fictitious type of egalitarianism that is fostered by the party system itself, but it is distasteful to the public.[28]

Although professional politicians have existed in Costa Rica since the nineteenth century, changes in their nature have accompanied the advent of the welfare state. Until the formation of political parties during the latter part of that century, candidates for congress ran as independents, but as parties were organized, aspirants for office came to identify themselves increasingly with them. Ten percent of the congressmen between 1821 and 1948 served in their posts for ten to thirty years. Manuel Antonio Bonilla Nava served thirty-four years, and Andrés Sáenz Llorente thirty-eight.[29] New electoral practices after the 1948 civil war banned reelection to congress during consecutive periods and virtually eliminated independent politicians by making them dependent on parties. Congressmen must now wait four years between terms and in the interim seek other public posts. The constitution allows presidents to serve only one term. Government, then, continues to be a way of life for many, but in another fashion since 1948.

This discussion of the emergence of the public sector as one of the principal powers in Costa Rican politics is reminiscent of some of the thoughts of Guillermo O'Donnell on the evolution of political systems that either incorporate middle and lower strata and allow them a voice in national politics or, on the other hand, exclude them from the political arena.[30] In the economic and political development of Argentina, he views three phases: an initial "oligarchic" stage, where no popular sectors emerge and exporting élites dominate the state and orient public policy to suit their own needs. This is followed by a "populist" period during which the state encourages industrialists to increase workers' incomes to promote sales.

Last comes "bureaucratic-authoritarianism," which excludes the general population from the political arena and permits the military, along with civilian technocrats closely associated with foreign capital, to eliminate electoral competition to further promote industrialization. The transition from one stage to another is the result of payoffs to nascent industrial groups. Labor is supported in exchange for political backing and technocrats counteract economic policies through intervention in political, economic, and social matters.

In Costa Rica, growth of the public sector has followed some of the patterns outlined by O'Donnell in the transition from an oligarchic stage (that existed with the coffee planters during the nineteenth century) to one that was populist in nature and has been developing since midtwentieth century among collectivist parties. Industrialization is linked to political change through foreign aid granted to emergent ruling groups. This has meant a transfer of power within the ruling class, from those involved in agriculture to others in industry and finance. In the process, political organizations play a role similar to what O'Donnell attributes to the coalition of the military and technocrats in Argentina. Costa Rica, then, presents a case of bureaucratic-authoritarianism that derives power from public employees rather than militarism.

The foregoing implies serious burdens for the economy. While productivity decreases in traditional areas, the welfare state and the party system grow through taxes levied on them. Growing national debt has caused constant currency devaluations, and the *colon*, worth eleven United States cents in 1979, was worth only 0.1 cents in 1988 and continues to fall. In spite of such calamities, the citizenry maintains lifestyles that deny the existence of problems of such magnitude. This suggests that it is living beyond its means.

Living beyond One's Means

An example of the way in which living beyond one's means can affect a society is provided by the social security system. Recently, Minister of the Treasury Fernando Naranjo Villalobos, expressed fear of chaos in the public sector as a result of a labor court ruling in favor of social security workers seeking salary increases and fringe benefits that the institution could not afford to pay. Even greater was his consternation over the possibility of the rest of the public sector making similar demands (as it has already done). Shortly after, the press announced that the social security retirement program was a time bomb that offered only two alternatives: bankruptcy for the state or social conflict when the state openly declared its incapacity to meet its obligations. A few days later, Minister Naranjo announced there were no funds to pay pensions in September 1988 and that this would affect teachers (who constitute the largest group) more drastically than other retired persons. While the law stipulates that retirement is at fifty years of age and that monthly payments must have been made for thirty, many find ways to retire much earlier. Pensions in 1988 cost the treasury four billion colones per year (10 percent of the central government's budget), and it is estimated that they will reach fifty billion by 1993. Jorge Woodbridge, president of the Chamber of Industry, warned of a crisis because consolidated public spending has increased from 19 to 53 percent of the gross internal product since the beginning of the 1970s; since 1950, employment in the public sector has gone from one out of twenty laborers to one out of five. He observed that average salaries in the public sector are 60 percent higher than in the private sector; social charges for the private sector have increased by 70 percent during the last fifteen years; and 90 percent of public spending is for consumption, while investment is decreasing.[31]

Government efforts to balance budgets—increasing taxation on established sectors, borrowing at home and abroad, and meeting obligations with bonds—have produced resentment among producers. Insecurity with the Sandinista government in Nicaragua, especially due to its role in training the Costa Rican left for subversion, also affects production. At the pace set by the nation's contemporary policies, debts that have heretofore passed from one administration to another can eventually be paid off only at the price of national sovereignty, with measures such as the one taken by the government when it authorized the construction near the Nicaraguan border of a landing strip for use by the United States armed forces. This last point was revealed in the congressional hearings on the Iran-Contra affair and subsequently had serious repercussions in relations between former President Monge and President Arias.[32]

There have been appeals to correct problems through a new constitution. The constitution of Costa Rica (and those of most Latin American nations) is based on its French and United States counterparts and does not respond to national realities. An example is the Costa Rican banking system, nationalized in 1948 for the purpose of distributing credit to a wider sector of the population. Twenty years later, state banks reluctantly admitted that the thinking behind that program was a failure because during the planning stages, the functional financing ties between large and small coffee producers were not taken into account. The traditional role of Costa Rica as a refuge for political exiles from other countries (asylum is guaranteed in the constitution) fostered political thought and encouraged democratic ideals during the past century and first part of the present one.[33] In the social convulsions of modern times, however, that constitutional right has converted the country into a Casablanca[34] where followers of Fidel Castro plotted against Fulgencio Batista, those of Juan Bosch against Rafael Leonidas Trujillo, and where Nicaraguan Sandinistas, Contras, and other aliens have used national territory in their struggles to regain power in their own countries. The question of political exile in modern times also has harmful effects on the country's labor force, as Nicaraguan and Salvadoran exiles seek asylum from contemporary upheaval in their own nations. Constitutions should offer viable rules in relationships among men, but to do this they must respond to norms and behavior accepted in a society. In this sense the current one could well stand amendment. Motivation of those calling for a constituent assembly, however, appears to be merely a ploy to enable former presidents to serve another term.

Those seeking to replace the traditional ruling class must view Costa Rica within a realistic perspective. The state is a bankrupt entity demanding exaggerated shares of national production. Political parties cultivate their clienteles and drain the state's coffers for their own benefit. The industrial sector is like a twenty-five year old person learning to swim with a father who has never let him go. Trade unions are trying to decide on whom to bet, and the left is divided. Traditional producers are footing the bill for most of these activities and are losing interest in everything. Such a situation has a devastating effect on society and one of the best ways to appreciate this is through the ways in which values have been changing. A starting point is the following true story.

The Changing Nature of Values

It was cold in Aspen, but there was plenty of snow and the skiing was excellent. Felipe released his T-bar, turned and undertook to get down to the restaurant as rapidly as he could. He had agreed to meet his wife and family at noon for lunch.

Once seated, the family laughed over the ridiculous spills and tumbles each had taken that morning. They devoured their meal and as they were enjoying the last glass of wine in the crowded restaurant, a man and a woman took a seat at a table next to theirs.

At Felipe's table everyone was speaking Spanish. The other couple started their conversation in a language that was not at all intelligible to them. At one point the man turned to Felipe and asked where he was from.

"Costa Rica," replied Felipe.

"Oh," said the man and resumed chatting with his companion in the same strange tongue.

After a while he turned again to Felipe:

"We're Persians and fled with the Shah. I was just commenting to my wife on how much we would have liked to settle in Costa Rica. But when we learned of some of our citizens who sought exile there we decided to look for a home in another place. I mean no offense to you, but that's the way we feel." [35]

Today few Costa Ricans have not had such experiences: "Costa Rica! Oh yes. That's where Vesco lived"; "Costa Rica! Isn't that where Traficante, the mafia chief, retired?"; "I'm told you can get some pretty good hookers in Costa Rica"; "I understand Costa Rica is the bridge for drugs between South America and the United States." Such references come up constantly in the media and the cinema, where they acquire added weight throughout the world. They are not limited to the United States, as can be seen in Cizia Zikë's novel *Or* (published in France in 1985), depicting Costa Rica as a country where drugs and corruption are rampant. When Costa Ricans hear this repeatedly, some feel indignation and shame. This ill repute has secondary effects that can be worse, for sensationalists present the Sandinistas as the "good guys" in Central America and Costa Ricans as the bad ones. To counteract this, President Luis Alberto Monge Alvarez spent the month of July 1984 in Europe with members of his cabinet trying to sway international public opinion in a more favorable direction. President Oscar Arias Sánchez did the same thing during the latter part of 1987. With time, however, the Costa Rican's shock turns into indifference and resignation.

Divisions among leaders about the correct response to economic stress have occurred several times since the beginning of the colonial period and have affected other social strata. Before Independence, when the province foundered in poverty due to the monopoly of profitable activities by Spain and Guatemala, some members of the traditional ruling class set an example for the rest of the population by engaging in contraband. Others from the same class stoically accepted their miserable level of living and reluctantly adhered to restrictions imposed by the crown. Though "nouveau riche" coffee planters emerged from the class toward midnineteenth century, the sobering experiences of a cholera epidemic (with a 10 percent mortality rate) and violent military confrontations with United States fili-buster William H. Walker in 1856 caused succeeding generations to become responsible people who introduced legislation that raised the national level of literacy to a degree surpassing that of other Isthmian nations.[36] These attitudes became identified with the first political parties toward the end of the nineteenth century, and marked the course of national politics for nearly one hundred years.[37] Whereas challenges to the status quo had tradi-tionally come from within the aristocracy, after the 1929 depression, emerg-ing ruling groups from other cultural heritages undermined the position of the planters. Largely as a result of this, the class has experienced a "withering away" or an extinction.

Recent value changes in ruling circles came to national attention with the Sabundra affair. That concerned a Hindu who, between 1958 and 1959, developed social relations at high levels with members of the banking world and caused heavy losses through swindling. He did this with com-plicity of members of the ruling class. Around 1960 the Pietrogrande affair implicated an Italian telephone company that ineptly bid for a public con-tract through high-level political connections. In the Teja affair a former Indian executive who sought refuge in Costa Rica was arrested in England bearing a Costa Rican diplomatic passport. Robert Vesco, a fugitive from United States justice, was invited to Costa Rica by President José Figueres and became involved in questionable economic activities. With the help of Figueres, Vesco came close to being granted Costa Rican citizenship but was forced to leave the country by President Rodrigo Carazo in 1978. Vesco was followed by the late Joe Traficante, number-two boss in the international Mafia, who purchased a home in the elegant district of Belo Horizonte and was pensioned under official government auspices. Then came controversial Iranian nationals who had fled with the Shah's family. Iranian sources link them with the Shah's sister and his secret police, the Savak.

Why did these people seek haven in Costa Rica? The answer involves money and power, but most of all the changing values of the Costa Ricans who helped and tolerated them. More was to come: the Saopim scandal concerned a large construction company that was awarded public con-tracts and was linked by the press to funding an important political party. The Spanish firm Pegasso placed a bid for public busses and won the con-tract, allegedly for political reasons. The Proin affair entailed companies and paper banks in the Caribbean; with the complicity of prominent fig-ures, it swindled funds and caused heavy losses for Costa Rican and United

States banks. The Lada Niva company involved prominent political and social figures who imported three hundred Soviet vehicles in violation of regulations; public opinion was highly critical. A recent scandal involved a $5 million swindle on the stock exchange. It has undermined confidence and revealed a huge black market in that currency.[38] All these scandals have involved prominent members of the ruling class and have had a common factor: the use of political power for personal gain.

The change of values is visible in the Costa Ricans' tolerance. "Affairs" occur almost weekly and people now simply comment, unimpressed, on the lamentable state of the country. Contraband has become a mainstay of some members of the ruling class. It has included alcoholic beverages, household appliances, arms (on a monumental scale after the Sandinistas started their war against Somoza and extended the conflict to the rest of Central America), and now drugs. A recent incident involving illicit use of some $10 million from the National Emergency Fund implicates important former public figures.[39]

These incidents have shaken national society to its bones and lead to questioning the legitimacy of the political system. Costa Rica has known corruption in the past, for there have been several important scandals. One concerned the disappearance, during the nineteenth century, of British loans to the government. Today, however, illegal activity is so frequent that in spite of huge quantities of money involved, the ruling class and the populace take it for granted. Corruption is a product of changing values but is encouraged by other factors. Foremost has been the lack of equilibrium between salaries and the cost of living. Excessive public spending has led to devaluations every two weeks during the last seven years. Printing of money has created inflation not commensurate with salary levels. A full-time state university professor with tenure, for example, earns three hundred to four hundred dollars a month, while one of the cheapest automobiles on the market (a Toyota Starlet) costs over thirteen thousand dollars, and an ordinary jeep runs close to fifty thousand. Elsewhere in the public sector salaries are slightly higher: a gardener on the public payroll earns close to three hundred a month, and salaries for white collar workers range from six hundred to fifteen hundred dollars.

As a result of the Central American conflict, foreign aid from the United States has increased substantially (see table 11). It has been used mainly to pay off overdue interest on foreign debt, to meet the need for foreign exchange for imports, and to pay for services contracted outside the country.[40] Much of it is going into the private sector. Such an astronomical infusion of money overwhelms a population whose salary levels remain low. Contrasts shatter hopes and produce a sense of injustice that induces people to redress grievances by doing things they would not do under normal circumstances. In addition, as the state bureaucracy grows, its regulations become increasingly complex and render the normal conduct of business despairingly complicated. Giving and receiving bribes becomes increasingly a way of getting around cumbersome requirements. Members of the ruling class set examples for other social categories and promote corruption.

Changes in values are also reflected in an orientation toward mediocrity, for citizens condemn things beyond their reach. Professional guilds to monopolize, at the expense of quality, a growing spectrum of activities, proliferate. For example, journalism can be legally practiced only by members of the journalism guild, who are normally graduates of the School of Journalism of the University of Costa Rica; teachers must join a guild (I have twice been forbidden to teach for a delay in paying my dues); and even politicians are vulnerable, for in the late 1970s, students attempted to restrict participation in certain public posts to graduates of the School of Political Science of the University of Costa Rica. Mediocrity can be seen in education, where excellent public schools degenerated disastrously after the 1948 civil war, precipitating an avalanche of private schools. Inadequately trained teachers were given jobs in public schools by the Ministry of Education and the poor preparation of their students became painfully clear at all levels. In a recent quiz at the third-year level in the School of Political Science of the University of Costa Rica, out of eighty-two students, only twenty-two knew the year of Costa Rica's independence from Spain. Two knew that the French Revolution had started in 1789. None knew when World War I occurred. Only ten knew when World War II ended, and none knew when it started (the majority placed it between the years 1946 and 1955). Five knew the name of the party that has ruled Mexico for half a century; ten believed that Pinochet was President of Argentina; forty-eight could not name the capital of Bolivia; seventy-six could not distinguish the nineteenth century from the eighteenth; only three could name four Costa Rican presidents during the nineteenth century; sixty-three did not know who was president of Costa Rica during the 1948 civil war; and ten knew the names of the current vice-presidents of Costa Rica.[41]

The minister of education who took office in 1986 ordered a nationwide evaluation of comprehension of Spanish and mathematics. In the last year of secondary school, only 1.5 percent of the students obtained the expected minimum grade in mathematics, and 5.6 percent in Spanish.[42] Parents and teachers alleged that students were scared and that the exams had been poorly prepared, but the source of the problem should be sought in the ethos of the welfare state, the mediocrity among public employees, and a condesending political party system.[43]

The welfare state has increasingly incorporated radical ideologies and personnel.[44] This tendency appeared as early as the 1930s when Ricardo Jiménez Oreamuno, a liberal (of conservative origins) who had been president of the republic three times, chose Manuel Mora Valverde, founder of the Communist Party of Costa Rica, as director of his fourth campaign for the presidency.[45] Since midtwentieth century the tendency toward ideological convergence has increased through the welfare state, where leaders whose political doctrines had previously clashed have joined forces to defend the institution that provides their swelling ranks with a means of livelihood. Members of the ruling class, for example, who before going on public payrolls had been owners of large and medium-sized properties, would never have accepted concepts such as agrarian reform. Others who had worked under the private banking system would have opposed nationalization of that institution, and architects, upon becoming state employees, saw their imagination limited to designing monotonous public housing projects.

The state has come to monopolize or control insurance, banking, railroads, telecommunications, and other activities. In addition, it has undertaken steps in that direction in shrimp farming, sugarcane cultivation, meat processing, fertilizer production, the manufacture of aluminum pots and pans, and such a wide variety of enterprises that it has been dubbed a "mess-hall manager."[46] Over and above extending its activities into many fields, the state has acted in ways that best suit the interests of its own bureaucracy. All phases of life have been affected, and repercussions on the economy suggest major problems with production in the future. The state is akin to a growing elephant standing on a matchbox (production). How much longer can the matchbox withstand the pressure?[47]

The Meaning of Class Awareness

This chapter has been a discussion of the Costa Rican coffee planters who emerged from a colonial nobility imbued with egalitarian values molded by poverty. Their progeny, as planters, saw their values reshaped by a plantation economy and produced trustworthy men who served in positions of authority and leadership. They developed an economic complex that brought general prosperity and material and political benefits to a large sector of the population. They held their position for a century and a half, but as their decline began, rivals appeared in the power vacuum they left. Today they have lost the authority that society once attributed to them as a ruling class. Their evolution suggests that values stemming from equality and authority have produced confusion that has undermined their position as a class. It also raises questions concerning the compatibility between equality and excellence.[48]

To the north of Costa Rica, as Indian populations become more important in the demographic composition of each society, there is an increasingly noticeable survival of Spanish aristocratic traits, for ruling classes imposed their social systems more strictly on larger native civilizations to maintain their superior status. Ruling classes in Guatemala and El Salvador can be expected to continue assuming recalcitrant stances in answer to class warfare instigated by rising popular sectors. Their Honduran and Costa Rican counterparts can be expected to cede to mounting popular pressures and to continue being pushed into the background. Sandinistas and Contras in the Nicaraguan ruling class can be expected to continue bickering among themselves over how to satisfactorily divide their economic and political pies. How they handle contemporary problems is the subject of the next and last chapter.

CHAPTER 8

Pointers for the Rest
of the Isthmus

This final chapter explores parallels and divergences among ruling classes in Central America, using certain aspects of Costa Rica as an example. Its purpose is to relate the two topics of the book: 1) that the configuration of those social categories, despite antagonisms amid their members, rests on lineage and ties of kinship and 2) that scarcity of economic resources —in the Central American ambience—can help spur the development of democracy, while abundance tends to lead to authoritarianism. Ruling classes themselves, consisting of descendants of colonial aristocracy united by kinship, are the link between the two phenomena, for since Independence, their progeny have used their heritage of power and wealth to organize these governments.

The relationship between ruling classes and forms of government that are determined either by scarcity or abundance of resources requires a brief summary. Members of those classes, even in modern times, are of noble ancestry and usually descend from conquistadors. Their forefathers were entitled to power and privileges not accessible by people from other social categories, and as they settled throughout the Isthmus, they not only came to rule over their respective territories, but also discovered that good land and ample supplies of labor were more plentiful in the north, and such advantages attracted settlers of higher social standing with more capital to invest in export agriculture, mining, cattle raising, and other activities. By starting and operating larger plantations, members of ruling classes amassed wealth and created wide economic gaps between themselves and other social strata. They were quick to discover that authoritarian government could best serve their economic interests, and this led them to organizing the state to serve production. To maintain order, they recruited armies from other social backgrounds and established dictatorships that reinforced their Spanish aristocratic traits. The heritages of the Indian cultures surrounding them, however, clashed with their own values and filled them with complexes. One important problem stemming from this conflict concerned racial features and color of the skin, for these became ingrained in their social system (see chapter 4). However, this cultural discord between Hispanic and indigenous values never affected their own awareness of their position of command. In southern territories, limited resources offered relatively little wealth, and the less pronounced extremes of wealth and poverty led to the emergence of more democratic traits. It did not affect the political status of ruling classes, however. Since production could not be efficiently organized, their members soon turned their attention to public posts that provided small but fixed sources of income and social prestige. This is particularly true of Costa Rica (by comparison with Nicaragua), where after the introduction of coffee toward the midnineteenth century, the egalitarian values inherited from the colonial period permeated the new plantation economy and ultimately made the ruling class lose awareness of its position as such.

The Costa Rican experience discussed in the preceding chapter brings to light several significant concepts. One concerns the emergence of groups that attain power through divisions within ruling classes. Another has to do with values formed by the different ways they have handled available resources, and how these either deterred them from or drove them toward seeking economic and political hegemony. Others deal with the effects of those values on ruling classes themselves as well as on other social strata. Yet another involves the legitimacy attributed by other sectors to ruling groups, and is generally contingent on the nature of benefits they reap from economic complexes. Further questions are raised: Is the state an institution conceived to serve the interests of production (as in the north), or should production serve the state (as in the south)? To what extent should political parties encourage or discourage development of welfare? Finally, there are conditions under which corruption sets in. Given the fact that all of the societies in question have had different ruling groups in power, production appears to be a good starting point toward understanding how the Costa Rican case can provide perspectives for other Isthmian countries.

Colonial Production

Three enterprises were important in Central America during the colonial period. In order of importance, these were indigo (principally in Guatemala and El Salvador), cacao (in Costa Rica), and mining (in Honduras). Indigo plantations were located on Pacific coastal areas, from the northwest corner of Guatemala, through El Salvador and parts of Honduras, as far south as Lake Nicaragua. Indigo cultivation eventually succumbed to taxes, to competition with Venezuela and the Philippines, and finally to substitutes.[1] The principal exporters were families from traditional ruling classes such as the Fermín Aycinenas in Guatemala,[2] and included many who signed the Declaration of Independence in 1821.[3] In Guatemala "las familias" (the Pavóns, the Piñols, and the Batres, among others) constituted an aristocracy based on birth and fortune.[4] Aristocratic creoles (nobles of Spanish descent born in America) encouraged independence, but with limited and provincial understandings of the issues confronting them. They were honest and had good intentions but solved few social and economic problems during the nineteenth century.[5] Despite a scarcity of cheap labor and a lack of capital to purchase slaves, the Honduran economy was supported by mining during the last two centuries of colonial rule, and towns like Tegucigalpa and Comayagua emerged as supply centers. Cattle raising and agriculture were also important.[6] In Costa Rica, cacao plantations, located on the Caribbean coast, required little labor. Cultivation started late by comparison with the rest of Central America but helped offset the penury caused by subsistence agriculture. The major share of all these interests was concentrated in the hands of colonial aristocracy, both Spanish and creole.

In terms of social values, all Central American countries can be situated on a scale between Guatemala on the one hand (highly stratified and with a visible mixture of Spanish aristocratic and Indian traits) and Costa Rica on the other (far more egalitarian and with little indigenous heritage). To illustrate the connection between cultures and numbers of aborigines, for example, Andalusians from the south of Spain were indolent by comparison with Catalonians from the north, and Spaniards ruling over many were less humble than those in command of only a few. Nicaragua, with its large Indian population, was more similar to Guatemala than to Costa Rica. As a result, egalitarianism, generally associated with the latter country, does not exist in the Costa Rican province of Guanacaste, which belonged to Nicaragua until 1824.

A brief look at each of the Central American republics will show how the use of resources affected producers' values and their awareness of themselves as members of ruling classes. Power has been held by conquistadors, miners, and cultivators of indigo, cochineal, sugarcane, coffee, and of many other products. In a sense, those groups can all be regarded as "people with greatest access to, and control of values,"[7] which at different times drove them to either seek or shun political and economic hegemony.

Guatemala

Guatemala has had numerous ruling groups since Independence, yet in seeking power and economic predominance, they have often tarnished the image of their entire class in the eyes of other strata. This, in turn, led to questioning their very legitimacy. In modern times, as the Central American political and social turmoil grows and United States and Soviet economic assistance to their Isthmian protégés increases, political parties in Guatemala tend to use the state to solve problems of unemployment and patronage, and even corruption.[8] How Guatemala will confront its problems requires delving further into the country's history. Value disorientation caused by antagonism between aristocratic Spanish arrogance and Indian submissiveness, and by the gradual darkening of the Spanish race, has not undermined self-awareness of its ruling class.

During the seventeenth century, the capital city of Antigua was one of the most important centers of prestige and authority in America. A great part of its seventy thousand inhabitants (more than lived in Barcelona, Spain, or any contemporaneous city in English America) were Spanish; while some families dated from the Conquest, others who arrived later were principally Basque aristocrats (which contrasts with the Andalusian roots of the Costa Rican population).[9] It was the political, religious, and above all, the cultural center of the Isthmus.[10] During the colonial period it (along with the rest of Central America) was poor by comparison with Mexico and Peru, and little effort was made to diversify the economy. While indigo cultivation was initially undertaken in Guatemala, after the destruction of Antigua by an earthquake in 1773,[11] the crop spread to other regions, particularly El Salvador and Nicaragua. It is significant that initial drives toward independence came from producers of that item,[12] for such an initiative indicates their relative weight in their societies.

The first years of independence presented serious problems for the ruling class, whose only experience in government had been through colonial municipalities. National unity was challenged by caudillos who spread chaos and even civil war throughout the land.[13] José Rafael Carrera Turcios,

born in a run-down neighborhood of Guatemala City in 1814 and lacking a formal education (he learned to read and write only after becoming
president), first served as a drummer boy in the army and later worked as a
swineherd. Endowed with both military and political prowess, he became
a peasant hero and converted a mob into a guerrilla army that forced the
government to escalate suppression.[14] He eventually emerged as the natural leader of a popular conservative movement against liberal Honduran
Gen. Francisco Morazán.[15] Upon becoming chief of state, Carrera was not
opposed by creole aristocracy, for in spite of being of peasant extraction,
he protected upper class interests against abuses by the liberals.[16]

During the nineteenth century and the first half of the twentieth, Guatemala was dominated fundamentally by five dictators. Carrera's conservative movement was followed by a liberal one under Justo Rufino Barrios, Manuel Estrada Cabrera, and Jorge Ubico Castañeda.[17] The dictators
favored different ruling groups, but the position of the traditional ruling
class was not seriously threatened until roughly midtwentieth century. Its
members are today confronted with a riptide of change that, allowed to
develop freely, would undoubtedly force them into a weak and intolerable
situation. Yet the specters of land and tax reform, falling production, stag-
gering debt, massive inflation, and other adverse factors that would seem
to point to their displacement as a ruling class have not dismayed them.
In fact it has made them close ranks and violently resist change. Why? The
answer lies in their perception of themselves as a ruling class that once
constituted a small white colony in the midst of a large indigenous population and vast extensions of fertile lands, gathering power and wealth.
Despite admixtures of their own caste with Indians, they have treated Indians harshly[18] and held positions of command that were never questioned
by members of other strata. During the nineteenth century German coffee
planters married into prominent families and, by so doing, disguised some
of those undesirable characteristics by "putting a little milk in the coffee."[19]
In the face of current adversity, members of the Guatemalan ruling class
respond violently to forces seeking to displace them. They feel that they
have made possible the economic and political existence of the country
and are proud of it.

The army is no longer under the control of the aristocracy as it was
before the advent of the civilian Christian Democratic administration of
Vinicio Cerezo, which confronts serious problems due to taxes, rising cost
of public services, reduced buying power, lack of housing, poor land distribution, and unemployment. Because the threat of agrarian reform is a
call to arms for members of the ruling class,[20] the government hesitates to

promote that type of change too hastily. Human rights, which are today being imposed from the outside world for political reasons, have never figured in their rules of the game. Change is in the air, yet the ruling class feels compelled to resist, and many of them have died in the process of maintaining their position. Although few recognize social injustice in their society,[21] most hope to regain their lost hegemony.

As with members of ruling classes in the other countries, many are engaged in agricultural production for export, and for this reason their capital is largely tied up in land. This forces them to remain there to protect their belongings and, in so doing, to confront the tides of change. They still form the backbone of the nation's productive system and know it. In recent times production has stagnated, real income has shrunk, unemployment has increased, living conditions have deteriorated, and labor is nearing what its leaders consider a long overdue vindication of their grievances. Strikes of the Red Cross, social security workers, the customs union, students, banana workers, and textile and bakery employees have caused the government to establish minimum wages, price controls, fixed electric rates, and to create a commission to investigate the disappearance of citizens.

For these reasons, the Christian Democrats face mounting tension. Right-wing parties are joining forces, and increasing unity among leftist political parties, labor groups, and the Catholic Church is becoming apparent. The right is called the "white hand" and the left is the "black hand." Antagonistic social relations and political tensions develop because of the centuries-old contempt of the ruling class. These problems point toward the reinstitution of autocratic rule such as Guatemala has known throughout most of its history. The right will probably not yield in Guatemala and if it does, it will go down fighting.[22]

El Salvador

Sharing a relative abundance of resources, the small ruling class of El Salvador has had a strong tradition of engaging in agricultural activities similar to those of Guatemala. Unlike Guatemala, however, Salvadoran families composing the ruling groups have tended to become involved in a wide variety of enterprises and for this reason it is more difficult to identify them with any single activity. In fact, they constitute an oligarchy that is not responsible to the many and has incited strong disapproval of other population sectors.[23] The "fourteen families" have been adept at organizing production and, contrary to Guatemalans and Costa Ricans, have made investments beyond national borders. Their emergence (as in Guatemala) has had to do with the presence of a large, submissive, and indifferent Indian population. In recent years those families have faced vigorous competition from foreign elements, especially Arabs, in commerce and trade. Like their counterparts in Guatemala, during the colonial period they sought money and power, and, with a smaller number of Indians to exploit, built a clearly stratified society, which they maintain with haughty indifference to others. The stripping of Indian lands began in the sixteenth century, and a mass assassination under the dictatorship of Maximiliano Hernández Martínez in the early 1930s enhanced their interests.

United States and Soviet economic assistance fosters explosive divisions within the population, with the former backing movements it does not appear to understand clearly, while the latter (along with Cuba) supports almost any insurgence against the existing order. Cuba has been quick to kindle class warfare, with the certainty that members of traditional ruling groups would abandon the country to military appointees, who would eventually betray the best interests of the upper class.

With Independence, the economy of El Salvador continued to develop around indigo, cochineal, agriculture in general, and cattle raising. The country's early history was marked by struggles between conservatives[24] and liberal proponents of union. Agitation subsided during the administrations of Francisco Dueñas (1863–71) and Rafael Zaldívar (1876–85), when coffee, commercialized around 1885, became important. Power remained in the hands of changing ruling groups, and coffee plantations flourished. Presidents—not normally from the ruling class—chose their successors, who have often been close relatives. Throughout most of the nineteenth century and well into the twentieth, politics was a struggle between conservatives and liberals, who succeeded themselves in office.[25] In 1886, the former regained power and held it until 1931, when the army became a strong political force through the coffee planter aristocracy.

A military dictator, Gen. Maximiliano Hernández Martínez, ruled from 1931 to 1944 and extended state control over coffee exports. His ruthless treatment of Indians and his confiscation of their lands in the name of the coffee aristocracy alienated the native population, reviving resentments against the entire ruling class, whose members continued to act with indifference. After a series of military governments and continuous civil unrest, a Christian Democratic administration headed by José Napoleon Duarte adopted unpopular measures for ruling groups when he nationalized sales of coffee, the country's most important export item. This led to court battles between producers and the state and to a regrouping of the right, similar to what occurred in Guatemala. Duarte also sought to bring distribution of electricity, among other commodities, under government control. The war between his government and insurgents, backed by Managua and Havana, rages on. The return to the country of two leftist leaders, poor weather, the 1986 earthquake, and the private sector's refusal to cooperate with government plans for improvements have contributed to general deterioration. As in the case of Guatemala, the attitude of the laboring class was strongly affected by the harsh treatment it received at the hands of the military, on behalf of the ruling class. Members of this last group closed ranks as their Guatemalan counterparts had done, and this only led to an escalation of problems over many issues.[26]

Land reform has been carried out largely through agrarian cooperatives that have proven worse than usual in Central America. Changes in land ownership have generally meant taking large productive areas out of operation and dividing them into minifundia with inadequate financing and no markets. Although coffee continues to be the mainstay of the economy, between 1979 and 1985, production fell almost 25 percent, taxes from that crop by almost 50 percent, and exports by about 40 percent.

The Salvadoran ruling class has had an advantage over its counterparts throughout the Isthmus, and that has been the mobility of many of its members. Taking advantage of abundant labor and land that has been good for export crops, planter groups after Independence became wealthy enough to extend their spheres of activities into the outside world. During the twentieth century, sons of planters learned the coffee business and then worked in investment banking firms in New York, where they established ties, and most of them spent more time away from El Salvador than in the country. When serious social upheaval first appeared, Salvadorans from that class were able to leave and settle in the United States or Europe.

Honduras

Honduras has had few (if any) national ruling groups since Independence and stands out in contrast with the rest of Central America in this respect. Families that formed the traditional ruling class were generally adept at cattle raising and mining, and were also leaders of the country's two main political parties (the conservatives and the liberals). Early in the twentieth century, however, their command waned as they lost hegemony to foreign banana corporations and to the army, which teamed up in pursuit of their best interests. The only remaining advantage of the aristocratic families turned out to be that the military sensed that benefits derive from the presence of civilians in government; since then, the ruling class has been trying to remain in the good graces of the army. As elsewhere, collectivist organizations of European origin have begun to make their appearance. Today Honduras (like Costa Rica) has been suffering from distorted values related to monetary handouts to its government as a result of its proximity to Nicaragua.

Like Costa Rica, Honduras was not blessed with abundant economic resources. No wide economic disparity arose between the gentry and the peons, and the two groups functioned with relative mutual trust. The aristocracy could not compete for labor with foreign capitalists, and self-awareness of their position as a ruling class is a thing of the past, due to the overwhelming presence of foreign investment and the army. How the Honduran will confront his problems requires delving further into the country's history.

During and after the colonial period, mining provided much of the country's revenue, although farming and cattle raising were important. In the 1570s, a silver strike in the highlands resulted in the establishment of a significant population center at Tegucigalpa. Following Independence, the conservatives took power and held on to it until the 1870s, when the liberal movement swept through the Isthmus. Since then, the nation has been ruled by strongmen and military juntas.[27]

The traditional Honduran ruling class, although displaced early in the twentieth century by foreign economic interests, did not cease to play an active and important role in politics. When the United Fruit Company and others became the main source of tax dollars, ruling class families still participated in politics, in both appointed and elected office, but in an uncomfortable position with regard to the army, which has the income and the power to run government. Recent crises and shake-ups within its ranks reveal the existence of a strong group of leaders who oppose the presence of the Contras and feel that the country should receive more benefits from the United States for the use of its territory as military bases.[28]

Honduras has enacted an agrarian reform program but has had difficulties implementing it. Peasants constitute the country's principal work force. Sixty percent of the population lives in rural areas, and only 16 percent of total land is cultivated. Over the past two decades young leftist insurgency movements have broken out; the principal one calls itself the Cinchoneros. Hondurans are disturbed at the extent to which their country has been drawn into the Central American conflict and at deepening poverty.

Despite the generally favorable shift in trade, economic indicators reveal serious problems facing the country. After more than a century of operating in Honduras, Rosario Resources, a subsidiary of a United

States mining corporation, ended operations, practically the last of that activity in the country. One of the principal factors in economic development has been the power of organized labor, and government efforts to establish a viable equilibrium between labor and management have been unsuccessful.[29]

The industrial sector is a serious problem for the country. Unions have presented a common front against business and state institutions due to the rise of so-called "solidarity" movements between labor and management (as in Costa Rica). There have been strikes of municipal and state employees, banana laborers, and others. Much of this tumultuous business atmosphere (again as in Costa Rica) has opened new possibilities for trade with the Soviet Union. On another front, while two major banana producers (Standard Fruit and United Brands) announced a profitable future, small national producers claim they are being squeezed out of business. The private sectors of Honduras and Costa Rica have been encouraged by AID to seek ways of getting public investment out of the hands of the state.[30]

What reasonable future can be expected for Honduras, given the position of its ruling class as described above? In general terms, the economy and production are in poor health, international problems exist with Nicaragua and the United States, labor appears to have reached an irreconcilable position with both government and private enterprise, the Catholic Church is pressing for land reform, and the government increasingly looks to foreign aid as a panacea for its problems. Good lands are scarce (except in coastal regions where bananas are cultivated and cattle are raised); capital is hard to come by; and as if this were not enough, neither the army nor foreign investment—let alone the ruling class—appears to have a firm control over the ship of state. Drug trafficking has set in on a large scale, as can be seen by the recent capture and expatriation to the United States of Juan Ramón Matta Ballesteros.[31] This intervention by the United States, although strongly criticized by political, military, and civilian elements in Honduras,[32] is a succinct manifestation of value changes such as the ones that have occurred in Costa Rica.

Nicaragua

Nicaragua has had numerous ruling groups since Independence, and like most other nations on the Isthmus, contrasts with Costa Rica. Its ruling class has been made up of the same traditional families as elsewhere, descended from the original Central American conquistadors. They too have been adept at organizing production and have generally gone unquestioned as economic and political leaders. The emerging ruling groups relied on a large yet apathetic Indian population, but when the latter declined during the colonial period, Nicaraguan aristocrats experienced an economic levelling almost as severe as their Costa Rican counterparts. Their goal was always power and economic predominance, and they blackened the image of their entire class by affronting other strata. The rest of the population regarded the economic and political systems they created with mistrust, which contrasted with the Costa Rican coffee complex, where the planters inspired greater confidence. As Central American political and social turmoil grows and as United States and Soviet economic assistance to their Isthmian protégés rises, political parties in Nicaragua will turn increasingly to the state as a source of employment, patronage obligations, and even corruption.

The Sandinista revolution that ousted the Somoza family represents the accession to power of another group within the traditional ruling class. In a system of frequent rotation of power, wealth and privilege had remained in the hands of the Somozas for too many years, principally due to the backing of successive United States political administrations. Calls from other social strata for changes in patterns of land tenure and wealth distribution were never as pressing as in El Salvador, for the real issue in Nicaragua was within the ruling class itself. Because the "outs" assume that they will some day again be the "ins," a number of prominent families have remained in the country since the fall of Somoza. In many cases, ties of kinship enabled members of the losing side to leave the country and return at will, and even to obtain political posts in the Sandinista administration. Huge debt, heavy public expenditures, uncertainty, and linkages with the Soviet Union affect the two Nicaraguan sides engaged in the conflict. A satisfactory outcome will probably present itself in the form of a settlement in which both sides (without any significant participation from other social sectors) can have their share of the economic and political benefits associated with running the state.

The Sandinista aim is to reduce public spending dramatically, increase exports, reduce imports, control speculation, and encourage production, but a variety of forces have cut Nicaragua's export income by 50 percent between 1983 and 1986. Furthermore, in 1986 alone, imports cost four times the amount earned by exports. Both public sector salaries and consumer prices have risen significantly while foreign exchange rates and public aid to the private sector have fallen. The idea has been to reduce monetarization, the steady growth rate in the supply of money, which is considered the principal cause of inflation. The Sandinista government, restricted by its own policies of "survival economics" introduced last year, is slashing public projects already underway.[33]

Socialist countries continue assisting Nicaragua (see table 2). Aid has been used for irrigating grain fields on the Pacific coast, a textile plant in Estelí, and two projects in Matagalpa, one to improve agricultural sales and the other for a dairy. It has also been destined for hydroelectric plants and a deepwater port in Bluefields, for gold mining, and for petroleum. Bilateral aid from Europe, however, is drying up. In 1985, the German Christian Democratic coalition government suspended it for political reasons and was followed by the governments of France and Holland. Canada and Spain, however, have reaffirmed their commitments to provide milk, food, agricultural supplies, and medicine.

The government hopes to increase revenues from tourism and coffee production. The output of sugar has dropped, due primarily to lack of fuel and spare parts for machinery, as well as to drought. Cuba has tried to help. Petroleum products have presented serious problems that seem to change quite frequently. Trade seems to be improving in some quarters, but industry has been plagued by production bottlenecks, depressions, scarcity of foreign exchange, liberal subsidy policies, and high public spending. Land distributed under the agrarian reform program has gone increasingly to individuals as opposed to cooperatives.

And what could the foregoing mean for ruling classes in Central America today? Probably in Guatemala and El Salvador they will resist change to the very end. Any leadership from other social origins will have a difficult time to make a go of it because most of those who know how to produce come from the traditional ruling classes. In Honduras, the ruling class will adapt to situations that best serve its interests. Both the military and foreign producers will play instrumental roles and, unfortunately, drug traffickers will rise in influence. In Nicaragua, the fight remains among ruling groups, which must seek a formula for dividing the political and economic pies among themselves. In Costa Rica, the traditional ruling class appears to have lost its position to new groups emerging in the public sector.

Final Considerations

The principal idea in this book is that the conquistadors left a heritage in Central American societies. It was a legacy in the form of a consensus on who the ruling classes were. Within the populations involved, tacit acceptance and recognition of the exclusive social, political, and economic attributes of those relatively small groups has continued over the course of close to five centuries and has come to be questioned by other sectors of societies only in recent times.

Destiny or fate has played a role in the trajectory of those classes, for the distribution of economic resources throughout the Isthmus has influenced ways of organizing production and of governing in their respective societies. It has even shaped values. Repercussions of that unequal distribution have created delicate and potentially explosive social situations. In Guatemala and El Salvador, the wide gap between social strata in terms of income, housing, access to medical facilities, electricity, and other consumer goods results from the concentration of wealth in the hands of small groups within ruling classes. In Costa Rica, a country with different values, the gap between strata is more narrow than in the northern republics, but both the government and individuals are heavily in debt. Social upheaval, then, has had its roots in different problems.

Political change has mirrored the economic interests of groups within the same ruling classes. Coffee planters displaced indigo and cochineal producers in Guatemala and El Salvador during the nineteenth century; industrialists and state bureaucrats displaced planters in Costa Rica toward mid-twentieth century; Arabs emerged economically, politically, and socially in contemporary Honduras; the Sandinistas are establishing an economic and political order in which they can benefit from the productive system as Somoza did before them. Industrialists, farmers, ranchers, bureaucrats, and financiers, then, compete with each other to establish political hegemony, and when they attain power they influence legislation to best suit their interests. Yet most of these opposing groups (even some minorities today) have a common factor: their members can usually trace their origins back to the conquistadors and colonial nobility. Descendants of colonial aristocracy are today found in all walks of life, in political parties representing the right, the center, and even the extreme left.

One reason for the difficulty in understanding this is due to the common mistake of associating class with wealth. Money has little to do with social position. It can provide some members of ruling classes with advantages over others, but kinship is the principal factor in relationships that open doors to political and economic opportunity. This does not mean that people from other strata do not have access to ruling classes and their activities, but when they do, it is generally through marriage, friendship, or a combination of both.

The United States and the Soviet Union have attempted to introduce wealth redistribution through credit and scholarship programs (among others) designed to reach the grass roots of Isthmian societies by offering opportunity to students from rural areas to study there. While the hope is that upon completion of their studies the students will return to their home towns, the social systems do not encourage this. Not only is it improbable that students will return to their rural homes after two or more years of graduate study in the United States, but most of them will in all probability have problems finding jobs anywhere in the country, due to lack of kinship ties with people in positions of command. The granting of credit to bring about change has meant limiting its use to either public or private sectors. In either case it has become a bone of contention among groups within ruling classes seeking economic and political hegemony.

For these reasons, revolution does not normally imply lasting change. The advent of the Sandinistas in Nicaragua is a good example. With few exceptions, the hierarchy of that movement has the same social background as those in the upper echelons of the Somocista regime they ousted. Their revolution seems to reflect change because they displaced an administration that had outworn its welcome, but the new regime is enjoying life-styles reminiscent of the Somoza order.

Implications for Central America: A Search for Its Own Solutions

Individual Central American countries must confront problems with their own solutions, understanding them in their own context, and not relying on imported interpretations. Most imported ideas have been failures throughout the region. The industrial movement has been an unsuccessful experience for all concerned except those directly making money out of the process. The idea was introduced after the Great Depression of 1929 as an import-substitution plan and has meant the production of inferior quality goods at high prices, decreased revenue for governments that must subsidize such activities, increased doubts about the legitimacy of political systems on the part of agricultural producers, unemployment due to excessive automation, and general disenchantment.

Even the concept of democracy, also imported, is open to question. Under the aegis of that notion, politicians find easy prey in illiterate and generally uneducated populations, with the result that liberty often becomes confused with libertinism. Does this mean that democratic ideals should not be pursued? Not at all. It means that unprepared populations cannot be duped into believing that general well-being, prosperity, and happiness will inevitably follow if land is redistributed through agrarian reform programs to cooperatives or individuals who do not have the means, the knowledge, or even the slightest chance of succeeding with uneconomical productive units. What better example is there than Mexico, Bolivia, and now El Salvador? The idea of cooperatives has also been imported, but these have worked only where they have been adopted by groups with cultural backgrounds that enable them to understand the value of that type of collective effort. Such groups are limited in number. Again, what better example of failure than El Salvador? Savings is a basic tenet of capitalism—and hence of democracy—and the media constantly advertise the need for investment. Most Central Americans not only lack any propensity to save but are incapable of meeting such basic requirements as adequate nutrition.

In spite of the foregoing failures—and the likelihood that foreign experts will downplay the uniqueness of each nation's problems—the five Central American nations tend to look to the outside world for advice and solutions for everything. Liberalism was imported and junked without giving it a chance to work; socialism was implanted without a bourgeoisie; communism was introduced without a proletariat. In this sense, Latin

America has been a battleground of defeated foreign ideas. To respond to their unique problems, Latin Americans must analyze their needs for themselves.

There is need for a serious reassessment of educational policies, for they are the starting point on Central America's tortuous journey toward development. Policies concerning education in Costa Rica, where literacy is somewhere near 90 percent, must be radically different in Guatemala, where half the people cannot read or write and many cannot speak the national language. Education at all levels has bounced back and forth between private and public hands with no lasting improvements, becoming increasingly concerned with job security for educators rather than with teaching. The basic tenet that economic considerations should not be obstacles to education at any level has been abused by both politicians and guilds involved with teaching, to the extent that education has more political than academic overtones.

Despite its striking ecological and human differences, the Isthmus is often regarded as a homogeneous group of societies where regional strategies can be applied to issues such as wealth distribution, education, birth control, production, and human rights. Such an outlook is often shared by Central Americans themselves and has led to many attempts to organize the Isthmus politically, economically, and even militarily. All the important ones have failed, which suggests dissimilarities significant enough to constitute permanent barriers to unity.

Implications for the Industrialized World: A Need for Foreign Policy

The world beyond the Isthmus, and particularly industrialized nations, needs to formulate foreign policy for each country individually, rather than following regional orientations within East-West political contexts. Goals set within these parameters have a better chance of leading to democratic societies. The United States (and Great Britain) cannot escape paying a price for problems presented by Nicaragua and for past experiences elsewhere in Central America. During events leading to the 1948 civil war in Costa Rica, the United States supported United Fruit Company interests, and this sparked nationalism within the opposition party headed by Figueres. When Figueres was elected president in 1953, one of his first measures was to increase taxes paid by that company from 5 to 30 percent of earnings. That was only a small part of the final price paid by the company, for to avoid further problems, it had to offer similar increases to the governments of all the other countries where it had holdings. In 1954, the United States played an important role in overthrowing the administration of Guatemalan President Jacobo Arbenz Guzmán, who had developed close ties with the Soviet Union and posed a threat for the United Fruit Company. This too set off a wave of nationalism in many parts of Latin America. In the decade of the 1980s, Nicaragua represents a repetition of much of the above, for United States political involvement in that country during the nineteenth century and its military interventions during the twentieth have led to many of today's problems.

Central America is of strategic interest to the United States, and the Nicaraguan question has been making headlines for over a decade, yet it is still treated as a bush-fire. Mutual interests need to be defined and implemented in a lasting and continuous policy, over and above problems with the Soviet Union. Supporting the Contras may not be a practical solution for many reasons, for an important question concerns who will assume control if and when they accomplish their objective of ousting the Sandinistas. The real issue is how to divide the political and economic pies between the two groups of the ruling class (the Sandinistas and the Contras), and they alone can solve it. Settlement will probably have to come over the bargaining table and whatever it takes to get them there is a step in the right direction. Regardless of the outcome of those negotiations, Nicaragua's demands will be high and may well be in the name of all of Central America, for the entire region has come to depend on foreign aid from the United States and the Soviet Union. The former must be prepared to compensate in the interest of its own national security. What this boils down to for the United States is that there is no such thing as a small enemy, but to know how to deal with him it is necessary to understand what makes him tick.

Appendixes

Introduction

The purpose of presenting these genealogical trees is to show the continued influence of conquistadors, nobles from the colonial period, and their descendants on Isthmian political systems. The appendixes show presidents and public figures in the families of the following colonial personages:

1. Conquistador Cristóbal de Alfaro.
2. Conquistador Juan Vázquez de Coronado.
3. Conquistador Jorge de Alvarado.
4. Nobleman José Antonio Lacayo de Briones and others.
5. Nobleman Antonio de la Quadra and others.

Members of colonial nobility, whose prerogatives included the right to change their names, did not always use the paternal surname followed by the maternal one, as is customary today. It was acceptable to use both independently, or to use the name of another member of the family or even a village, depending on prestige and particularly on circumstances surrounding birth (children born out of wedlock constitute a good example of the latter). In the New Kingdom of Granada, for example, the noble family of Jaramillo changed its name to that of Zafra, its native village. Toward the beginning of the colonial period, such alterations were quite common, which explains why brothers at times had different family names (Castro Tosi 1963–64: 71). In these genealogical trees, except in those cases where individuals have significantly altered what is today considered normal usage, the paternal surname is followed by the maternal one. Other pertinent remarks:

1. In all of the marriages the names above the line are those of consan-

guineal descendants of the conquistador (or the noble), while those below are related by affinity.

2. A surname followed by a (1) or a (2) means that the person was a first or second spouse.

In each of appendixes 1–3, the first page is a guide-sheet showing an abbreviated family tree of a conquistador on the left (where presidents are represented by a number) and a column of names on the right (where presidents are shown by country, in alphabetical order). Each guide-sheet is followed by pages with columns listing the name and generation number of each president along with those of his forefathers who link him to the conquistador.

In appendixes 4 and 5, the first page is also a guide-sheet with an abbreviated family tree of a noble Nicaraguan family from the colonial period (and in both cases several similar families linked to them) on the left. In those trees, Nicaraguan presidents before the Sandinistas are represented by a "P" and a number, and Sandinistas are represented by an "S" and a number. Both categories (presidents and Sandinistas) appear in a column on the right of the page. Following each guide-sheet are pages listing each individual, by generation, and his relationship with the colonial noble. Attention should be paid to the number denoting each generation, for in many instances several people from the same generation are presented in a single column.

Appendix 6 (where congressmen descended from Vázquez de Coronado are listed) consists of seven parts. Each congressman is represented by a number, and Part I indicates the location of branches presented in the other parts. How each congressman is related to the conquistador can be seen in S. Stone, *Dinastía*, appendix 5.

Sources

The principal sources used were the following: Robert Luján 1955; Sanabria Martínez 1957; Fernández Peralta 1958; Castro Tosi 1963–64, 1964, 1975; Vivas Benard 1967; Aparicio y Aparicio and Falla Sánchez 1969; Aparicio y Aparicio 1969, 1969–70, 1971–72; Falla Sánchez 1969–70; Zavala Urtecho 1970; Ordóñez y Jonama 1971–72; Guirola Leal 1971–72; Fernández Piza 1975; Samuel Stone 1975, 1979, 1981; Fernández Alfaro 1976, 1979.

In addition, the National Archives of Guatemala and Costa Rica were frequently consulted, as were the following people: Rosa Font Frutos de Schütt, Rosa Veiga Pinto de Jiménez, Joaquín Fernández Alfaro, Ricardo Fernández Peralta, and Mario Fernández Piza.

ALFARO FAMILY TREE · 153

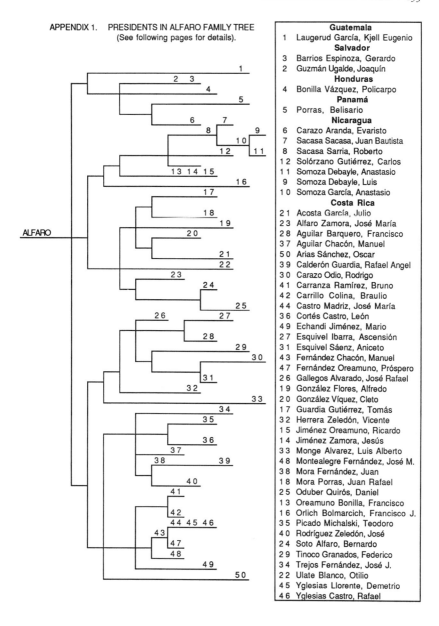

APPENDIX 1.   PRESIDENTS IN ALFARO FAMILY TREE
(See following pages for details).

Guatemala
1 Laugerud García, Kjell Eugenio
Salvador
3 Barrios Espinoza, Gerardo
2 Guzmán Ugalde, Joaquín
Honduras
4 Bonilla Vázquez, Policarpo
Panamá
5 Porras, Belisario
Nicaragua
6 Carazo Aranda, Evaristo
7 Sacasa Sacasa, Juan Bautista
8 Sacasa Sarria, Roberto
12 Solórzano Gutiérrez, Carlos
11 Somoza Debayle, Anastasio
9 Somoza Debayle, Luis
10 Somoza García, Anastasio
Costa Rica
21 Acosta García, Julio
23 Alfaro Zamora, José María
28 Aguilar Barquero, Francisco
37 Aguilar Chacón, Manuel
50 Arias Sánchez, Oscar
39 Calderón Guardia, Rafael Angel
30 Carazo Odio, Rodrigo
41 Carranza Ramírez, Bruno
42 Carrillo Colina, Braulio
44 Castro Madriz, José María
36 Cortés Castro, León
49 Echandi Jiménez, Mario
27 Esquivel Ibarra, Ascensión
31 Esquivel Sáenz, Aniceto
43 Fernández Chacón, Manuel
47 Fernández Oreamuno, Próspero
26 Gallegos Alvarado, José Rafael
19 González Flores, Alfredo
20 González Víquez, Cleto
17 Guardia Gutiérrez, Tomás
32 Herrera Zeledón, Vicente
15 Jiménez Oreamuno, Ricardo
14 Jiménez Zamora, Jesús
33 Monge Alvarez, Luis Alberto
48 Montealegre Fernández, José M.
38 Mora Fernández, Juan
18 Mora Porras, Juan Rafael
25 Oduber Quirós, Daniel
13 Oreamuno Bonilla, Francisco
16 Orlich Bolmarcich, Francisco J.
35 Picado Michalski, Teodoro
40 Rodríguez Zeledón, José
24 Soto Alfaro, Bernardo
29 Tinoco Granados, Federico
34 Trejos Fernández, José J.
22 Ulate Blanco, Otilio
45 Yglesias Llorente, Demetrio
46 Yglesias Castro, Rafael

APPENDIX 1

1 KJELL E. LAUGERUD GARCIA	2, 3 JOAQUIN E. GUZMAN UGALDE GERARDO BARRIOS ESPINOZA	4 POLICARPO BONILLA VASQUEZ
Generations:		
0) Cristóbal de Alfaro Catalina Gutiérrez Xaramillo	0) Cristóbal de Alfaro Catalina Gutiérrez Xaramillo	0) Cristóbal de Alfaro Catalina Gutiérrez Xaramillo
1) María de Alfaro Cristóbal de Cháves	1) María de Alfaro Cristóbal de Cháves	1) María de Alfaro Cristóbal de Cháves
2) Ana Cháves de Alfaro Diego López de Ortega	2) Ana Cháves de Alfaro Diego López de Ortega	2) Ana Cháves de Alfaro Diego López de Ortega
3) Laureana López de Ortega a) Tomás de Umaña b) Cristóbal Tenorio	3) Juana de Ortega Juan de Vidamartel	3) Juana de Ortega Juan de Vidamartel
4) Juana J. Tenorio Azofeifa Fco. Rodríguez Castro	4) Catalina de Vidamartel Pedro de Alvarado y Vera	4) Catalina de Vidamartel Pedro de Alvarado y Vera
5) Miguel C. Castro Tenorio Micaela Trejos Fernández	5) Juan de Alvarado Vidamartel Juana Ma. Galagarza	5) Gil de Alvarado Vidamartel Josefa González del Camino
6) José Francisco de Castro Trejos Josefa R. de Alvarado S.	6) Rita Alvarado Faustino Ugalde Sandoval	6) Domingo Alvarado González Estéfana Salmón-Pacheco
7) Juan Ant. Castro Alvarado Ana M. J. I. Hidalgo Oreamuno	7) Fermina Ugalde Alvarado Manuel Antonio Guzmán Garlindo	7) Juana Alvarado Pacheco José Fco. Bonilla Morales
8) Darío Castro Hidalgo Teodora Hidalgo	8) JOAQUIN E. GUZMAN UGALDE Paula Saldós	8) Policarpo Bonilla Alvarado Rosa Girón
9) Joaquina Castro Hidalgo José Zúñiga	9) Adela Guzmán Saldós GERARDO BARRIOS ESPINOZA	9) Inocente Bonilla Girón Juana Vázquez
10) Juan R. Zúñiga Castro Isabel de Coronado		10) POLICARPO BONILLA VAZQUEZ Emma Bonilla Lardizábal
11) Teresa Zúñiga Coronado ? Losi		
12) Helen Losi Zúñiga KJELL E. LAUGERUD GARCIA		

APPENDIX 1

5	6	7, 8
BELISARIO PORRAS	EVARISTO CARAZO ARANDA	ROBERTO SACASA SARRIA
		JUAN BAUTISTA SACASA SACASA

Generations:

0) Cristóbal de Alfaro	0) Cristóbal de Alfaro	0) Cristóbal de Alfaro
Catalina Gutiérrez Xaramillo	Catalina Gutiérrez Xaramillo	Catalina Gutiérrez Xaramillo
1) María de Alfaro	1) María de Alfaro	1) María de Alfaro
Cristóbal de Cháves	Cristóbal de Cháves	Cristóbal de Cháves
2) Ana Cháves de Alfaro	2) Ana Cháves de Alfaro	2) Ana Cháves de Alfaro
Diego López de Ortega	Diego López de Ortega	Diego López de Ortega
3) Juana de Ortega	3) Juana de Ortega	3) Ma. Cháves Ramiro-Corajo
Juan de Vidamartel	Juan de Vidamartel	a) Juan Astúa
		b) Tomás Andrés Polo
4) Catalina de Vidamartel	4) Catalina de Vidamartel	4) Francisca Astúa
Pedro de Alvarado y Vera	Pedro de Alvarado y Vera	Juan Bonilla Pereira
5) Pedro de Alvarado Vidamartel	5) Pedro de Alvarado Vidamartel	5) Ana Ant. Bonilla Astúa
Angela de Guevara	Angela de Guevara	Manuel Sáenz Vázquez
6) Pedro de Alvarado Guevara	6) Pedro de Alvarado Guevara	6) Bárbara Sáenz Bonilla
Manuela de Baeza	Manuela de Baeza	Cecilio Romero
7) Manuela Fra. Alvarado Baeza	7) Jacoba Alvarado Baeza	7) Casimira Romero Sáenz
Antonio de la Fuente	Francisco Carazo Soto	Mno. Montealegre Balmaceda
8) María Feliciana de la Fuente	8) Lorenzo Carazo Alvarado	8) Francisca Montealegre Romero
Ignacio Llorente y Arcedo	María del Rosario Aranda	Ramón Sarria
9) Ma. Petronila Llorente Lafuente	9) EVARISTO CARAZO ARANDA	9) Casimira Sarria Montealegre
Joaquín Iglesias	Engracia Hurtado	Juan Bautista Sacasa Méndez
10) Ramona Yglesias Llorente		10) ROBERTO SACASA SARRIA
Fco. de P. Gutiérrez Peña-M.		Angela Sacasa Cuadra
11) Ramona Gutiérrez Iglesias		11) JUAN BAUTISTA SACASA SACASA
Angel Anselmo Castro Méndez		
12) Alicia Castro Gutiérrez		
BELISARIO PORRAS		

APPENDIX 1

9 ANASTASIO SOMOZA GARCIA	10, 11 ANASTASIO SOMOZA DEBAYLE LUIS SOMOZA DEBAYLE	12 CARLOS SOLORZANO GUTIERREZ

Generations:

0) Cristóbal de Alfaro Catalina Gutiérrez Xaramillo	0) Cristóbal de Alfaro Catalina Gutiérrez Xaramillo	0) Cristóbal de Alfaro Catalina Gutiérrez Xaramillo
1) María de Alfaro Cristóbal de Cháves	1) María de Alfaro Cristóbal de Cháves	1) María de Alfaro Cristóbal de Cháves
2) Ana Cháves de Alfaro Diego López de Ortega	2) Ana Cháves de Alfaro Diego López de Ortega	2) Ana Cháves de Alfaro Diego López de Ortega
3) María Cháves Ramiro-Corajo a) Juan Astúa b) Tomás Andrés Polo	3) María Cháves Ramiro-Corajo a) Juan Astúa b) Tomás Andrés Polo	3) María Cháves Ramiro-Corajo a) Juan Astúa b) Tomás Andrés Polo
4) Francisca Astúa Juan Bonilla Pereira	4) Francisca Astúa Juan Bonilla Pereira	4) Francisca Astúa Juan Bonilla Pereira
5) Ana Antonia Bonilla Astúa Manuel Sáenz Vásquez	5) Ana Antonia Bonilla Astúa Manuel Sáenz Vázquez	5) Ana Antonia Bonilla Astúa Manuel Sáenz Vázquez
6) Bárbara Sáenz Bonilla Cecilio Romero	6) Bárbara Sáenz Bonilla Cecilio Romero	6) Bárbara Sáenz Bonilla Cecilio Romero
7) Casimira Romero Sáenz Mariano Montealegre Balmaceda	7) Casimira Romero Sáenz Mariano Montealegre Balmaceda	7) Casimira Romero Sáenz Mariano Montealegre Balmaceda
8) Francisca Montealegre Romero Ramón Sarria	8) Francisca Montealegre Romero Ramón Sarria	8) G. Montealegre Romero Vicente Solórzano
9) Casimira Sarria Montealegre Juan Bautista Sacasa Méndez	9) Casimira Sarria Montealegre Juan Bautista Sacasa Méndez	9) Francisco Solórzano Montealegre Felipa Zavala Uscola
10) ROBERTO SACASA SARRIA Angela Sacasa Cuadra	10) ROBERTO SACASA SARRIA Angela Sacasa Cuadra	10) Ana J. Solórzano Zavala Heliodoro Rivas Fitorio
11) Casimira Sacasa Sacasa Luis H. Debayle	11) Casimira Sacasa Sacasa Luis H. Debayle	11) Leonor Rivas Solórzano CARLOS SOLORZANO GUTIERREZ
12) Salvadora Debayle Sacasa ANASTASIO SOMOZA GARCIA	12) Salvadora Debayle Sacasa ANASTASIO SOMOZA GARCIA	
13) LUIS SOMOZA DEBAYLE Isabel Urcuyo Rodríguez	13) ANASTASIO SOMOZA DEBAYLE Hope Portocarrero Debayle	

APPENDIX 1

13, 14, 15	16	17
FSCO. MA. OREAMUNO BONILLA	FSCO. J. ORLICH BOLMARCICH	TOMAS GUARDIA GUTIERREZ
JESUS JIMENEZ ZAMORA		
RICARDO JIMENEZ OREAMUNO		

Generations:

0) Cristóbal de Alfaro
Catalina Gutiérrez Xaramillo

1) María de Alfaro
Cristóbal de Cháves

2) Francisco Cháves Alfaro
Francisca Zúñiga Ramiro-Corajo

3) María Cháves Ramiro
a) Juan Astúa
b) Tomás Andrés Polo

4) Francisca Astúa
Juan Bonilla Pereira

5) José Bonilla Astúa
Manuela Sáenz

6) Andrés Bonilla Sáenz
María Laya-Bolívar

7) Justa Bonilla Laya-Bolívar
Isidro Oriamuno Alvarado

8) FSCO. MA. OREAMUNO BONILLA
Agustina Gutiérrez Peña Monje

9) Emida. Oreamuno Gutiérrez
JESUS JIMENEZ ZAMORA

10) RICARDO JIMENEZ OREAMUNO
a) Beatriz Zamora López
b) María Eugenia Badía C.

0) Cristóbal de Alfaro
Catalina Gutiérrez Xaramillo

1) María de Alfaro
Cristóbal de Cháves

2) Francisco Cháves Alfaro
Francisca Zúñiga Ramiro-Corajo

3) María Cháves Ramiro
a) Juan Astúa
b) Tomás Andrés Polo

4) Vicente Andrés Polo Cháves
Alfonsa Bonilla Grados

5) María Polo Bonilla
Estanislao Castro Porras

6) Nicolasa Castro Polo
José Manuel Quirós

7) Juan Manuel Quirós Castro
Teresa Josefa Castro Cascante

8) Calixto Quirós Castro
Ramona Jiménez Soto

9) Ascención Quirós Jiménez
Bartola Montero Zamora

10) Rafaela Quirós Montero
Evaristo Quirós Solera

11) Zeneida Quirós Quirós
Salustio Camacho Muñoz

12) Marita Camacho Quirós
FSCO. J. ORLICH BOLMARCICH

0) Cristóbal de Alfaro
Catalina Gutiérrez Xaramillo

1) María de Alfaro
Cristóbal de Cháves

2) Francisco Cháves Alfaro
Francisca Zúñiga Ramiro-Corajo

3) Gregorio Cháves Ramiro
Leonor de los Ríos

4) Nicolás de Alfaro
a) María de Morera
b) Juana Sibaja

5) Juana Alfaro Morera
Nicolás González Oviedo

6) Nicolasa González Alfaro
Alfonso Porras Sibaja

7) Manuela J. Porras González
Santiago Flores Paniagua

8) Manuela Gertrudis Flores Porras
Anselmo Gutiérrez Ruíz

9) María Gutiérrez Flores
Rudecindo de la Guardia Robles

10) TOMAS GUARDIA GUTIERREZ
a) Perfecta Barrios
b) E. Solórzano

APPENDIX 1

18	19	20
JUAN RAFAEL MORA PORRAS	ALFREDO GONZALEZ FLORES	CLETO GONZALEZ VIQUEZ

Generations:

0) Cristóbal de Alfaro Catalina Gutiérrez Xaramillo	0) Cristóbal de Alfaro Catalina Gutiérrez Xaramillo	0) Cristóbal de Alfaro Catalina Gutiérrez Xaramillo
1) María de Alfaro Cristóbal de Cháves	1) María de Alfaro Cristóbal de Cháves	1) María de Alfaro Cristóbal de Cháves
2) Francisco Cháves Alfaro Francisca Zúñiga Ramiro-Corajo	2) Francisco Cháves Alfaro Francisca Zúñiga Ramiro-Corajo	2) Francisco Cháves Alfaro Francisca Zúñiga Ramiro-Corajo
3) Gregorio Cháves Ramiro-Corajo Leonor de los Ríos	3) Gregorio Cháves Ramiro-Corajo Leonor de los Ríos	3) Gregorio Cháves Ramiro-Corajo Leonor de los Ríos
4) Nicolás de Alfaro a) María de Morera b) Juana Sibaja	4) Nicolás de Alfaro a) María de Morera b) Juana Sibaja	4) Nicolás de Alfaro a) María de Morera b) Juana Sibaja
5) Juana Alfaro Morera Nicolás González Oviedo	5) Juana Alfaro Morera Nicolás González Oviedo	5) Juana Alfaro Morera Nicolás González Oviedo
6) Nicolasa González Alfaro Alonso de Porras Sibaja	6) Isidro González Alfaro Manuela E. Rodríguez Martínez	6) José N. González Alfaro María Concepción Ulloa
7) Juan Agus. Porras González Juana González de León	7) Isidro M. González Rodríguez Juana Ma. Cháves Aguilar	7) Francisco González Ulloa Antonia Pérez Mairena
8) José A. Porras González Josefa Ulloa González	8) María González Cháves Miguel González Alfaro	8) Cleto González Pérez Aurora Viquez Murillo
9) Ana Benita Porras Ulloa Camilo Mora Alvarado	9) Lorenzo González González Baltasara Pérez Zamora	9) CLETO GONZALEZ VIQUEZ Adela Herrán Bonilla
10) JUAN RAFAEL MORA PORRAS Inés Aguilar Cueto	10) Domingo González Porras Elemberta Flores Zamora	
	11) ALFREDO GONZALEZ FLORES Delia Morales Gutiérrez	

APPENDIX 1

21 JULIO ACOSTA GARCIA	22 OTILIO ULATE BLANCO	23 JOSE MARIA ALFARO ZAMORA

Generations:

0) Cristóbal de Alfaro Catalina Gutiérrez Xaramillo	0) Cristóbal de Alfaro Catalina Gutiérrez Xaramillo	0) Cristóbal de Alfaro Catalina Gutiérrez Xaramillo
1) María de Alfaro Cristóbal de Cháves	1) María de Alfaro Cristóbal de Cháves	1) María de Alfaro Cristóbal de Cháves
2) Francisco Cháves Alfaro Francisca Zúñiga Ramiro-Corajo	2) Francisco Cháves Alfaro Francisca Zúñiga Ramiro-Corajo	2) Francisco Cháves Alfaro Francisca Zúñiga Ramiro-Corajo
3) Gregorio Cháves Ramiro Leonor de los Ríos	3) Gregorio Cháves Ramiro Leonor de los Ríos	3) Gregorio Cháves Ramiro Leonor de los Ríos
4) Nicolás de Alfaro a) María de Morera b) Juana Sibaja	4) Nicolás de Alfaro a) María de Morera b) Juana Sibaja	4) Nicolás de Alfaro a) María de Morera b) Juana Sibaja
5) Juana Alfaro Morera Nicolás González Oviedo	5) Rafael Alfaro Morera Jsfa. Nic. Arias Hidalgo	5) José Antonio Alfaro Sibaja María Manuela González Godoy
6) José Nicolás González Alfaro María Concepción Ulloa	6) Fermín Alfaro Arias Antonio Huesca	6) José Trinidad Alfaro González María Josefa Arias Ugalde
7) María González Ulloa José A. Zumbado Valverde	7) Manuel Alfaro Huesca Micaela González	7) Antonio Alfaro Arias Ma. Damiana Zamora Flores
8) Nicolás Zumbado González Francisca Moya Hidalgo	8) Ma. Petronila Alfaro González Francisco González Brenes	8) JOSE MARIA ALFARO ZAMORA
9) Nicolasa Zumbado Moya Juan García Carrillo	9) Adolfo González Alfaro N. Ulate	
10) Jesús García Zumbado Juan Vicente Acosta Cháves	10) Ildefonso González Ulate Ermida Blanco Rojas	
11) JULIO ACOSTA GARCIA Elena Gallegos Rosales	11) OTILIO ULATE BLANCO	

APPENDIX 1

24 BERNARDO SOTO ALFARO	25 DANIEL ODUBER QUIROS	26 JOSE RAFAEL GALLEGOS ALVARADO

Generations:

0) Cristóbal de Alfaro Catalina Gutiérrez Xaramillo	0) Cristóbal de Alfaro Catalina Gutiérrez Xaramillo	0) Cristóbal de Alfaro Catalina Gutiérrez Xaramillo
1) María de Alfaro Cristóbal de Cháves	1) María de Alfaro Cristóbal de Cháves	1) María de Alfaro Cristóbal de Cháves
2) Francisco Cháves Alfaro Francisca Zúñiga Ramiro-Corajo	2) Francisco Cháves Alfaro Francisca Zúñiga Ramiro-Corajo	2) Ana Cháves de Alfaro Diego López de Ortega
3) Gregorio Cháves Ramiro Leonor de los Ríos	3) Gregorio Cháves Ramiro Leonor de los Ríos	3) Juana de Ortega Juan de Vida Martel
4) Nicolás de Alfaro a) María de Morera b) Juana Sibaja	4) Nicolás de Alfaro a) María de Morera b) Juana Sibaja	4) Catalina de Vida Martel Pedro de Alvarado y Vera
5) José Antonio Alfaro Sibaja Maria Manuela González Godoy	5) José Antonio Alfaro Sibaja Maria Manuela González Godoy	5) Pedro de Alvarado Angela de Guevara
6) Andrés Abel. Alfaro González María Godínez Barrantes	6) Andrés Abel. Alfaro González María Godínez Barrantes	6) Lucía G. Alvarado Guevara Felipe Gallegos Trigo
7) Ambrosio Alfaro Godínez Ma. Lorenza López Herrera	7) Ambrosio Alfaro Godínez Ma. Lorenza López Herrera	7) JOSE RAF. GALLEGOS ALVARADO Ma. Ignacia Sáenz Ulloa
8) Manuel Alfaro López Narcisa Muñoz González	8) Manuel Alfaro López Narcisa Muñoz González	
9) Joaquina Alfaro Muñoz Apolinar Soto Quesada	9) Joaquina Alfaro Muñoz Apolinar Soto Quesada	
10) BERNARDO SOTO ALFARO Pacífica Fernández Guardia	10) Eloisa Soto Alfaro Fco. Oduber Keckmayer	
	11) Porfirio Oduber Soto Ana María Quirós Quirós	
	12) DANIEL ODUBER QUIROS Marjorie Elliott Sypher	

APPENDIX 1

27 ASCENSION ESQUIVEL IBARRA	28 FRANCISCO AGUILAR BARQUERO	29 FEDERICO TINOCO GRANADOS

Generations:

0) Cristóbal de Alfaro Catalina Gutiérrez Xaramillo	0) Cristóbal de Alfaro Catalina Gutiérrez Xaramillo	0) Cristóbal de Alfaro Catalina Gutiérrez Xaramillo
1) María de Alfaro Cristóbal de Cháves	1) María de Alfaro Cristóbal de Cháves	1) María de Alfaro Cristóbal de Cháves
2) Ana Cháves de Alfaro Diego López de Ortega	2) Ana Cháves de Alfaro Diego López de Ortega	2) Ana Cháves de Alfaro Diego López de Ortega
3) Juana de Ortega Juan de Vida Martel	3) Juana de Ortega Juan de Vida Martel	3) Juana de Ortega Juan de Vida Martel
4) Catalina de Vidamartel Pedro de Alvarado y Vera	4) Catalina de Vidamartel Pedro de Alvarado y Vera	4) Catalina de Vidamartel Pedro de Alvarado y Vera
5) Pedro de Alvarado Angela de Guevara	5) Pedro de Alvarado Angela de Guevara	5) Pedro de Alvarado Angela de Guevara
6) Nicolasa de Alvarado y Guevara José Nicolás Bonilla	6) Nicolasa de Alvarado y Guevara José Nicolás Bonilla	6) Pedro de Alvarado y Guevara Manuela de Baeza Espinoza
7) Pedro León Bonilla Alvarado María Silvestra Salmón-Pacheco	7) Pedro León Bonilla Alvarado María Silvestra Salmón-Pacheco	7) María Francisca Alvarado Baeza Antonio de la Fuente
8) Félix Bonilla Salmón-Pacheco a) Catalina Nava b) J. Aguilar	8) Félix Bonilla Salmón-Pacheco a) Catalina Nava b) J. Aguilar	8) Ma. Feliciana de la Fuente Ignacio Llorente y Arcedo
9) Bárbara Bonilla Nava Francisco de la Guardia Robles	9) Francisco Aguilar Cubero María Sacramento Barquero	9) María P. Llorente y La Fuente Joaquín Yglesias
10) Adela Guardia Bonilla Jesús Salazar Aguado	10) FRANCISCO AGUILAR BARQUERO	10) María Joaq. Yglesias Llorente Saturnino Tinoco López
11) a) Adela Salazar Guardia b) Cristina Salazar Guardia ASCENCION ESQUIVEL IBARRA		11) Federico Tinoco Yglesias Guadalupe Granados Bonilla
		12) FEDERICO TINOCO GRANADOS María Fernández LaCappellain

APPENDIX 1

30 RODRIGO CARAZO ODIO	31 ANICETO ESQUIVEL SAENZ	32 VICENTE HERRRERA ZELEDON

Generations:

0) Cristóbal de Alfaro Catalina Gutiérrez Xaramillo	0) Cristóbal de Alfaro Catalina Gutiérrez Xaramillo	0) Cristóbal de Alfaro Catalina Gutiérrez Xaramillo
1) María de Alfaro Cristóbal de Cháves	1) María de Alfaro Cristóbal de Cháves	1) María de Alfaro Cristóbal de Cháves
2) Ana Cháves de Alfaro Diego López de Ortega	2) Ana Cháves de Alfaro Diego López de Ortega	2) Ana Cháves de Alfaro Diego López de Ortega
3) Juana de Ortega Juan de Vida Martel	3) Juana de Ortega Juan de Vida Martel	3) Juana de Ortega Juan de Vida Martel
4) Catalina de Vidamartel Pedro de Alvarado y Vera	4) Catalina de Vidamartel Pedro de Alvarado y Vera	4) Catalina de Vidamartel Pedro de Alvarado y Vera
5) Pedro de Alvarado Vidamartel Angela de Guevara	5) Pedro de Alvarado Vidamartel Angela de Guevara	5) Juana P. Alvarado Vidamartel Juan Sancho de Castañeda
6) Pedro de Alvarado Guevara Manuela de Baeza Espinoza	6) Pedro de Alvarado Guevara Manuela de Baeza Espinoza	6) Ana J. Sancho Alvarado Julián García de Ergueta
7) Jacoba Alvarado Baeza Francisco Carazo Soto	7) Jacoba Alvarado Baeza Francisco Carazo Soto	7) M. J. Nicolás García Sancho Josefa S. Ramírez Otárola
8) Joaquín Carazo Alvarado Ana Francisca Bonilla Alvarado	8) Joaquín Carazo Alvarado Ana Francisca Bonilla Alvarado	8) M. J. Pilar García Ramírez Atanasio Gutiérrez Lizaurzábal
9) Manuel José Carazo Bonilla María Toribia Peralta Echeverría	9) Manuel José Carazo Bonilla María Toribia Peralta Echeverría	9) Guadalupe Gutiérrez García VICENTE HERRERA ZELEDON
10) Mariano Carazo Peralta Liboria Quesada Calvo	10) Isaura Carazo Peralta ANICETO ESQUIVEL SAENZ	
11) Enrique Carazo Quesada Catalina Paredes Zúñiga		
12) Mario Carazo Paredes Julieta Odio Cooper		
13) RODRIGO CARAZO ODIO Estrella Zeledón Lizano		

APPENDIX 1

33 LUIS ALBERTO MONGE ALVAREZ	34 JOSE JOAQUIN TREJOS FERNANDEZ	35 TEODORO PICADO MICHALSKI

Generations:

0) Cristóbal de Alfaro Catalina Gutiérrez Xaramillo	0) Cristóbal de Alfaro Catalina Gutiérrez Xaramillo	0) Cristóbal de Alfaro Catalina Gutiérrez Xaramillo
1) María de Alfaro Cristóbal de Cháves	1) María de Alfaro Cristóbal de Cháves	1) María de Alfaro Cristóbal de Cháves
2) Ana Cháves de Alfaro Diego López de Ortega	2) Ana Cháves de Alfaro Diego López de Ortega	2) Ana Cháves de Alfaro Diego López de Ortega
3) Juana de Ortega Juan de Vida Martel	3) Laureana López de Ortega a) Tomás de Umaña b) Cristóbal Tenorio	3) Laureana López de Ortega a) Tomás de Umaña b) Cristóbal Tenorio
4) Manuela de Vidamartel José Escalante y Paniagua	4) Juan de Umaña Josefa Corrales Guzmán	4) Juan de Umaña Josefa Corrales Guzmán
5) José Escalante Paniagua Mariana de Torres	5) Ma. Josefa Umaña Corrales Manuel Felipe Fernández Acosta	5) María Josefa Umaña Corrales Manuel Felipe Fernández Acosta
6) Teresa Escalante Paniagua Cayetano de Sandoval	6) Manuel José Fernández Umaña Agueda de Alvarado Valverde	6) José Cornelio Fernández Umaña Josefa de Salazar Castro
7) Josefa de Sandoval Pedro de Ugalde Rodríguez	7) Gregorio Fernández Alvarado Trinidad Quesada Reyes	7) José L. Fernández Salazar Sebastiana Bonilla de la Peña
8) Manuel de Jesús Ugalde Sandoval Francisca Bogantes	8) José Fco. Fernández Quesada Juana Alvarado Madrigal	8) León Fernández Bonilla Isabel de la Guardia Gutiérrez
9) Jerónimo Ugalde Bogantes Ramona Murillo Herrera	9) Ceferino Fernández Alvarado Manuela de Aguilar y Fernández	9) Clemencia Fernández Guardia José Antonio Lara Von Chamier
10) Rafael Ugalde Murillo Manuela Ma. Quesada Benavides	10) Emilia Fernández Aguilar Juan Trejos Quirós	10) Mercedes Lara Fernández TEODORO PICADO MICHALSKI
11) Custodia Quesada Ugalde Prudencio Monge Esquivel	11) JOSE JOA. TREJOS FERNANDEZ Clara Fonseca Guardia	
12) Pedro Gerardo Monge Quesada Elisa Alvarez Vargas		
13) LUIS ALB. MONGE ALVAREZ Doris Yankelewitz		

APPENDIX 1

36	37	38, 39
LEON CORTES CASTRO	MANUEL AGUILAR CHACON	JUAN MORA FERNANDEZ
		RAFAEL ANGEL CALDERON GUARDIA

Generations:

0) Cristóbal de Alfaro Catalina Gutiérrez Xaramillo	0) Cristóbal de Alfaro Catalina Gutiérrez Xaramillo	0) Cristóbal de Alfaro Catalina Gutiérrez Xaramillo
1) María de Alfaro Cristóbal de Cháves	1) María de Alfaro Cristóbal de Cháves	1) María de Alfaro Cristóbal de Cháves
2) Ana Cháves de Alfaro Diego López de Ortega	2) Ana Cháves de Alfaro Diego López de Ortega	2) Ana Cháves de Alfaro Diego López de Ortega
3) Laureana López de Ortega a) Tomás de Umaña b) Cristóbal Tenorio	3) Laureana López de Ortega a) Tomás de Umaña b) Cristóbal Tenorio	3) Laureana López de Ortega a) Tomás de Umaña b) Cristóbal Tenorio
4) Juan de Umaña Josefa Corrales Guzmán	4) Juan de Umaña Josefa Corrales Guzmán	4) Juan de Umaña Josefa Corrales Guzmán
5) María Josefa Umaña Corrales Manuel Felipe Fernández Acosta	5) María Josefa Umaña Corrales Manuel Felipe Fernández Acosta	5) María Josefa Umaña Corrales Manuel Felipe Fernández Acosta
6) J. Cornelio Fernández Umaña Josefa de Salazar Castro	6) Eulalia Fernández Umaña Hermenegildo Aguilar Siles	6) Lucía Fernández Umaña J. M. Mora Salado-Valverde
7) José León Fernández Salazar Sebastiana Bonilla de la Peña	7) Miguel A. Aguilar Fernández Josefa de la Luz Chacón Aguilar	7) JUAN MORA FERNANDEZ Juana Castillo Palacios
8) Ramón Fernández Bonilla Ma. Josefa Pérez Rodríguez	8) MANUEL AGUILAR CHACON Inés Cueto de la Llana	8) Frutos Mora del Castillo Juana Monge
9) Fco. Eulogio Fernández Pérez Luisa Rodríguez Quesada		9) Juana Mora Monge C. de la Guardia Barrios
10) Julia Fernández Rodríguez LEON CORTES CASTRO		10) Ana María Guardia Mora Rafael Calderón Muñoz
		11) RAFAEL A. CALDERON GUARDIA a) Ivonne Clays b) Rosario Fournier

APPENDIX I

	40	41	42

40 JOSE JOAQ. RODRIGUEZ ZELEDON **41** BRUNO CARRANZA RAMIREZ **42** BRAULIO CARRILLO COLINA

Generations:

40	41	42
0) Cristóbal de Alfaro Catalina Gutiérrez Xaramillo	0) Cristóbal de Alfaro Catalina Gutiérrez Xaramillo	0) Cristóbal de Alfaro Catalina Gutiérrez Xaramillo
1) María de Alfaro Cristóbal de Cháves	1) María de Alfaro Cristóbal de Cháves	1) María de Alfaro Cristóbal de Cháves
2) Ana Cháves de Alfaro Diego López de Ortega	2) Ana Cháves de Alfaro Diego López de Ortega	2) Ana Cháves de Alfaro Diego López de Ortega
3) Laureana López de Ortega a) Tomás de Umaña b) Cristóbal Tenorio	3) Laureana López de Ortega a) Tomás de Umaña b) Cristóbal Tenorio	3) Laureana López de Ortega a) Tomás de Umaña b) Cristóbal Tenorio
4) Juan de Umaña Josefa Corrales Guzmán	4) Cristóbal Tenorio Azofeifa Juana J. Rodríguez Castro	4) Cristóbal Tenorio Azofeifa Juana J. Rodríguez Castro
5) Ma. Josefa Umaña Corrales Ml. Felipe Fernández Acosta	5) Ma. Catharina Tenorio Azofeifa Pedro N. Fernández Acosta	5) Ma. Catharina Tenorio Azofeifa Pedro N. Fernández Acosta
6) Lucía Fernández Umaña J. M. Mora-Salado Valverde	6) María Fernández Tenorio José Manuel Carranza	6) María Fernández Tenorio José Manuel Carranza
7) Feliciana Mora Fernández Eusebio Rodríguez Calvo	7) Miguel Carranza Fernández Joaquina Ramírez García	7) Miguel Carranza Fernández Joaquina Ramírez García
8) Sebastián Rodríguez Mora Francisca Zeledón Mora	8) BRUNO CARRANZA RAMIREZ Jerónima Montealegre Fernández	8) Froilana Carranza Ramírez BRAULIO CARRILLO COLINA
9) JOSE JOA. RODRIGUEZ ZELEDON Luisa Alvarado Carrillo		

APPENDIX 1

43, 44, 45, 46	47	48
MANUEL FERNANDEZ CHACON	PROSPERO FERNANDEZ OREAMUNO	JOSE M. MONTEALEGRE FERNANDEZ
JOSE MARIA CASTRO MADRIZ		
DEMETRIO YGLESIAS LLORENTE		
RAFAEL YGLESIAS CASTRO		

Generations:

0) Cristóbal de Alfaro	0) Cristóbal de Alfaro	0) Cristóbal de Alfaro
Catalina Gutiérrez Xaramillo	Catalina Gutiérrez Xaramillo	Catalina Gutiérrez Xaramillo
1) María de Alfaro	1) María de Alfaro	1) María de Alfaro
Cristóbal de Cháves	Cristóbal de Cháves	Cristóbal de Cháves
2) Ana Cháves de Alfaro	2) Ana Cháves de Alfaro	2) Ana Cháves de Alfaro
Diego López de Ortega	Diego López de Ortega	Diego López de Ortega
3) Laureana López de Ortega	3) Laureana López de Ortega	3) Laureana López de Ortega
a) Tomás de Umaña	a) Tomás de Umaña	a) Tomás de Umaña
b) Cristóbal Tenorio	b) Cristóbal Tenorio	b) Cristóbal Tenorio
4) Cristóbal Tenorio Azofeifa	4) Cristóbal Tenorio Azofeifa	4) Cristóbal Tenorio Azofeifa
Juana J. Rodríguez Castro	Juana J. Rodríguez Castro	Juana J. Rodríguez Castro
5) Ma. Catharina Tenorio Azofeifa	5) Ma. Catharina Tenorio Azofeifa	5) Ma. Catharina Tenorio Azofeifa
Pedro Nicolás Fernández Acosta	Pedro Nicolás Fernández Acosta	Pedro Nicolás Fernández Acosta
6) Félix Fernández Tenorio	6) Félix Fernández Tenorio	6) Félix Fernández Tenorio
a) Petronila Chacón Aguilar	a) Petronila Chacón Aguilar	a) Petronila Chacón Aguilar
b) Evarista Hidalgo Oreamuno	b) Evarista Hidalgo Oreamuno	b) Evarista Hidalgo Oreamuno
7) MANUEL FERNANDEZ CHACON	7) MANUEL FERNANDEZ CHACON	7) Jerónima Fernández Chacón
Dolores Oreamuno Muñoz	Dolores Oreamuno Muñoz	Mariano Montealegre Bustamante
8) Pacifica Fernández Oreamuno	8) PROSP. FERNANDEZ OREAMUNO	8) J. M. MONTEALEGRE FERNANDEZ
JOSE MARIA CASTRO MADRIZ	Cristina Guardia Gutiérrez	Ana María Mora Porras
9) Eudoxia Castro Fernández		
DEMETRIO YGLESIAS LLORENTE		
10) RAFAEL YGLESIAS CASTRO		
Manuela Rodríguez Alvarado		

APPENDIX 1

49	50
MARIO ECHANDI JIMENEZ	OSCAR ARIAS SANCHEZ

Generations:

0) Cristóbal de Alfaro Catalina Gutiérrez Xaramillo	0) Cristóbal de Alfaro Catalina Gutiérrez Xaramillo
1) María de Alfaro Cristóbal de Cháves	1) María de Alfaro Cristóbal de Cháves
2) Ana Cháves de Alfaro Diego López de Ortega	2) Ana Cháves de Alfaro Diego López de Ortega
3) Laureana López de Ortega a) Tomás de Umaña b) Cristóbal Tenorio	3) Laureana López de Ortega a) Tomás de Umaña b) Cristóbal Tenorio
4) Cristóbal Tenorio Azofeifa Juana J. Rodríguez Castro	4) Juana Tenorio Azofeifa Francisco Rodríguez Castro
5) Ma. Catharina Tenorio Azofeifa Pedro Nicolás Fernández Acosta	5) Miguel C. Castro Tenorio Micaela Trejos Fernández
6) José Cipriano Fernández Tenorio Basilia Ramírez García	6) José Fco. de Castro Trejos Josefa Rafaela de Alvarado S.
7) Práxedes Fernández Ramírez José Ma. Jiménez Carranza	7) Juan Antonio Castro Alvarado Ana M. J. Irinea Hidalgo Oreamuno
8) José Ma. Jiménez Fernández Teresa Rucavado Bonilla	8) Bartolo Castro Hidalgo Mercedes Bolandi Hidalgo
9) Josefa Jiménez Rucavado Alberto Echandi Montero	9) Ignacia Castro Bolandi Jacinto Trejos Gutiérrez
10) MARIO ECHANDI JIMENEZ Olga Benedictis Antonelli	10) Luisa Trejos Castro Juan Rafael Arias Bonilla
	11) Juan Rafael Arias Trejos Lilliam Sánchez Cortés
	12) OSCAR ARIAS SANCHEZ Margarita Penón Góngora

APPENDIX 2

PRESIDENTS IN VAZQUEZ FAMILY TREE
(See following pages for details.)

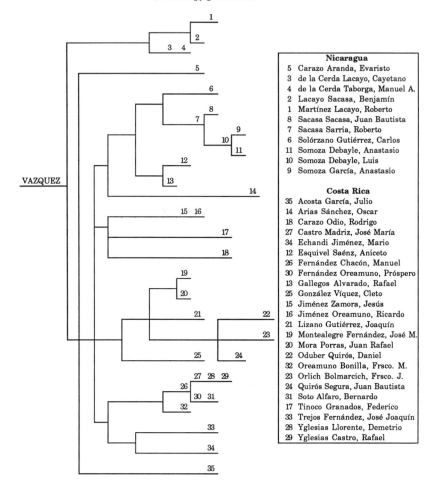

Nicaragua

5 Carazo Aranda, Evaristo
3 de la Cerda Lacayo, Cayetano
4 de la Cerda Taborga, Manuel A.
2 Lacayo Sacasa, Benjamín
1 Martínez Lacayo, Roberto
8 Sacasa Sacasa, Juan Bautista
7 Sacasa Sarria, Roberto
6 Solórzano Gutiérrez, Carlos
11 Somoza Debayle, Anastasio
10 Somoza Debayle, Luis
9 Somoza García, Anastasio

Costa Rica

35 Acosta García, Julio
14 Arias Sánchez, Oscar
18 Carazo Odio, Rodrigo
27 Castro Madriz, José María
34 Echandi Jiménez, Mario
12 Esquivel Saénz, Aniceto
26 Fernández Chacón, Manuel
30 Fernández Oreamuno, Próspero
13 Gallegos Alvarado, Rafael
25 González Víquez, Cleto
15 Jiménez Zamora, Jesús
16 Jiménez Oreamuno, Ricardo
21 Lizano Gutiérrez, Joaquín
19 Montealegre Fernández, José M.
20 Mora Porras, Juan Rafael
22 Oduber Quirós, Daniel
32 Oreamuno Bonilla, Frsco. M.
23 Orlich Bolmarcich, Frsco. J.
24 Quirós Segura, Juan Bautista
31 Soto Alfaro, Bernardo
17 Tinoco Granados, Federico
33 Trejos Fernández, José Joaquín
28 Yglesias Llorente, Demetrio
29 Yglesias Castro, Rafael

APPENDIX 2

1,2 ROBERTO MARTINEZ LACAYO BENJAMIN LACAYO SACASA	3,4 CAYETANO DE LA CERDA LACAYO MANUEL A. DE LA CERDA TABORGA	5 EVARISTO CARAZO ARANDA

Generations:

0) Juan Vázquez de Coronado Anaya Isabel Arias Dávila	0) Juan Vázquez de Coronado Anaya Isabel Arias Dávila	0) Juan Vázquez de Coronado Anaya Isabel Arias Dávila
1) Gonzálo Vázquez de Coronado A. Ana Rodríguez del Padrón	1) Gonzálo Vázquez de Coronado A. Ana Rodríguez del Padrón	1) Gonzálo Vázquez de Coronado A. Ana Rodríguez del Padrón
2) Diego Vázquez de Coronado R. Francisca del Castillo Hoces	2) Diego Vázquez de Coronado Francisca del Castillo Hoces	2) Andrea Vázquez de Coronado Diego Peláez de Lermos
3) Gertrudis Vázquez de Coronado Pedro Ocón y Trillo	3) Gertrudis Vázquez de Coronado Pedro Ocón y Trillo	3) Antonia Vázquez Peláez Sebastián Pereira Cardoso
4) María Ocón y Trillo Vázquez Diego Vázquez de Montiel	4) María Ocón y Trillo Vázquez Diego Vázquez de Montiel	4) Isabel Pereira Vázquez José Sandoval Ocampo
5) Diego Vázquez Ocón y Trillo Sebastiana Echavarría Navarro	5) Diego Vázquez Ocón y Trillo Sebastiana Echavarría Navarro	5) Inés Ocampo Golfín José Guevara Maldonado
6) Micaela Vázquez y Echavarría Simón Lacayo de Briones y Pomar	6) Micaela Vázquez y Echavarría Simón Lacayo de Briones y Pomar	6) Alvaro Guevara Sandoval María Sáenz Vázquez
7) Gabriel Lacayo Vázquez Manuela Marenco Alarcón	7) Gabriel Lacayo Vázquez Manuela Marenco Alarcón	7) Angela Guevara Sáenz Pedro Alvarado Vidamartel
8) José Antonio Lacayo Marenco Pilar Agüero	8) Francisca Lacayo Marenco Blas de la Cerda Aguilar	8) Pedro Alvarado Guevara Manuel Baeza Maroto
9) Fernando Lacayo Agüero Pastora Bermúdez Cerda	9) CAYETANO DE LA CERDA LACAYO María de Jesús Taborga	9) Jacoba Alvarado Baeza Francisco Carazo Soto
10) Daniel Lacayo Bermúdez Encarnación Sacasa Cuadra	10) MAN. A. DE LA CERDA TABORGA	10) Lorenzo Carazo Alvarado María del Rosario Aranda Muñoz
11) BENJAMIN LACAYO SACASA		11) EVARISTO CARAZO ARANDA Engracia Hurtado

11) Emelina Lacayo Sacasa
Roberto Martínez Moya

12) ROBERTO MARTINEZ LACAYO

APPENDIX 2

6	7, 8, 9, 10, 11
CARLOS SOLORZANO GUTIERREZ	ROBERTO SACASA SARRIA
	JUAN BAUTISTA SACASA SACASA
	ANASTASIO SOMOZA GARCIA
	LUIS SOMOZA DEBAYLE
	ANASTASIO SOMOZA DEBAYLE

Generations:

0) Juan Vázquez de Coronado Anaya
Isabel Arias Dávila

0) Juan Vázquez de Coronado Anaya
Isabel Arias Dávila

(FROM PREVIOUS COLUMN)
12) Casimira Sacasa Sacasa
Luis Debayle Pallais

1) Gonzálo Vázquez de Coronado A.
Ana Rodríguez del Padrón

1) Gonzálo Vázquez de Coronado A.
Ana Rodríguez del Padrón

13) Salvadora Debayle Sacasa
ANASTASIO SOMOZA GARCIA

2) Andrea Vázquez de Coronado
Diego Peláez de Lermos

2) Andrea Vázquez de Coronado
Diego Peláez de Lermos

14) LUIS SOMOZA DEBAYLE
Isabel Urcuyo Rodríguez

3) María Peláez Vázquez de Coronadc
Jerónimo Retes López Ortega

3) María Peláez Vázquez de Coronado
Jerónimo Retes López Ortega

14) ANASTSIO SOMOZA DEBAYLE
Hope Portocarrero Debayle

4) María Retes Peláez
Francisco Ramiro Corajo

4) María Retes Peláez
Francisco Ramiro Corajo

5) María Vázquez Ramiro
Pedro José Sáenz

5) María Vázquez Ramiro
Pedro José Sáenz

6) Manuel Sáenz Vázquez
Antonia Bonilla Astúa

6) Manuel Sáenz Vázquez
Antonia Bonilla Astúa

7) Bárbara Sáenz Bonilla
Cecilio Romero

7) Bárbara Sáenz Bonilla
Cecilio Romero

8) Casimira Romero Sáenz
Mariano Montealegre Balmaceda

8) Casimira Romero Sáenz
Mariano Montealegre Balmaceda

9) Gertrudis Montealegre Romero
Vicente Solórzano Pérez

9) Francisca Montealegre Romero
Ramón Sarria

10) Frsco. Solórzano Montealegre
Felipa Zavala

10) Casimira Sarria Montealegre
Juan Bautista Sacasa Méndez

11) Ana Joaquina Solórzano Zavala
Heliodoro Rivas Fitoria

11) ROBERTO SACASA SARRIA
Angela Sacasa Cuadra

12) Leonor Rivas Solórzano
CARLOS SOLORZANO GUTIERREZ

12) JUAN BTA. SACASA SACASA
María Argüello Manning
(CONTINUES NEXT COLUMN)

APPENDIX 2

12, 13 ANICETO ESQUIVEL SAENZ RAFAEL GALLEGOS ALVARADO	14 OSCAR ARIAS SANCHEZ

Generations:

0) Juan Vázquez de Coronado Anaya Isabel Arias Dávila	0) Juan Vázquez de Coronado Anaya Isabel Arias Dávila	(FROM PREVIOUS COLUMN) 13) Luisa Trejos Castro Juan R. Arias Bonilla
1) Gonzálo Vázquez de Coronado A. Ana Rodríguez del Padrón	1) Gonzálo Vázquez de Coronado A. Ana Rodríguez del Padrón	14) Juan R. Arias Trejos Lilliam Sánchez Cortés
2) Andrea Vázquez de Coronado Diego Peláez de Lermos	2) Andrea Vázquez de Coronado Diego Peláez de Lermos	15) OSCAR ARIAS SANCHEZ Margarita Penón Góngora
3) María Peláez Vázquez de C. Jerónimo Retes López Ortega	3) María Peláez Vázquez de C. Jerónimo Retes López Ortega	
4) María Retes Peláez Francisco Ramiro Corajo	4) María Retes Peláez Francisco Ramiro Corajo	
5) María Vázquez Ramiro Pedro José Sáenz	5) Juana Ramíro Corajo Isidro González Correa	
6) Manuel Sáenz Vázquez Antonia Bonilla Astúa	6) Catalina González Ramiro Domingo García Fernández	
7) Tiburcio Sáenz Vázquez Juana M. Alvarado Alvarado	7) Efigenia García González Francisco Orlamuno Vázquez	
8) Manuel J. Sáenz Alvarado Ma. Cayetana Ulloa Guzmán	8) José Ant. Oreamuno García Ma. E. Muñoz de la Trinidad	
9) Ursula Sáenz Ulloa Narciso Esquivel Salazar	9) Ana Rita Oreamuno Muñoz Tomás B. Hidalgo Bonilla	
9) María Ignacia Sáenz Ulloa RAFAEL GALLEGOS ALVARADO	10) Ana M. Hidalgo Oreamuno Juan Antonio Castro Alvarado	
10) ANICETO ESQUIVEL SAENZ Isaura Carazo Peralta	11) Bartolo Castro Hidalgo Mercedes Bolandi Hidalgo	
	12) Ignacia Castro Bolandi Jacinto Trejos Gutiérrez (CONTINUES NEXT COLUMN)	

APPENDIX 2

15, 16 JESUS JIMENEZ ZAMORA RICARDO JIMENEZ OREAMUNO	17 FEDERICO TINOCO GRANADOS	18 RODRIGO CARAZO ODIO

Generations:

0) Juan Vázquez de Coronado Anaya Isabel Arias Dávila	0) Juan Vázquez de Coronado Anaya Isabel Arias Dávila	0) Juan Vázquez de Coronado Anaya Isabel Arias Dávila
1) Gonzálo Vázquez de Coronado A. Ana Rodríguez del Padrón	1) Gonzálo Vázquez de Coronado A. Ana Rodríguez del Padrón	1) Gonzálo Vázquez de Coronado A. Ana Rodríguez del Padrón
2) Andrea Vázquez de Coronado Diego Peláez de Lermos	2) Andrea Vázquez de Coronado Diego Peláez de Lermos	2) Andrea Vázquez de Coronado Diego Peláez de Lermos
3) María Peláez Vázquez Jerónimo Retes López O.	3) María Peláez Vázquez Jerónimo Retes López O.	3) María Peláez Vázquez Jerónimo Retes López O.
4) Ana Retes Peláez Juan Echavarría Navarro	4) Ana Retes Peláez Juan Echavarría Navarro	4) Ana Retes Peláez Juan Echavarría Navarro
5) Juana Echavarría Retes Francisco Arlegui Armendaris	5) María Echavarría Retes José Pérez de Muro	5) Antonia Echavarría Retes José Guzmán
6) Manuel A. Arlegui Echavarría Gertrudis de Hoces Navarro	6) Agueda Pérez Echavarría José Casasola y Córdoba	6) José M. Guzmán Echavarría Micaela Bonilla Vargas
7) Gabriela Arlegui de Hoces Juan Rodríguez Robredo	7) Josefa Casasola Pérez Bernardo García Miranda	7) José M. Echavarría Gertrudis Sarmiento Rosa
8) Ana P. Rodríguez Arlegui José Ant. Jiménez Bonilla	8) Agueda M. García Miranda ?	8) A. M. Echavarría Sarmiento A. Mateo Camacho Angulo
9) Ramón Jiménez Robredo Joaquina Zamora Coronado	9) Joaquina Yglesias García ?	9) Félix Echavarría María Práxedes Alvarado Carazo
10) JESUS JIMENEZ ZAMORA Esmeralda Oreamuno Gutiérrez	10) Joaquín Yglesias ?	10) Ma. E. Echavarría Alvarado Enrique Cooper Sandoval
11) RICARDO JIMENEZ OREAMUNO a) Beatriz Zamora b) María Eugenia Calvo Badia	11) Ma. Joaqna. Yglesias Llorente Saturnino Tinoco López	11) Elena Cooper Echeverría Manuel Francisco Odio
	12) Federico Tinoco Yglesias Lupita Granados Bonilla	12) Julieta Odio Cooper Mario Carazo Paredes
	13) FEDERICO TINOCO GRANADOS María Fernández Le Cappellain	13) RODRIGO CARAZO ODIO Estrella Zeledón Lizano

APPENDIX 2

19,20	21
JOSE M. MONTEALEGRE FERNANDEZ	JOAQUIN LIZANO GUTIERREZ
JUAN RAFAEL MORA PORRAS	

Generations:

0) Juan Vázquez de Coronado Anaya Isabel Arias Dávila	0) Juan Vázquez de Coronado Anaya Isabel Arias Dávila
1) Gonzálo Vázquez de Coronado A. Ana Rodríguez del Padrón	1) Gonzálo Vázquez de Coronado A. Ana Rodríguez del Padrón
2) Andrea Vázquez de Coronado Diego Peláez de Lermos	2) Andrea Vázquez de Coronado Diego Peláez de Lermos
3) María Peláez Vázquez Jerónimo Retes López O.	3) María Peláez Vázquez Jerónimo Retes López O.
4) Jerónima Retes Peláez Pedro Lorenzo Venegas	4) Jerónima Retes Peláez Pedro Lorenzo Venegas
5) Lorenza J. Venegas Retes Francisco Martínez Gamboa	5) Lorenza J. Venegas Retes Francisco Martínez Gamboa
6) María J. Martínez Venegas Pedro González de León S.	6) María J. Martínez Venegas Pedro González de León S.
7) Juana M. González Martínez a) Agustín Porras González b) Antonio Matías Sandoval	7) Juana M. González Martínez a) Agustín Porras González b) Antonio Matías Sandoval
8) Jesús Antonio Porras González Josefa Ulloa González	8) Matías Sandoval González María Manuela Porras
9) Ana Benita Porras Ulloa Camilo Mora Alvarado	9) Casimira Sandoval Porras Pedro Antonio Solares
10) Ana María Mora Porras J.M. MONTEALEGRE FERNANDEZ	10) Florencia Solares Sandoval Nicolás Ulloa
10) JUAN RAFAEL MORA PORRAS Inés Aguilar Cueto	11) Matilde Ulloa Solares JOAQUIN LIZANO GUTIERREZ

APPENDIX 2

22 DANIEL ODUBER QUIROS		23 FRANCISCO J. ORLICH BOLMARCICH

Generations:

0) Juan Vázquez de Coronado Anaya Isabel Arias Dávila	(FROM PREVIOUS COLUMN) 13) Pedro Quirós Jiménez Dolores Aguilar Castro	0) Juan Vázquez de Coronado Isabel Arias Dávila
1) Gonzálo Vázquez de Coronado A. Ana Rodríguez del Padrón	14) Mario Quirós Aguilar Justo Quirós Montero	1) Gonzálo Vázquez de Coronado Ana Rodríguez del Padrón
2) Andrea Vázquez de Coronado Diego Peláez de Lermos	15) Ana Ma. Quirós Quirós Porfirio Oduber Soto	2) Andrea Vázquez de Coronado Diego Peláez de Lermos
3) María Peláez Vázquez Jerónimo Retes López O.	16)DANIEL ODUBER QUIROS Marjorie Elliot	3) María Peláez Vázquez Jerónimo Retes López
4) Jerónima Retes Peláez Pedro Lorenzo Venegas		4) Jerónima Retes Peláez Pedro Lorenzo Venegas
5) Lorenza J. Venegas Retes Fco. Martínez Gamboa		5) Lorenza J. Venegas Retes Fco. Martínez Gamboa
6) Ma. J. Martínez Venegas Pedro González de León S.		6) Ma. J. Martínez Venegas Pedro González de León S.
7) Juana González Martínez a) Agustín Porras González b) Antonio Matías Sandoval		7) Juana González Martínez a) Agustín Porras González b) Antonio Matías Sandoval
8) Petronila Porras González Ambrosio de Castro Arias		8) Petronila Porras González Ambrosio de Castro Arias
9) Estanislao Castro Porras María Polo Bonilla		9) Estanislao Castro Porras María Polo Bonilla
10) Nicolasa Castro Polo José MI. Quirós Arrieta		10) Nicolasa Castro Polo José MI. Quirós Arrieta
11) Juan MI. Quirós Castro Josefa T. Castro Cascante		11) Juan Manuel Quirós Castro Josefa T. Castro Cascante
12) Calixto Quirós Castro Ramona Jiménez Soto (CONTINUES NEXT COLUMN)		12) Calixto Quirós Castro Ramona Jiménez Soto (CONTINUES NEXT PAGE)

APPENDIX 2

	24 JUAN BAUTISTA QUIROS SEGURA	25 CLETO GONZALEZ VIQUEZ
Generations:		
(CONT.. FROM PREVIOUS PAGE)	0) Juan Vázquez de Coronado	0) Juan Vázquez de Coronado
13) Ascención Quirós Jiménez	Isabel Arias Dávila	Isabel Arias Dávila
Bartola Montero Zamora		
	1) Gonzalo Vázquez de Coronado A.	1) Gonzalo Vázquez de Coronado A.
14) Rafaela Quirós Montero	Ana Rodríguez del Padrón	Ana Rodríguez del Padrón
Evaristo Quirós Solera		
	2) Andrea Vázquez de Coronado	2) Andrea Vázquez de Coronado
15) Zeneida Quirós Quirós	Diego Peláez de Lermos	Diego Peláez de Lermos
Salustión Camacho Muñoz		
	3)Ma. Peláez Vázquez de Coronado	3)Ma. Peláez Vázquez de Coronado
16) Marita Camacho Quirós	Jerónimo Retes López	Jerónimo Retes López
FCO. J. ORLICH BOLMARCICH		
	4) Jerónima Retes Peláez	4) Jerónima Retes Peláez
	Pedro Lorenzo Venegas	Pedro Lorenzo Venegas
	5) Lorenza Venegas Retes	5) Lorenza Venegas Retes
	Francisco Martínez Gamboa	Francisco Martínez Gamboa
	6) María Martínez Venegas	6) Bernarda Martínez Venegas
	Pedro González de León	Juan de Villar y Hevia
	7) Juana González Martínez	7) Antonia de Villar Hevia Mart.
	a) Agustín Porras González	Hermenegildo Gutiérrez Ochoa
	b) Antonio Matías Sandoval	
	8) Petronila Porras González	8) María Gutiérrez de Ochoa
	Ambrosio de Castro Arias	José Murillo de Campos
	9) Estanislao Castro Porras	9) Josefa Murillo Gutiérrez
	María Polo Bonilla	Casimiro Víquez Ugalde
	10) Nicolasa Castro Polo	10) Aurora Víquez Murillo
	José Ml. Quirós Arrieta	Cleto González Pérez
	11) Juan Manuel Quirós Castro	11) CLETO GONZALEZ VIQUEZ
	Josefa Castro Cascante	Adela Herrán Bonilla
	12) Calixto Quirós Castro	
	Ramona Jiménez Soto	
	13) Pablo Quirós Jiménez	
	Mercedes Segura Masís	
	14) JUAN BTA. QUIROS SEGURA	

APPENDIX 2

26, 27, 28, 29	30, 31	32
MANUEL FERNANDEZ CHACON JOSE MARIA CASTRO MADRIZ DEMETRIO YGLESIAS LLORENTE RAFAEL YGLESIAS CASTRO	PROSPERO FERNANDEZ OREAMUNO BERNARDO SOTO ALFARO	FRANCISCO MA. OREAMUNO BONILLA

Generations:

0) Juan Vázquez de Coronado Isabel Arias Dávila	0) Juan Vázquez de Coronado Isabel Arias Dávila	0) Juan Vázquez de Coronado Isabel Arias Dávila
1) Gonzálo Vázquez de Coronado A. Ana Rodríguez del Padrón	1) Gonzálo Vázquez de Coronado A. Ana Rodríguez del Padrón	1) Gonzálo Vázquez de Coronado A. Ana Rodríguez del Padrón
2) Andrea Vázquez de Coronado Diego Peláez de Lermos	2) Andrea Vázquez de Coronado Diego Peláez de Lermos	2) Andrea Vázquez de Coronado Diego Peláez de Lermos
3) María Peláez Vázquez de Coronad Jerónimo Retes López	3) María Peláez Vázquez de Coronad Jerónimo Retes López	3) María Peláez Vázquez de Coronad Jerónimo Retes López
4) Petronila Retes Peláez José Alvarado y Vera	4) Petronila Retes Peláez José Alvarado y Vera	4) Petronila Retes Peláez José Alvarado y Vera
5) Rafaela Alvarado Retes Esteban de Moya	5) Rafaela Alvarado Retes Esteban de Moya	5) Rafaela Alvarado Retes Esteban de Moya
6) Petronila Moya Alvarado Juan F. Ibarra Calvo	6) Petronila Moya Alvarado Juan F. Ibarra Calvo	6) Petronila Moya Alvarado Juan F. Ibarra Calvo
7) María Catalina Ibarra Moya José Antonio Oreamuno Vázquez	7) María Catalina Ibarra Moya José Antonio Oreamuno Vázquez	7) María Catalina Ibarra Moya José Antonio Oreamuno Vázquez
8) Romualdo José Oreamuno Ibarra Antonia Mía. Alvarado López	8) Romualdo José Oreamuno Ibarra Antonia Mía. Alvarado López	8) Romualdo José Oreamuno Ibarra Antonia Mía. Alvarado López
9) José Greg. Oreamuno Alvarado Juana Muñoz Gómez	9) José Greg. Oreamuno Alvarado Juana Muñoz Gómez	9) Isidro Oreamuno Alvarado Justa Bonilla Laya-Bolíva
10) Dolores Oreamuno Muñoz MANUEL FERNANDEZ CHACON	10) Dolores Oreamuno Muñoz MANUEL FERNANDEZ CHACON	10) FCO.MA. OREAMUNO BONILLA Agustina Gutiérrez Peña
11) Pacífica Fernández Oreamuno JOSE MARIA CASTRO MADRIZ	11) PROS. FERNANDEZ OREAMUNO Cristina Guardia Gutiérrez	
12) Eudoxia Castro Fernández DEMETRIO YGLESIAS LLORENTE	12) Pacífica Fernández Guardia BERNARDO SOTO ALFARO	
13) RAFAEL YGLESIAS CASTRO Manuela Rodríguez Alvarado		

APPENDIX 2

33	34	35
JOSE JOAQUIN TREJOS FERNANDEZ	MARIO ECHANDI JIMENEZ	JULIO ACOSTA GARCIA

Generations:

0) Juan Vázquez de Coronado Anaya Isabel Arias Dávila	0) Juan Vázquez de Coronado Anaya Isabel Arias Dávila	0) Juan Vázquez de Coronado Anaya Isabel Arias Dávila
1) Gonzálo Vázquez de Coronado A. Ana Rodríguez del Padrón	1) Gonzálo Vázquez de Coronado A. Ana Rodríguez del Padrón	1) Gonzálo Vázquez de Coronado A. Ana Rodríguez del Padrón
2) Andrea Vázquez de Coronado Diego Peláez de Lermos	2) Andrea Vázquez de Coronado Diego Peláez de Lermos	2) Andrea Vázquez de Coronado Diego Peláez de Lermos
3) María Peláez Vázquez Jerónimo Retes López de O.	3) María Peláez Vázquez Jerónimo Retes López de O.	3) Juan Peláez Vázquez de C. María Madrigal López
4) Petronila Retes Peláez José Alvarado y Vera	4) Petronila Retes Peláez José Alvarado y Vera	4) María Peláez Madrigal Pedro Solano
5) Antonio Alvarado Retes Juana Aguirre Grado	5) Antonio Alvarado Retes Juana Aguirre Grado	5) Mariana Solano Peláez Fco. Falla de la Vega
6) Miguel Alvarado Aguirre María Mag. Valverde Echavarría	6) Miguel Alvarado Aguirre María Mag. Valverde Echavarría	6) Dionisia Falla Solano Manuel García Argueta
7) Agueda Alvarado Valverde Ml. José Fernández Umaña	7) Benita Alvarado Valverde Felipe Fernández Umaña	7) Josefa García Falla Vega ?
8) Gregorio Fernández Alvarado Ma. Trinidad Quesada Reyes	8) Narcisa Alvarado Fernández Luis Aguilar Rodríguez	8) Mateo García Falla Vega Ma. Josefa García Masís
9) José Fco. Fernández Quesada Juana Alvarado Madrigal	9) Silves. Aguilar Fernández Pedro Montero Sáenz	9) Esteban García García Ana Petr. Carrillo Colina
10) Ceferino Fernández Alvarado Manuela Aguilar Fernández	10) Ana Montero Aguilar Laureno Echandi Morales	10) Juan J. García Carrillo Nicolasa Zumbado Mora
11) Emilia Fernández Aguilar Juan Trejos Quirós	11) Alberto Echandi Montero Josefa Jiménez Rucavado	11) Jesús García Zumbado Juan Vicente Acosta Cháves
12) JOSE JOAQ. TREJOS FERNANDEZ Clara Fonseca Guardia	12) MARIO ECHANDI JIMENEZ Olga Benedictis Antonelli	12) JULIO ACOSTA GARCIA Elena Gallegos Rosales

APPENDIX 3

PRESIDENTS IN ALVARADO FAMILY TREE
(See following pages for details.)

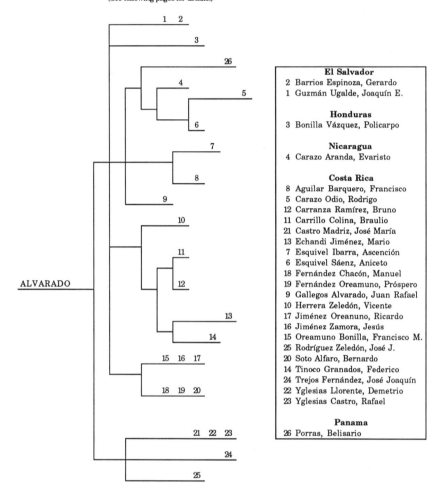

El Salvador
2 Barrios Espinoza, Gerardo
1 Guzmán Ugalde, Joaquín E.

Honduras
3 Bonilla Vázquez, Policarpo

Nicaragua
4 Carazo Aranda, Evaristo

Costa Rica
8 Aguilar Barquero, Francisco
5 Carazo Odio, Rodrigo
12 Carranza Ramírez, Bruno
11 Carrillo Colina, Braulio
21 Castro Madriz, José María
13 Echandi Jiménez, Mario
7 Esquivel Ibarra, Ascención
6 Esquivel Sáenz, Aniceto
18 Fernández Chacón, Manuel
19 Fernández Oreamuno, Próspero
9 Gallegos Alvarado, Juan Rafael
10 Herrera Zeledón, Vicente
17 Jiménez Oreanuno, Ricardo
16 Jiménez Zamora, Jesús
15 Oreamuno Bonilla, Francisco M.
25 Rodríguez Zeledón, José J.
20 Soto Alfaro, Bernardo
14 Tinoco Granados, Federico
24 Trejos Fernández, José Joaquín
22 Yglesias Llorente, Demetrio
23 Yglesias Castro, Rafael

Panama
26 Porras, Belisario

APPENDIX 3

1,2 JOAQUIN EUFR. GUZMAN UGALDE GERARDO BARRIOS ESPINOZA	3 POLICARPO BONILLA VAZQUEZ	4 EVARISTO CARAZO ARANDA

Generations:

0) Jorge de Alvarado Contreras Luisa Estrada Gutiérrez	0) Jorge de Alvarado Contreras Luisa Estrada Gutiérrez	0) Jorge de Alvarado Contreras Luisa Estrada Gutiérrez
1) Jorge Alvarado Estrada Catalina Carvajal Villafañe	1) Jorge Alvarado Estrada Catalina Carvajal Villafañe	1) Jorge Alvarado Estrada Catalina Carvajal Villafañe
2) Jorge Alvarado Carvajal Juana Benavides	2) Jorge Alvarado Carvajal Juana Benavides	2) Jorge Alvarado Carvajal Juana Benavides
3) Gil Alvarado Benavides Juana Vera Sotomayor	3) Gil Alvarado Benavides Juana Vera Sotomayor	3) Gil Alvarado Benavides Juana Vera Sotomayor
4) Pedro Alvarado Vera Catalina Vidamartel López	4) Pedro Alvarado Vera Catalina Vidamartel López	4) Pedro Alvarado Vera Catalina Vidamartel López
5) Juan MI. Alvarado Jirón Juana Ma. Galarza	5) Gil Alvarado Vidamartel Josefa González del Camino	5) Pedro Alvarado Vidamartel Angela Guevara
6) Rita Alvarado Galarza Faustino Ugalde Sandoval	6) Domingo Alvarado González Estéfana Salmón-Pacheco	6) Pedro Alvarado Guevara Manuela Baeza Espinoza
7) Fermina Ugalde Alvarado Manuel A. Guzmán Garlindo	7) Juana Alvarado Pacheco José Fco. Bonilla Morales	7) Jacoba Alvarado Baeza Francisco Carazo Soto
8) JOAQUIN EUFR. GUZMAN UGALDE a) Paula Saldós b) Ana Martorell Peña	8) Policarpo Bonilla Alvarado Rosa Girón	8) Lorenzo Carazo Alvarado Ma. del Ros. Aranda Muñoz
9) Adela Guzmán Saldós GERARDO BARRIOS ESPINOZA	9) Inocente Bonilla Girón Juana Vázquez	9) EVARISTO CARAZO ARANDA Engracia Hurtado
	10) POLICARPO BONILLA VAZQUEZ Emma Gutiérrez Lardizábal	

APPENDIX 3

5 RODRIGO CARAZO ODIO	6 ANICETO ESQUIVEL SAENZ	7 ASCENCION ESQUIVEL IBARRA
Generations:		
0) Jorge de Alvarado Contreras Luisa Estrada Gutiérrez	0) Jorge de Alvarado Contreras Luisa Estrada Gutiérrez	0) Jorge de Alvarado Contreras Luisa Estrada Gutiérrez
1) Jorge Alvarado Estrada Catalina Carvajal Villafañe	1) Jorge Alvarado Estrada Catalina Carvajal Villafañe	1) Jorge Alvarado Estrada Catalina Carvajal Villafañe
2) Jorge Alvarado Carvajal Juana Benavides	2) Jorge Alvarado Carvajal Juana Benavides	2) Jorge Alvarado Carvajal Juana Benavides
3) Gil Alvarado Benavides Juana Vera Sotomayor	3) Gil Alvarado Benavides Juana Vera Sotomayor	3) Gil Alvarado Benavides Juana Vera Sotomayor
4) Pedro Alvarado Vera Catalina Vidamartel López	4) Pedro Alvarado Vera Catalina Vidamartel López	4) Pedro Alvarado Vera Catalina Vidamartel López
5) Pedro Alvarado Vidamartel Angela Guevara	5) Pedro Alvarado Vidamartel Angela Guevara	5) Pedro Alvarado Vidamartel Angela Guevara
6) Pedro Alvarado Guevara Manuela Baeza Espinoza	6) Pedro Alvarado Guevara Manuela Baeza Espinoza	6) Nicolasa Alvarado Guevara José Nicolás de Bonilla
7) Jacoba Alvarado Baeza Francisco Carazo Soto	7) Jacoba Alvarado Baeza Francisco Carazo Soto	7) Pedro L. Bonilla Alvarado Silvestra Salmón-Pacheco
8) Joaquín Carazo Alvarado Ana Fca. Bonilla Alvarado	8) Joaquín Carazo Alvarado Ana Fca. Bonilla Alvarado	8) Félix Bonilla Pacheco a) Catalina Nava López del Corral b) J. Aguilar
9) Manuel J. Carazo Bonilla Ma. Toribia Peralta Echeverría	9) Manuel J. Carazo Bonilla Ma. Toribia Peralta Echeverría	9) Bárbara Bonilla Nava Francisco Guardia Robles
10) Mariano Carazo Peralta Liboria Quesada Calvo	10) Isaura Carazo Peralta ANICETO ESQUIVEL SAENZ	10) Adela Guardia Bonilla Jesús Salazar Aguado
11) Enrique Carazo Quesada Catalina Paredes Zúñiga		11) a) Adela Salazar Aguado b) Cristina Salazar Aguado ASCENSION ESQUIVEL IBARRA
12) Mario Carazo Paredes Julieta Odio Cooper		
13) RODRIGO CARAZO ODIO Estrella Zeledón Lizano		

APPENDIX 3

8	9	10
FRANCISCO AGUILAR BARQUERO	JOSE RAFAEL GALLEGOS ALVARADO	VICENTE HERRERA ZELEDON

Generations:

0) Jorge de Alvarado Contreras Luisa Estrada Gutiérrez	0) Jorge de Alvarado Contreras Luisa Estrada Gutiérrez	0) Jorge de Alvarado Contreras Luisa Estrada Gutiérrez
1) Jorge Alvarado Estrada Catalina Carvajal Villafañe	1) Jorge Alvarado Estrada Catalina Carvajal Villafañe	1) Jorge Alvarado Estrada Catalina Carvajal Villafañe
2) Jorge Alvarado Carvajal Juana Benavides	2) Jorge Alvarado Carvaja Juana Benavides	2) Jorge Alvarado Carvaja Juana Benavides
3) Gil Alvarado Benavides Juana Vera Sotomayor	3) Gil Alvarado Benavides Juana Vera Sotomayor	3) Gil Alvarado Benavides Juana Vera Sotomayor
4) Pedro Alvarado Vera Catalina Vidamartel López	4) Pedro Alvarado Vera Catalina Vidamartel López	4) Pedro Alvarado Vera Catalina Vidamartel López
5) Pedro Alvarado Vidamartel Angela Guevara	5) Pedro Alvarado Vidamartel Angela Guevara	5) Juana Alvarado Vidamartel Juan Sancho Castañeda
6) Nicolasa Alvarado Guevara José Nicolás de Bonilla	6) Ma. Josefa Alvarado Guevara ?	6) Ana Jfa. Sancho Alvarado Julián García Ergueta
7) Pedro L. Bonilla Alvarado M. Silvestra Salmón-Pacheco	7) Lucía Alvarado Felipe Gallegos Trigo	7) José Ml. García Sancho Salvadora Ramírez Otárola
8) Félix Bonilla Pacheco a) Catalina Nava López del Corral b) J. Aguilar	8) JOSE R. GALLEGOS ALVARADO Ma. Ignacia Sáenz Ulloa	8) Ma. Jfa. García Ramírez Atan. Gutiérrez Lizaurzábal
9) Francisco Aguilar Cubero María Sacramento Barquero		9) Guadalupe Gutiérrez García VICENTE HERRERA ZELEDON
10) FRANCISCO AGUILAR BARQUERO		

APPENDIX 3

11, 12 BRAULIO CARRILLO COLINA BRUNO CARRANZA RAMIREZ	13 MARIO ECHANDI JIMENEZ	14 FEDERICO TINOCO GRANADOS

Generations:

0) Jorge de Alvarado Contreras Luisa Estrada Gutiérrez	0) Jorge de Alvarado Contreras Luisa Estrada Gutiérrez	0) Jorge de Alvarado Contreras Luisa Estrada Gutiérrez
1) Jorge Alvarado Estrada Catalina Carvajal Villafañe	1) Jorge Alvarado Estrada Catalina Carvajal Villafañe	1) Jorge Alvarado Estrada Catalina Carvajal Villafañe
2) Jorge Alvarado Carvajal Juana Benavides	2) Jorge Alvarado Carvajal Juana Benavides	2) Jorge Alvarado Carvajal Juana Benavides
3) Gil Alvarado Benavides Juana Vera Sotomayor	3) Gil Alvarado Benavides Juana Vera Sotomayor	3) Gil Alvarado Benavides Juana Vera Sotomayor
4) Pedro Alvarado Vera Catalina Vidamartel López	4) Pedro Alvarado Vera Catalina Vidamartel López	4) Pedro Alvarado Vera Catalina Vidamartel López
5) Juana Alvarado Vidamartel Juan Sancho Castañeda	5) Juana Alvarado Vidamartel Juan Sancho Castañeda	5) Juana Alvarado Vidamartel Juan Sancho Castañeda
6) Ana Josefa Sancho Alvarado Julián García Ergueta	6) Ana Josefa Sancho Alvarado Julián García Ergueta	6) Ana Josefa Sancho Alvarado Julián García Ergueta
7) Bárbara García Sancho Francisco Ramírez Castillo	7) Bárbara García Sancho Francisco Ramírez Castillo	7) Bárbara García Sancho Francisco Ramírez Castillo
8) Joaquina Ramírez García Miguel Carranza Fernández	8) Basilia Ramírez García Cipriano Fernández Tenorio	8) Basilia Ramírez García Cipriano Fernández Tenorio
9) Froilana Carranza Ramírez BRAULIO CARRILLO COLINA	9) Práxedes Fernández Ramírez José Ma. Jiménez Maldonado	9) José A. Fernández Ramírez Merced. Acuña Diez-Dobles
9) BRUNO CARRANZA RAMIREZ Jerma. Montealegre Fernández	10) José Ma. Jiménez Fernández Josefa Rucavado Bonilla	10) Mauro Fernández Acuña Ada Le Cappellain Agnew
	11) Josefa Jiménez Rucavado Alberto Echandi Montero	11) Ma. Fernández LeCappellain FEDERICO TINOCO GRANADOS
	12) MARIO ECHANDI JIMENEZ Olga Benedictis Antonelli	

ALVARADO FAMILY TREE · 183

APPENDIX 3

15, 16, 17 F. M. OREAMUNO BONILLA JESUS JIMENEZ ZAMORA RICARDO JIMENEZ OREAMUNO	18, 19, 20 MANUEL FERNANDEZ CHACON PROSPERO FERNANDEZ OREAMUNO BERNARDO SOTO ALFARO	21, 22, 23 JOSE M. CASTRO MADRIZ DEMETRIO YGLESIAS LLORENTE RAFAEL YGLESIAS CASTRO
Generations: 0) Jorge de Alvarado Contreras Luisa Estrada Gutiérrez	0) Jorge de Alvarado Contreras Luisa Estrada Gutiérrez	0) Jorge de Alvarado Contreras Luisa Estrada Gutiérrez
1) Jorge Alvarado Estrada Catalina Carvajal Villafañe	1) Jorge Alvarado Estrada Catalina Carvajal Villafañe	1) Jorge Alvarado Estrada Catalina Carvajal Villafañe
2) Jorge Alvarado Carvajal Juana Benavides	2) Jorge Alvarado Carvajal Juana Benavides	2) Jorge Alvarado Carvajal Juana Benavides
3) Gil Alvarado Benavides Juana Vera Sotomayor	3) Gil Alvarado Benavides Juana Vera Sotomayor	3) Gil Alvarado Benavides Juana Vera Sotomayor
4) Pedro Alvarado Vera Catalina Vidamartel López	4) Pedro Alvarado Vera Catalina Vidamartel López	4) José Alvarado Vera Petronila Retes Vásquez
5) José Alvarado Vidamartel Ursula López Conejo	5) José Alvarado Vidamartel Ursula López Conejo	5) Antonio Alvarado Retes Juana Aguirre Grado
6) Antonia Ma. Alvarado López Romualdo Oreamuno Ibarra	6) Antonia Ma. Alvarado López Romualdo Oreamuno Ibarra	6) Miguel Alvarado Aguirre Magdalena Valverde Echavarría
7) Isidro Oreamuno Alvarado Justa Bonilla Laya-Bolívar	7) Gregor. Oreamuno Alvarado Juana Muñoz de la Trinidad	7) Petronila Alvarado Valverde José Antonio Castro Umaña
8) FCO. M. OREAMUNO BONILLA Agustina Gutiérrez Lizaurzábal	8) Dolores Oreamuno Muñoz MANUEL FERNANDEZ CHACON	8) Francisco Castro Alvarado María de la Trinidad Ramírez
9) Esmeralda Oreamuno Gutiérrez JESUS JIMENEZ ZAMORA	9) PROSP. FERNANDEZ OREAMUNO Cristina Guardia Gutiérrez	9) José Ramón Castro Ramírez Lorenza Madriz Linares
10) RICDO. JIMENEZ OREAMUNO a) Beatriz Zamora b) Ma. E. Badía	10) Pacíf. Fernández Guardia BERNARDO SOTO ALFARO	10) JOSE MARIA CASTRO MADRIZ Pacifica Fernández Oreamuno
		11) Eudoxia Castro Fernández DEMETRIO YGLESIAS LLORENTE
		12) RAFAEL YGLESIAS CASTRO Manuela Rodríguez Alvarado

APPENDIX 3

24	25	26
JOSE JOAQ. TREJOS FERNANDEZ	JOSE JOAQUIN RODRIGUEZ ZELEDON	BELISARIO PORRAS

Generations:

0) Jorge de Alvarado Contreras Luisa Estrada Gutiérrez	0) Jorge de Alvarado Contreras Luisa Estrada Gutiérrez	0) Jorge de Alvarado Contreras Luisa Estrada Gutiérrez
1) Jorge Alvarado Estrada Catalina Carvajal Villafañe	1) Jorge Alvarado Estrada Catalina Carvajal Villafañe	1) Jorge Alvarado Estrada Catalina Carvajal Villafañe
2) Jorge Alvarado Carvajal Juana Benavides	2) Jorge Alvarado Carvajal Juana Benavides	2) Jorge Alvarado Carvajal Juana Benavides
3) Gil Alvarado Benavides Juana Vera Sotomayor	3) Gil Alvarado Benavides Juana Vera Sotomayor	3) Gil Alvarado Benavides Juana Vera Sotomayor
4) José Alvarado Vera Petronila Retes Vásquez	4) José Alvarado Vera Petronila Retes Vásquez	4) Pedro Alvarado Vera Catalina Vidamartel López
5) Antonio Alvarado Retes Juana Aguirre Grado	5) Antonio Alvarado Retes Juana Aguirre Grado	5) Pedro Alvarado Angela Guevara
6) Miguel Alvarado Aguirre Magdalena Valverde Echavarría	6) Miguel Alvarado Aguirre Magdalena Valverde Echavarría	6) Pedro Alvarado Guevara Manuela Baeza
7) Agueda Alvarado Valverde Manuel José Fernández Umaña	7) J. Felipe Alvarado Valverde María Santos Fernández	7) Francisca Alvarado Baeza Antonio de la Fuente
8) Gregorio Fernández Alvarado María de la Trinidad Oda Reyes	8) Fco. Alvarado Fernández Francisca Velasco Marín	8) Ma. Feliciana de la Fuente Ignacio Llorente y Arcado
9) José Francisco Fernández Oda Juana Alvarado Madrigal	9) Cruz Alvarado Velasco Manuela Carrillo Morales	9) M. Pet. Llorente y LaFuente Joaquín Yglesias
10) Ceferino Fernández Alvarado Manuela Aguilar Fernández	10) Luisa Alvarado Carrillo JOSE J. RODRIGUEZ ZELEDON	10) Ramona Yglesias Llorente Francisco de Paula Gutiérrez
11) Emilia Fernández Aguilar Juan Trejos Quirós		11) Ramona Gutiérrez Yglesias Angel A. Castro Méndez
12) JOSE J. TREJOS FERNANDEZ Clara Fonseca Guardia		12) Alicia Castro Gutiérrez BELISARIO PORRAS

APPENDIX 4

LACAYO AND RELATED FAMILIES: OLD ORDER PRESIDENTS AND SANDINISTAS
(See following pages for details.)

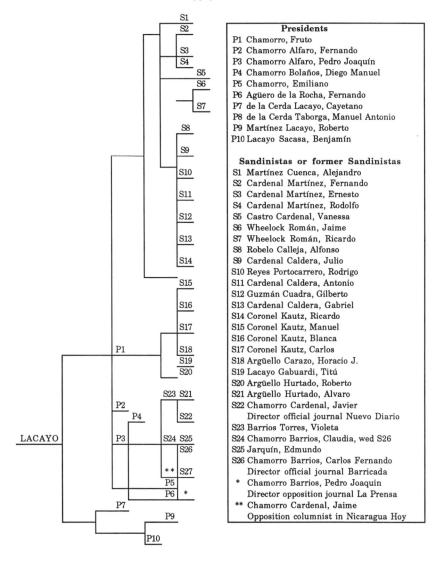

Presidents

P1 Chamorro, Fruto
P2 Chamorro Alfaro, Fernando
P3 Chamorro Alfaro, Pedro Joaquín
P4 Chamorro Bolaños, Diego Manuel
P5 Chamorro, Emiliano
P6 Agüero de la Rocha, Fernando
P7 de la Cerda Lacayo, Cayetano
P8 de la Cerda Taborga, Manuel Antonio
P9 Martínez Lacayo, Roberto
P10 Lacayo Sacasa, Benjamín

Sandinistas or former Sandinistas

S1 Martínez Cuenca, Alejandro
S2 Cardenal Martínez, Fernando
S3 Cardenal Martínez, Ernesto
S4 Cardenal Martínez, Rodolfo
S5 Castro Cardenal, Vanessa
S6 Wheelock Román, Jaime
S7 Wheelock Román, Ricardo
S8 Robelo Calleja, Alfonso
S9 Cardenal Caldera, Julio
S10 Reyes Portocarrero, Rodrigo
S11 Cardenal Caldera, Antonio
S12 Guzmán Cuadra, Gilberto
S13 Cardenal Caldera, Gabriel
S14 Coronel Kautz, Ricardo
S15 Coronel Kautz, Manuel
S16 Coronel Kautz, Blanca
S17 Coronel Kautz, Carlos
S18 Argüello Carazo, Horacio J.
S19 Lacayo Gabuardi, Titú
S20 Argüello Hurtado, Roberto
S21 Argüello Hurtado, Alvaro
S22 Chamorro Cardenal, Javier
    Director official journal Nuevo Diario
S23 Barrios Torres, Violeta
S24 Chamorro Barrios, Claudia, wed S26
S25 Jarquín, Edmundo
S26 Chamorro Barrios, Carlos Fernando
    Director official journal Barricada
  * Chamorro Barrios, Pedro Joaquin
    Director opposition journal La Prensa
** Chamorro Cardenal, Jaime
    Opposition columnist in Nicaragua Hoy

APPENDIX 4

P1	P1	P1
S1	S2,3,4,	S5,6,7

Generations:

0) José Ant. Lacayo de Briones Bárbara Rosa Pomar y Villegas	0) José Ant Lacayo de Briones Bárbara Rosa Pomar y Villegas	0) José Ant Lacayo de Briones Bárbara Rosa Pomar y Villegas
1) Gregoria Lacayo y Pomar Diego Chamorro Sotomayor	1) Gregoria Lacayo y Pomar Diego Chamorro Sotomayor	1) Gregoria Lacayo y Pomar Diego Chamorro Sotomayor
2) Fernando Chamorro Lacayo Bárbara Argüello del Castillo	2) Fernando Chamorro Lacayo Bárbara Argüello del Castillo	2) Fernando Chamorro Lacayo Bárbara Argüello del Castillo
3) Pedro Joaq. Chamorro Argüello Jfa. Mgta. Alfaro Monterrosa	3) Pedro Joaq. Chamorro Argüello Jfa. Mgta. Alfaro Monterrosa	3) Pedro Joaq. Chamorro Argüello Jfa. Mgta. Alfaro Monterrosa
4) FRUTO CHAMORRO - P1 Mercedes Avilés Alfaro (2) whose brother was:	4) FRUTO CHAMORRO - P1 Mercedes Avilés Alfaro (2) whose brother was:	4) FRUTO CHAMORRO - P1 Mercedes Avilés Alfaro (2) whose brother was:
5) Agustín Avilés Alfaro ? Briceño	5) Agustín Avilés Alfaro ? Briceño	5) Agustín Avilés Alfaro ? Briceño
6)Magdalena Avilés Briceño Juan Ignacio Urtecho Cabistán	6)Magdalena Avilés Briceño Juan Ignacio Urtecho Cabistán	6)Magdalena Avilés Briceño Juan Ignacio Urtecho Cabistán
7) Agustina Urtecho Avilés Ernesto Martínez Moya	7) Agustina Urtecho Avilés Ernesto Martínez Moya	7) Agustina Urtecho Avilés Ernesto Martínez Moya
8) Alejandro Martínez Urtecho Carmen Cuenca Cruz	8) Esmeralda Martínez Urtecho Rodolfo Cardenal Argüello	8) Esmeralda Martínez Urtecho Rodolfo Cardenal Argüello whose brother is:
		8) Carlos Cardenal Argüello ? Martínez
9) ALEJ. MARTINEZ CUENCA - S1	9) FER. CARDENAL MARTINEZ - S2	9) Nora Cardenal Martínez Francisco Castro
	9) ERN. CARDENAL MARTINEZ - S3	
	9) ROD. CARDENAL MARTINEZ - S4	
		10) VSA. CASTRO CARDENAL - S5 JAIME WHEELOCK ROMAN - S6
		10) RDO. WHEELOCK ROMAN - S7

APPENDIX 4

P1 S 8,9,10,11	S 12,13	P1 S 14,15,16,17
Generations:		
0) José Ant Lacayo de Briones Bárbara Rosa Pomar y Villegas	(FROM PREVIOUS COLUMN)	0) José Ant Lacayo de Briones Bárbara Rosa Pomar y Villegas
	9) Virginia Cardenal Caldera	
1) Gregoria Lacayo y Pomar Diego Chamorro Sotomayor	GILBERTO GUZMAN CUADRA-S12	1) Gregoria Lacayo y Pomar Diego Chamorro Sotomayor
	9) GABR. CARDENAL CALDERA -S13	
2) Fernando Chamorro Lacayo Bárbara Argüello del Castillo		2) Fernando Chamorro Lacayo Bárbara Argüello del Castillo
3) Pedro Joaq. Chamorro Argüello Jfa. Mgta. Alfaro Monterrosa		3) Pedro Joaq. Chamorro Argüello Jfa. Mgta. Alfaro Monterrosa
4) FRUTO CHAMORRO - P1 Mercedes Avilés Alfaro (2) whose brother was:		4) FRUTO CHAMORRO - P1 Mercedes Avilés Alfaro (2) whose brother was:
5) Agustín Avilés Alfaro ? Briceño		5) Agustín Avilés Alfaro ? Briceño
6)Magdalena Avilés Briceño Juan Ignacio Urtecho Cabistán		6)Magdalena Avilés Briceño Juan Ignacio Urtecho Cabistán
7) Agustina Urtecho Avilés Ernesto Martínez Moya		7) Blanca Urtecho Avilés Manuel Coronel Matus
8) Esmeralda Martínez Urtecho Rodolfo Cardenal Argüello whose brother is:		8) José Coronel Urtecho María Kautz Gross
		9) RICARDO CORONEL KAUTZ - S14 Silvia Pichardo Godoy
8) Julio Cardenal Argüello ? Caldera		
		9) MANUEL CORONEL KAUTZ - S15 Vida Novoa Callejas
9) Indiana Cardenal Caldera ALFONSO ROBELO CALLEJA - S8		
		9) BLANCA CORONEL KAUTZ - S16 Carlos Maturana
9) JULIO CARDENAL CALDERA - S9 Ma. Isabel Reyes Portocarrero		
		9) CARLOS CORONEL KAUTZ - S17
9) Ma. Isabel Cardenal Caldera RGO. REYES PORTOCARRERO-S10		
9) ANT. CARDENAL CALDERA -S11 (CONTINUES NEXT COLUMN)		

APPENDIX 4

P1	P1	P2,3,4
S 18,19	S 20,21	S 22,23,24,25,26

Generations:

0) José Ant Lacayo de Briones	0) José Ant Lacayo de Briones	0) José Ant Lacayo de Briones
Bárbara Rosa Pomar y Villegas	Bárbara Rosa Pomar y Villegas	Bárbara Rosa Pomar y Villegas
1) Gregoria Lacayo y Pomar	1) Gregoria Lacayo y Pomar	1) Gregoria Lacayo y Pomar
Diego Chamorro Sotomayor	Diego Chamorro Sotomayor	Diego Chamorro Sotomayor
2) Fernando Chamorro Lacayo	2) Fernando Chamorro Lacayo	2) Fernando Chamorro Lacayo
Bárbara Argüello del Castillo	Bárbara Argüello del Castillo	Bárbara Argüello del Castillo
3) Pedro Joaq. Chamorro Argüello	3) Pedro Joaq. Chamorro Argüello	3) Pedro Joaq. Chamorro Argüello
Jfa. Mgta. Alfaro Monterrosa	Jfa. Mgta. Alfaro Monterrosa	Jfa. Mgta. Alfaro Monterrosa
4) FRUTO CHAMORRO - P1	4) FRUTO CHAMORRO - P1	4) FERN. CHAMORRO ALFARO - P2
Mercedes Avilés Alfaro (2)	Mercedes Avilés Alfaro (2)	Ana Argüello Arellana
5) Mercedes J. Chamorro Avilés	5) Mercedes J. Chamorro Avilés	4) PE. J. CHAMORRO ALFARO - P3
José Miguel Bolaños Bedaña	José Miguel Bolaños Bedaña	Luz Bolaños Bendaña
6) Pastora Bolaños Chamorro	6) Pastora Bolaños Chamorro	5) D. M. CHAMORRO BOLANOS -P4
Gustavo Alberto Argüello Lugo	Gustavo Alberto Argüello Lugo	
		5) Pedro José Chamorro Bolaños
7)Felipe Argüello Bolaños	7) Gustavo Adolfo Argüello Bolaños	Dominga Zelaya
Lois Carazo Arellana	Carmen Hurtado Cárdenas	
		6) Pedro Joaquín Chamorro Zelaya
8) HOR. J. ARGUELLO CARAZO-S18	8) ROB. ARGUELLO HURTADO - S20	Margarita Cardenal Argüello
TITU LACAYO GABUARDI -S19	Ma. del Socorro Leiva Urcuyo	
		7) JAV. CHAMORRO CARDENAL-S22
	8) ALV. ARGUELLO HURTADO - S21	
		7) Pedro Joaq. Chamorro Cardenal
		VIOLETA BARRIOS TORRES - S23
		7) Jaime Chamorro Cardenal - **
		8) CLAU. CHAMORRO BARRIOS-S24
		EDMUNDO JARQUIN -S25
		8) C. F. CHAMORRO BARRIOS -S26
		8) Pe. Joaq. Chamorro Barrios - *

APPENDIX 4

P5	P6	P7,8

Generations:

P5	P6	P7,8
0) José Ant Lacayo de Briones Bárbara Rosa Pomar y Villegas	0) José Ant Lacayo de Briones Bárbara Rosa Pomar y Villegas	0) José Ant Lacayo de Briones Bárbara Rosa Pomar y Villegas
1) Gregoria Lacayo y Pomar Diego Chamorro Sotomayor	1) Gregoria Lacayo y Pomar Diego Chamorro Sotomayor	1) Simón Lacayo y Palacios Micaela Vázquez y Montiel
2) Fernando Chamorro Lacayo Bárbara Argüello del Castillo	2) Fernando Chamorro Lacayo Bárbara Argüello del Castillo	2) Gabriel Lacayo Montiel Manuela Marenco Alarcón
3) Pedro Joaq. Chamorro Argüello Jfa. Mgta. Alfaro Monterrosa	3) Pedro Joaq. Chamorro Argüello Jfa. Mgta. Alfaro Monterrosa	3) Francisca Lacayo Marenco Blas de la Cerda Aguilar
4) PE. J. CHAMORRO ALFARO - P3 Luz Bolaños Bendaña	4) Dionisio Chamorro Alfaro Mercedes Oreamuno Abaunza	4) CAY. DE LA CERDA LACAYO -P7 Ma. de Jesús Taborga
5) Dominga Chamorro Domingo Chamorro	5) Margarita Chamorro Oreamuno Octavio César Abaunza	5) M. A. DE LA CERDA TABORGA-P8
6) Salvador Chamorro Chamorro	6) Julio César Chamorro Amanda Chamorro Pasos	
7) EMILIANO CHAMORRO - P5	7) Margarita César Chamorro FERN. AGUERO DE LA ROCHA -P6	

APPENDIX 4

P 9,10

Generations:
0) José Ant Lacayo de Briones
   Bárbara Rosa Pomar y Villegas

1) Simón Lacayo y Palacios
   Micaela Vázquez y Montiel

2) Gabriel Lacayo Montiel
   Manuela Marenco Alarcón

3) José Antonio Lacayo Marenco
   Pilar Agüero

4) Fernando Lacayo Agüero
   Pastora Bermúdez Cerda

5) Daniel Lacayo Bermúdez
   Encarnación Sacasa Cuadra

6) BENJAMIN LACAYO SACASA-P10

6) Emelina Lacayo Sacasa
   Roberto Martínez Moya

7) ROBERTO MARTINEZ LACAYO-P9

APPENDIX 5

CUADRA AND RELATED FAMILIES: OLD ORDER PRESIDENTS AND SANDINISTAS
(See following pages for details.)

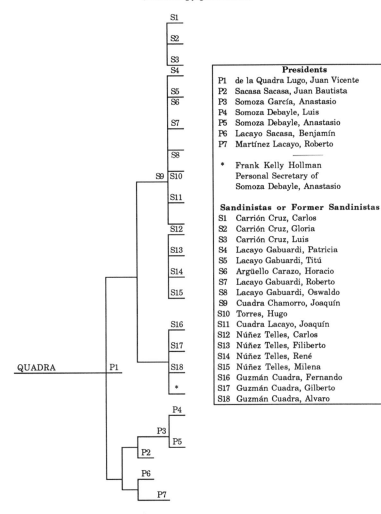

Presidents
P1 de la Quadra Lugo, Juan Vicente
P2 Sacasa Sacasa, Juan Bautista
P3 Somoza García, Anastasio
P4 Somoza Debayle, Luis
P5 Somoza Debayle, Anastasio
P6 Lacayo Sacasa, Benjamín
P7 Martínez Lacayo, Roberto

* Frank Kelly Hollman
    Personal Secretary of
    Somoza Debayle, Anastasio

Sandinistas or Former Sandinistas
S1 Carrión Cruz, Carlos
S2 Carrión Cruz, Gloria
S3 Carrión Cruz, Luis
S4 Lacayo Gabuardi, Patricia
S5 Lacayo Gabuardi, Titú
S6 Argüello Carazo, Horacio
S7 Lacayo Gabuardi, Roberto
S8 Lacayo Gabuardi, Oswaldo
S9 Cuadra Chamorro, Joaquín
S10 Torres, Hugo
S11 Cuadra Lacayo, Joaquín
S12 Núñez Telles, Carlos
S13 Núñez Telles, Filiberto
S14 Núñez Telles, René
S15 Núñez Telles, Milena
S16 Guzmán Cuadra, Fernando
S17 Guzmán Cuadra, Gilberto
S18 Guzmán Cuadra, Alvaro

APPENDIX 5

P1	P2	P 3,4,5

Generations:

0) Antonio de la Quadra Sebastiana de Gutiérrez	0) Antonio de la Quadra Sebastiana de Gutiérrez	0) Antonio de la Quadra Sebastiana de Gutiérrez
1) Santiago de la Quadra Gregoria Sánchez	1) Santiago de la Quadra Gregoria Sánchez	1) Santiago de la Quadra Gregoria Sánchez
2) José Mig. de la Quadra Sánchez Juana Agustina de Montenegro	2) José Mig. de la Quadra Sánchez Juana Agustina de Montenegro	2) José Mig. de la Quadra Sánchez Juana Agustina de Montenegro
3) Dionisio de la Quadra Montenegro Ana Norberta Ruy Lugo	3) Dionisio de la Quadra Montenegro Ana Norberta Ruy Lugo	3) Dionisio de la Quadra Montenegro Ana Norberta Ruy Lugo
4) J. VTE. DE LA QUADRA LUGO - P1	4) Manuela de la Quadra Lugo Salvador Sacasa Méndez	4) Manuela de la Quadra Lugo Salvador Sacasa Méndez
	5) Angela Sacasa Cuadra Roberto Sacasa Sarria	5) Angela Sacasa Cuadra Roberto Sacasa Sarria
	6) JUAN BTA. SACASA SACASA - P2	6) Casimira Sacasa Sacasa Luis H. Debayle
		7) Salvadora Debayle Sacasa ANASTASIO SOMOZA GARCIA - P3
		8) LUIS SOMOZA DEBAYLE - P4 Isabel Rodríguez Urcuyo
		8) ANASTASIO SOMOZA DEBAYLE P5 Hope Portocarrero Debayle

APPENDIX 5

P 6	P 7	S 1 - 9
Generations:		Generation:
0) Antonio de la Quadra Sebastiana de Gutiérrez	0) Antonio de la Quadra Sebastiana de Gutiérrez	0) Antonio de la Quadra Sebastiana de Gutiérrez
1) Santiago de la Quadra Gregoria Sánchez	1) Santiago de la Quadra Gregoria Sánchez	1) Santiago de la Quadra Gregoria Sánchez
2) José Mig. de la Quadra Sánchez Juana Agustina de Montenegro	2) José Mig. de la Quadra Sánchez Juana Agustina de Montenegro	2) José Mig. de la Quadra Sánchez Juana Agustina de Montenegro
3) Dionisio de la Quadra Montenegro Ana Norberta Ruy Lugo	3) Dionisio de la Quadra Montenegro Ana Norberta Ruy Lugo	3) Dionisio de la Quadra Montenegro Ana Norberta Ruy Ligo
4) Manuela de la Quadra Lugo Salvador Sacasa Méndez	4) Manuela de la Quadra Lugo Salvador Sacasa Méndez	4) José Joaquín Quadra Lugo Virginia Pasos Arellano
6) Encarnación Sacasa Cuadra Daniel Lacayo Bermúdez	6) Encarnación Sacasa Cuadra Daniel Lacayo Bermúdez	5) José Demetrio Cuadra Pasos Mercedes Zavala Barberena
7) BENJAMIN LACAYO SACASA - P6	7) Ernelina Lacayo Sacasa Roberto Martínez Moya	6) Joaquín Cuadra Zavala Cristina Chamorro Benard
	8) ROBERTO MARTINEZ LACAYO-P7	7) JOAQUIN CUADRA CHAMORRO-S9 Maruca Lacayo Hurtado
		8) Cristina Cuadra Lacayo OSWDO. LACAYO GABUARDI - S8 whose brother and sisters are:
		8) ROBERTO LACAYO GABUARDI-S7
		8) TITU LACAYO GABUARDI - S5 HORACIO ARGUELLO CARAZO - S6
		8) PATRICIA LACAYO GABUARDI-S4 LUIS CARRION CRUZ - S3 whose brother and sister are:
		8) GLORIA CARRION CRUZ - S2
		8) CARLOS CARRION CRUZ - S1

APPENDIX 5

S 9 - 15   S 16 - 18

---

0) Antonio de la Quadra
   Sebastiana de Gutiérrez

0) Antonio de la Quadra
   Sebastiana de Gutiérrez

1) Santiago de la Quadra
   Gregoria Sánchez

1) Santiago de la Quadra
   Gregoria Sánchez

2) José Mig. de la Quadra Sánchez
   Juana Agustina de Montenegro

2) José Mig. de la Quadra Sánchez
   Juana Agustina de Montenegro

3) Dionisio de la Quadra Montenegro
   Ana Norberta Ruy Ligo

3) Dionisio de la Quadra Montenegro
   Ana Norberta Ruy Ligo

4) José Joaquín Quadra Lugo
   Virginia Pasos Arellano

4) José Joaquín Quadra Lugo
   Virginia Pasos Arellano

5) José Demetrio Cuadra Pasos
   Mercedes Zavala Barberena

5) José Demetrio Cuadra Pasos
   Mercedes Zavala Barberena

6) Joaquín Cuadra Zavala
   Cristina Chamorro Benard

6) Adán Cuadra Zavala
   Angela Lacayo

7) JOAQUIN CUADRA CHAMORRO-S9
   Maruca Lacayo Hurtado

7) Amalia Cuadra Lacayo
   Horacio Guzmán Benard

8) María Lucía Cuadra Lacayo
   HUGO TORRES   - S10

8) FERN. GUZMAN CUADRA   - S16

8) GILBER. GUZMAN CUADRA - S17
   Virginia Cardenal Caldera

8) JOAQUIN CUADRA LACAYO - S11

8) Berta Cecilia Cuadra Lacayo
   CARLOS NUNEZ TELLES   - S12
   whose brothers and sister are:

8) ALVARO GUZMAN CUADRA - S18

8) María Eugenia Guzmán Cuadra
   Frank Kelly Holman   ·

8) FILIBERTO NUNEZ TELLES - S13

8) RENE NUNEZ TELLES   - S14

8) MILENA NUNEZ TELLES   - S15

APPENDIX 6

Part I. COSTA RICAN CONGRESSMEN DESCENDED FROM VAZQUEZ
(Source: Stone, Dinastía, Appendix 5.)

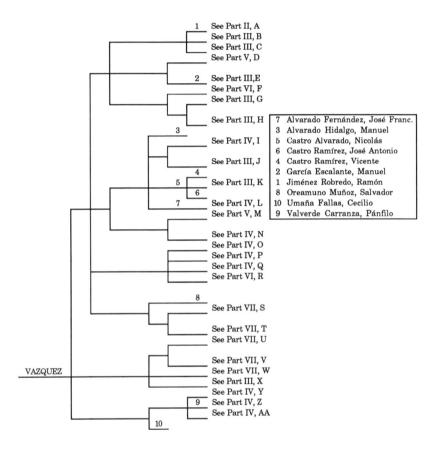

APPENDIX 6

Part II. COSTA RICAN CONGRESSMEN
DESCENDED FROM VAZQUEZ
(Source: Stone, Dinastía, Appendix 5.)

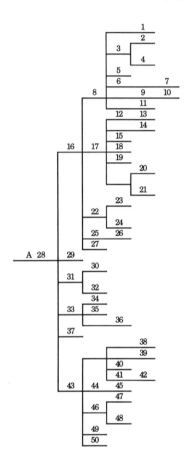

26	Aguilar, Joaquín
10	Chacón Jiménez, Luis Manuel
9	Chacón Pacheco, Nelson
23	Echeverría Aguilar, Manuel
39	Fallas Sibaja, Carlos Luis
29	García Oreamuno, Pedro
21	González Herrán, Manuel Antonio
35	Gutiérrez Zaldós, Atanasio
7	Jiménez Borbón, Manuel
2	Jiménez Flores, Gonzalo
46	Jiménez Oreamuno, Alfredo
25	Jiménez Oreamuno, Francisco
22	Jiménez Oreamuno, José M.
44	Jiménez Oreamuno, Manuel de Jesús
27	Jiménez Oreamuno, Nicolás
49	Jiménez Oreamuno, Ricardo
8	Jiménez Oreamuno. Manuel Vicente
3	Jiménez Ortiz, Carlos María
6	Jiménez Ortiz, Manuel Francisco
5	Jiménez Ortiz, Roberto
1	Jiménez Ramírez, Guillermo
28	Jiménez Robredo, Ramón
45	Jiménez Rojas, Nicómedes
32	Jiménez Sáenz, Roberto
4	Jiménez Sancho, Eugenio
24	Jiménez Sancho, José Miguel
40	Jiménez Tinoco, Mario
31	Jiménez Zamora, Agapito
43	Jiménez Zamora, Jesús
16	Jiménez Zamora, José Manuel
47	Jiménez Zavaleta, Arnoldo
48	Jiménez Zavaleta, Claudio
14	Orlich Zamora, Romano
30	Padilla Romero, Julio
37	Peralta Chavarría, Mauricio
36	Peralta Sancho, Leonidas
38	Reuben Aguilera, William
33	Sancho Alvarado, Félix
34	Sancho Jiménez, Enrique
50	Tinoco Yglesias, Demetrio
11	Villalobos Dobles, Jorge Nilo
13	Volio Guardia, Arturo
12	Volio Jiménez, Arturo
15	Volio Jiménez, Claudio María
42	Volio Jiménez, Fernando
18	Volio Jiménez, Jorge
17	Volio Llorente, Carlos
20	Volio Mata, Alfredo
41	Volio Sancho, Fernando
19	Volio Tinoco, Carlos

APPENDIX 6

Part III. COSTA RICAN CONGRESSMEN
DESCENDED FROM VAZQUEZ
(Source: Stone, Dinastía, Appendix 5.)

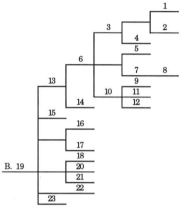

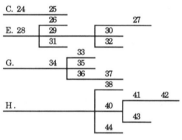

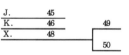

49	Acosta García, Julio
50	Acosta García, Raúl
12	Brenes Mata, Andrés
36	Carazo Bonilla, Manuel José
37	Carazo Peralta, Juan Manuel
16	Carranza Ramírez, Ramón
46	Castro Bonilla, Manuel
39	Chavarría Diez-Dobles, Ramón
44	Chavarría Mora, Francisco
38	Chavarría Mora, José Ramón
40	Chavarría Mora, Nicolás
32	Escalante Durán, Carlos Manuel
30	Escalante Durán, Manuel
45	Fernández Alvarado, Máximo
17	Fernández Oreamuno, Joaquín
22	Figueroa Oreamuno, Eusebio
2	Gallegos Yglesias, Felipe
48	García Carrillo, Juan J.G.
26	García Escalante, Juan Vicente
28	García Escalante, Manuel
31	García-Escalante Nava, Alejandro
29	García-Escalante Nava, Manuel
23	Hidalgo Muñoz, Joaquín
14	Jiménez Zamora, Manuel
4	Mata Oreamuno, Guillermo
3	Mata Valle, Félix
15	Ñeco, Juan
18	Oreamuno Carazo, Desiderio
6	Oreamuno Carazo, Rafael
20	Oreamuno Carazo, Ricardo
9	Oreamuno Flores, Alberto
13	Oreamuno Jiménez, Félix
19	Oreamuno Muñoz, Joaquín
10	Oreamuno Ortiz, Nicolás
43	Peña Chavarría, Antonio
35	Peralta Chavarría, José Manuel
33	Peralta Chavarría, Luciano
25	Peralta López, Francisco
34	Peralta López, Manuel María
11	Robles Troyo, Miguel Angel
42	Rossi Chavarría, Jorge
41	Rossi Monge, Jorge
8	Salazar Fábrega, Mario
1	Salazar Mata, Roberto
7	Salazar Oreamuno, Carlos Manuel
5	Salazar Oreamuno, Rogelio
21	Sancho Alvarado, Alejandro
24	Torre Romero, Manuel
27	Trejos Escalante, Fernando

APPENDIX 6

Part IV. COSTA RICAN CONGRESSMEN
DESCENDED FROM VAZQUEZ
(Source: Stone, Dinastía, Appendix 5.)

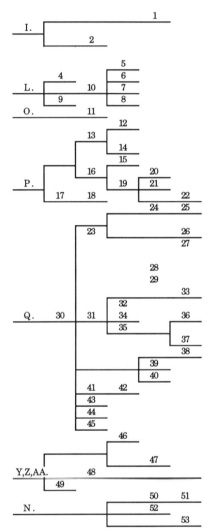

3 Alvarado Fernández, Francisco.
4 Alvarado Velasco, Cruz
9 Alvarado Velasco, Lucas
29 Argüello de Vars, Manuel
2 Astúa Aguilar, José
5 Baudrit González, Fabio
28 Beeche Argüello, Eduardo
36 Brenes Gutiérrez, Ramiro
38 Cañas Escalante, Alberto
40 Cañas Iraeta, Antonio
27 Castro Beeche, Ricardo
39 Castro Beeche, Ricardo
41 Chamorro Gutiérrez, José Antonio
42 Chamorro Mora, Diego
1 Echandi Jiménez, Mario
53 Espinach Escalante, Carlos
33 Gallegos Sáenz, Rafael
51 González Luján, Claudio
48 González Ramírez, Alejandro
50 González Rucavado, Claudio
45 Gutiérrez Peñamonje, Manuel Joaquín
6 Gutiérrez Ross, Agustín
47 Guzmán López-Calleja., Vesalio
7 Jiménez Delgado, Franklin
19 Lizano Gutiérrez, Joaquín
22 Lizano Hernández, Alberto
20 Lizano Ulloa, Carlos
21 Lizano Ulloa, Rafael
46 López-Calleja Umaña, Francisco
24 Loría Yglesias, Pedro
37 Marshall Jiménez, Francisco José
31 Montealegre Fernández, José María
35 Montealegre Mora, José María
34 Montealegre Mora, Manuel
30 Mora Alvarado, Camilo
43 Mora Porras, José Joaquín
23 Mora Porras, Juan Rafael
44 Mora Porras, Miguel
25 Morales de Echeverría, Graciela
8 Moreno Cañas, Ricardo
10 Moreno, Inocente
13 Moya Murillo, Rafael
14 Moya Solares, Rafael
12 Moya, Carlos Fabián
11 Quirós, Ramón
32 Rojas Vargas, Edgar
52 Rucavado Gómez, Otto
18 Sandoval Jiménez, Venancio
17 Sandoval Porras, Matías
15 Ulloa Solares, Juan José
16 Ulloa, Nicolás
26 Valladares Mora, Rafael Angel
49 Valverde Carranza, Pánfilo

APPENDIX 6

Part V.   COSTA RICAN CONGRESSMEN
DESCENDED FROM VAZQUEZ
(Source: Stone, Dinastía, Appendix 5.)

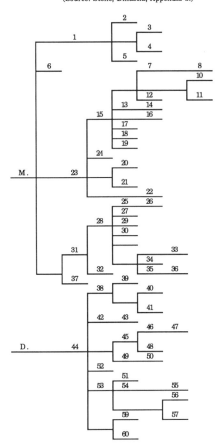

6	Bonilla Laya-Bolívar, Santiago
10	Brenes Gutiérrez, Ramiro
56	Brenes Gutiérrez, Ramiro
17	Castro Fernández, José María
18	Castro Fernández, Moisés
19	Castro Fernández, Ramón
15	Castro Madríz, José María
3	Escalante Durán, Manuel
33	Fallas Sibaja, Carlos Luis
23	Fernández Chacón, Manuel
20	Fernández Güell, Rogelio
21	Fernández Güell, Victor
24	Fernández Oreamuno, Joaquín
38	Gutiérrez Peñamonje, Fsco. de Paula
40	Gutiérrez Ross, Agustín
41	Gutiérrez Ross, Fsco. de Paula
39	Gutiérrez Yglesias, Ezequiel
25	Jiménez Oreamuno, Alfredo
27	Jiménez Oreamuno, Manuel de Jesús
29	Jiménez Oreamuno, Ricardo
34	Jiménez Tinoco, Mario
28	Jiménez Zamora, Jesús
26	Jiménez Zavaleta, Arnoldo
12	Lara Avellán, Gerardo
51	Lara Avellán, Gerardo
58	Loría Vega, Ramón
60	Loría Yglesias, Pedro
59	Loría Yglesias, Ramón
11	Marshall Jiménez, Francisco José
57	Marshall Jiménez, Francisco José
31	Oreamuno Bonilla, Francisco María
32	Oreamuno Gutiérrez, Francisco
14	Orozco Castro, Carlos
13	Orozco González, Rafael
1	Peralta de la Vega, José María
2	Peralta Echeverría, Bernardino
5	Peralta Echeverrría, José María
4	Peralta Esquivel, José Joaquín
42	Saborío Alfaro, Pedro
43	Saborío Yglesias, Carlos
37	Sandoval Jiménez, Venancio
22	Soto Fernández, Máximo
8	Tattenbach Yglesias, Christian
55	Tattenbach Yglesias, Christian
47	Tinoco Castro, Demetrio
50	Tinoco Granados, Federico
46	Tinoco Gutiérrez, Demetrio
48	Tinoco Gutiérrez, Ricardo
30	Tinoco Yglesias, Demetrio
45	Tinoco Yglesias, Demetrio
49	Tinoco Yglesias, Federico
16	Velásquez Castro, Miguel Angel
36	Volio Jiménez, Fernando
35	Volio Sancho, Fernando
7	Yglesias Castro, Rafael
54	Yglesias Castro, Rafael
53	Yglesias Llorente, Demetrio
9	Yglesias Llorente, Demetrio
52	Yglesias Llorente, Francisco María
44	Yglesias, Joaquín

APPENDIX 6

Part VI.   COSTA RICAN CONGRESSMEN
DESCENDED FROM VAZQUEZ
(Source: Stone, Dinastía, Appendix 5.)

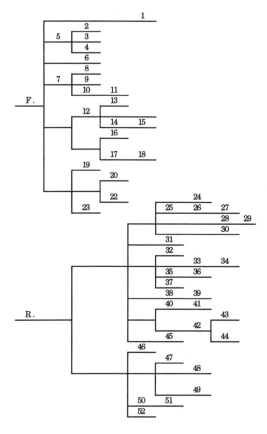

24 Acosta Valverde, Adán
52 Alvarado García, Alejandro
42 Camacho Muñoz, Salustio
44 Camacho Quirós, Adriano
 1 Carazo Odio, Rodrigo
15 Carro Zúñiga, Alfonso
38 Cordero Quirós, Francisco
39 Cordero Zúñiga, Hernán
46 Durán Cartín, Carlos
 8 Echavarría Aguilar, Juan F.
 9 Echavarría Aguilar, Manuel
 7 Echavarría Alvarado, Fsco. de P.
22 Escalante Durán, Manuel
48 Fournier Acuña, Fernando
49 Fournier Jiménez, Fabio
47 Fournier Quirós, Ricardo
37 García Aragón, Luis
50 Guardia Gutiérrez, Victor
51 Guardia Quirós, Victor
35 Leiva Quirós, Genaro
36 Leiva Quirós, Mario
33 Leiva Reyes, Roberto
34 Leiva Runnebaum, Rodolfo
31 Maroto Quirós, Marco Tulio
30 Oduber Quirós, Daniel
43 Orlich Bolmarcich, Francisco J.
21 Peralta Alvarado, Bernardino
19 Peralta Echavarría, Bernardo
23 Peralta Echavarría, José M.
20 Peralta Esquivel, José Joaquín
11 Pinto Echavarría, Fernando
10 Pinto Fernández, Alberto
25 Quirós Aguilar, Pedro
41 Quirós Fonseca, Napoleón
27 Quirós Maroto, Sergio
40 Quirós Montero, José
26 Quirós Quirós, Roberto
45 Quirós Segura, Juan Bta.
32 Quirós Troyo, Man. de J.
 5 Sáenz Carazo, Luis Diego
 3 Sáenz Echavarría, Frsco.
 2 Sáenz Echavarría, Manuel
18 Salazar Fábrega, Mario
17 Salazar Oreamuno, Carlos M.
16 Salazar Oreamuno, Rogelio
 4 Sánz Echavarría, Frcsco. V.
14 Solera Oreamuno, Jorge Luis
13 Solera Oreamuno, Juan Ma.
12 Solera Rodríguez, Juan Ma.
29 Trejos Fonseca, Juan José
28 Trejos Quirós, Juan
 6 Vargas Pacheco, José María

APPENDIX 6

Part VII. COSTA RICAN CONGRESSMEN
(Source: Stone, Dinastía, Appendix 5.)

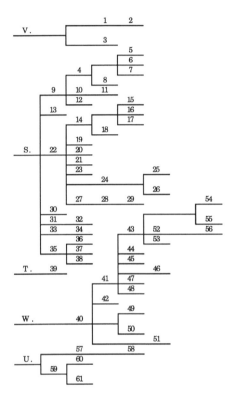

54 Brenes Gutiérrez, Ramiro
44 Castro Fernández, José María
47 Castro Fernández, Moisés
48 Castro Fernández, Ramón
41 Castro Madriz, José María
25 Escalante Durán, Manuel
28 Esquivel Carazo, Roberto
18 Esquivel Carrillo, José Joaquín
6 Esquivel Carrillo, José Joaquín
16 Esquivel Carrillo, José Joaquín
24 Esquivel Flores, Fabián
27 Esquivel Sáenz, Aniceto
21 Esquivel Sáenz, Camilo
7 Esquivel Sáenz, Jaime
17 Esquivel Sáenz, Jaime
5 Esquivel Sáenz, Julio
15 Esquivel Sáenz, Julio
20 Esquivel Sáenz, Macedonio
14 Esquivel Sáenz, Manuel de Jesús
19 Esquivel Sáenz, Manuel María
8 Esquivel Sáenz, Miguel Narciso
23 Esquivel Sáenz, Miguel Narciso
22 Esquivel Salazar, Narciso
40 Fernández Chacón, Manuel
49 Fernández Güell, Rogelio
50 Fernández Güell, Victor
42 Fernández Oreamuno, Joaquín
30 Fernández Tenorio, Cipriano
35 Gallegos Alvarado, Rafael
36 Gallegos Sáenz, Rafael
61 García Aragón Alejandro
60 García Aragón, Luis
59 García, Fernando
32 Jiménez Zamora, Agapito
53 Lara Avellán, Gerardo
55 Marshall Jiménez, Francisco José
37 Montealegre Fernández, Francisco
38 Montealegre Fernández, Mariano
45 Orozco González, Rafael
1 Ortiz Frutos, Francisco
2 Ortiz Odio , Ernesto
3 Pacheco Frutos, Juan Félix
58 Patiño Troyo, Manuel
26 Peralta Esquivel, José Joaquín
29 Peralta Esquivel, José Joaquín
39 Ramírez Ulloa, Santiago
57 Rojas Troyo, José Ramón
34 Sáenz Carazo, Luis Diego
11 Sáenz Esquivel, Carlos
4 Sáenz Llorente, Andrés
12 Sáenz Llorente, Pascual
10 Sáenz Llorente, Vicente
13 Sáenz Ulloa, Anselmo
33 Sáenz Ulloa, Diego María
9 Sáenz Ulloa, Francisco Javier
31 Sáenz Ulloa, José Nicolás
51 Soto Fernández, Maximiliano
56 Tattenbach Yglesias, Christian
46 Velásquez Castro, Miguel Angel
52 Yglesias Castro, Rafael
43 Yglesias Llorente, Demetrio

Kinship among Conquistadors

(C = Conquistador)
(m = married)

I
Alvarado Contreras Family
Six brothers and their progeny:
A. Pedro de Alvarado Contreras (C) m.
1. Luisa Xicoténcatl
2. Francisca de la Cueva Villacreces
3. Beatriz de la Cueva Villacreces
   a daughter:
   a) Leonor Alvarado Xicoténcatl m.
   1. Pedro Portocarrero (C)
   2. Francisco de la Cueva Villacreces (C)
B. Jorge de Alvarado Contreras (C) m.
1. Lucía Xicoténcatl
2. Luisa Estrada
   sons and daughters:
   a) ? m.
      Gonzalo Alvarado Chaves (C)
   b) Francisca Alvarado m.
      Francisco Girón y Nieto (C)
   c) Jorge Alvarado Estrada (C) m.
      Catalina Carvajal Villafañe, daughter of
      Angel de Villafañe (C)
C. Gonzalo de Alvarado Contreras (C)
D. Gómez de Alvarado Contreras (C)
E. Juan de Alvarado Contreras
F. Juan Alvarado (brother by) (C)

II
Pedrarias Davila Family
Two first cousins and their sons:
A. Pedro Arias de Avila (C) m.
   Isabel de Bobadilla y Peñalosa
   Daughter:
   1) Isabel Arias de Peñalosa m.

    a. Vasco Núñez de Balboa (C)
    b. Rodrigo de Contreras (C)
B. Gaspar Arias de Avila (C) m.
  Juana Robleto
  Daughter:
    1) Giné de Robleto y Arias Dávila
    Carlos Bonifaz (C)

III
Sancho de Barahona Family
Sancho de Barahona (C) m.
  Isabel Escobar
  Son and daughter:
    a) Sancho Barahona (C) m.
    Isabel Loaiza
    b) Leonor Barahona Escobar m.
      1. Juan de Cavallón (C)
      2. Juan de Cuellar y Mosía (C)

SOURCES: Edgar Juan Aparicio y Aparicio, *Conquistadores de Guatemala y fundadores de familias Guatemaltecas* (Mexico City, second edition, 1961). See also Gonzalo Fernández de Oviedo, *Historia general y natural de las Indias* (Asunción: Editorial Guaranía, 1944–45); and Antonio de Herrera, *Historia general de los hechos castellanos en las islas y tierrafirme del Mar Océano* (Madrid: Tipografía de Archivos, 1934–57).

Notes

Preface

1. Samuel Stone, *La dinastía de los conquistadores: La crisis del poder en la Costa Rica contemporánea* (1975). Samuel Stone, "Le café et le développement du Costa Rica," paper presented at the Centre d'Etudes Economiques, Politiques, et Sociales, Institut des Hautes Etudes de l'Amérique Latine, Université de Paris, 1966; subsequently *"Los cafetaleros:* Une étude de la classe des grands planteurs de café au Costa Rica" (Doctorat de Troisième Cycle, Université de Paris [Sorbonne], 1968). This dissertation was later published in abbreviated form in Spanish, under the title "Los cafetaleros: Un estudio de la clase de grandes caficultores de Costa Rica," *Revista de ciencias jurídicas* 13 (1969).

Introduction

1. *Enciclopedia Barsa*, 1958, 7:406; *The New Columbia Encyclopaedia*, 1975, p. 1156; *Encyclopaedia Britannica* Yearbook, 1988, p. 610.

2. *Encyclopaedia Britannica* Yearbook, 1988, pp. 579, 590, 610, 615, 669.

3. Miguel D'Escoto Brockmann, in Introduction to Richard Millett, *Guardianes de la dinastía*, 1979, p. 13.

4. Enrique Tierno Galván, *Actas de las Cortes de Cádiz*, 1964. See introductory chapter and articles on elections under the Constitution of Cádiz.

5. Samuel Stone, "Las convulsiones del Istmo Centroamericano: Raíces de un conflicto entre elites," *Estudios* 1 (1979): 9, 10.

6. This explanation was lightheartedly (but quite seriously) given to the CIAPA staff by former United States ambassador to Costa Rica, Lewis A. Tambs.

7. This comment was made to the CIAPA staff by President Rodrigo Carazo Odio in 1978.

8. The élitist concepts expressed here are based fundamentally on Percy Cohen, *Modern Social Theory*, 1968; and Carlo Marletti, "Clases y elites políticas: Teorías y análisis," in *Cuestiones de sociología.* ed. Francesco Alberoni, 1971, p. 345. Names usually associated with élitist doctrine are those of Gaetano Mosca, Vilifredo

Pareto, Robert Michels, James Burnham, C. Wright Mills, and Karl Marx. See Cohen, p. 27.

9. See Karl Wittfogel, *El despotismo oriental*, 1966.

10. Stone, *Dinastía*.

11. Judging the number of presidents is difficult due to coups d'état, revolutions, and vice presidents serving temporarily as chiefs of state. I have included only those who exercised power for prolonged periods of time.

12. His brother, Francisco, generally known in the United States as Coronado, was a conquistador of the Southwest and Mexico. Rules governing primogeniture had unexpected consequences, for younger sons were obliged to take desperate measures to fend for themselves. In the present case, upon learning that their older brother, Gonzalo, had inherited the family fortune, both went to America. See Herbert E. Bolton, *Coronado: Knight of Pueblos and Plains*, 1949, pp. 19, 20. My 1975 book, *Dinastía*, mistakenly said Juan's bride was a sister of Pedrarias; she was his first cousin.

13. F. Webster McBryde, *Encyclopaedia Britannica*, 1986, 15:693, 94.

Chapter 1

1. This is an adaptation of Miguel León-Portilla, ed., *Visión de los vencidos: Relaciones indígenas de la Conquista*, 7th ed., 1976, pp. 198–203.

2. Samuel Stone, "Los cafetaleros: Un estudio de la clase de grandes caficultores de Costa Rica," *Revista de Ciencias Jurídicas* 13 (1969): 167–75.

3. For a similar impression concerning marriages between first cousins in the ruling class in Nicaragua (and in all social classes), see Shirley Christian, *Nicaragua: Revolution in the Family*, 1985, p. 4. A similar idea is conveyed by the many genealogical studies on Guatemala and El Salvador in the *Revista de la Academia Guatemalteca de Estudios Genealógicos, Heráldicos, e Históricos*, where detailed social backgrounds of spouses are given for Guatemalan and Salvadoran families with more frequency than is the case for Costa Rican families in the *Revista de la Academia Costarricense de Ciencias Genealógicas*.

4. Samuel Stone, "Production and Politics in Central America's Convulsions," *Journal of Latin American Studies* 15, part 2 (November 1983): 453–69.

5. See Antonello Gerbi, *La naturaleza de las Indias nuevas*, 1978, pp. 365, 374–75. Gerbi quotes Juan Contreras, the Marqués de Lozoya, *Los orígenes del imperio: La España de Fernando e Isabel*, 1939, p. 184, who admired the fact that medieval culture continued into the Spanish Renaissance without interruption. For the encomienda and the repartimiento, see *Diccionario enciclopédico hispano americano*, no date; *Enciclopedia Barsa*, 1958; Silvio Zavala, *El mundo americano en la época colonial*, 1967; *The New Columbia Encyclopaedia*, 1975; Pilar Sanchiz Ochoa, *Los hidalgos de Guatemala: Realidad y apariencia en un sistema de valores*, 1976; William L. Sherman, *Forced Slave Labor in Sixteenth-Century Central America*, 1979; *Encyclopaedia Britannica*, 1986; Stephen Webre, "Las compañías de milicia y la defensa del Istmo Centroamericano en el siglo XVII," *Mesoamérica* 8,14 (1987): pp. 512, 513; and Murdo J. MacLeod, *Spanish Central America*, 1973, chap. 3.

6. MacLeod, *Spanish Central America*, pp. 49, 55.

7. Samuel Stone, *Dinastía*, part 2. The pre-Independence roots of this type of monopoly, as they apply to Costa Rican colonial society, are dealt with in some detail.

8. Manuel Rubio Sánchez, *Comercio de y entre las provincias de Centroamérica*, 1973,

pp. 338–64. These data were taken from *Pensamiento vivo de José Cecilio del Valle,* ed. Rafael Heliodoro Valle, 1971, pp. 115–19.

9. Edgar Juan Aparicio y Aparicio, "La familia de Arzú," *Revista de la Academia Guatemalteca de Estudios Genealógicos, Heráldicos, e Históricos* 3,4 (1969–70):69–113. "La familia Cabarrrús," ibid., pp. 321–45; see also Mercedes Guirola Leal de Acuña Durán, "La familia Durán," ibid., 5–6 (1971–72):199–334; Edgar Juan Aparicio y Aparicio and Juan José Falla Sánchez, "La familia Maestre," ibid., 2 (1969):335–82.

10. See Luis Mariñas Otero, *Las constituciones de Guatemala,* 1958, p. 137.

11. For a similar although slightly different interpretation of the liberal and conservative movements, see Christian, *Nicaragua,* p. 5.

12. Ciro Flamarion S. Cardoso and Héctor Pérez Brignoli, *Centroamérica y la economía occidental 1520–1930,* 1977, pp. 175, 206, 295. See also by the same authors *Historia económica de América Latina* 2, 1979, 29–63. These authors underscore the significance of those reforms for the Isthmus.

13. Cardoso and Pérez, *Centroamérica,* pp. 176, 273, 285–89.

14. Samuel Stone, *Dinastía,* pp. 190–94.

15. Héctor Pérez Brignoli, *Breve historia de Centro América,* 1985, pp. 42 (map 6), 92 (map 11), 103 (map 13).

16. For details on the death of Molina, see *La Nación* (San José, Costa Rica) 1 February 1980, p. 19A.

17. Félix Belly, *A travers l'Amérique Centrale,* 1867, 1:147.

18. Mario Monteforte Toledo, in *Centro América,* 1972, 2:192, gives the salary of Ydígoras as one million dollars. The salaries of both presidents were given in *Time* or *Newsweek* magazines circa 1960, but my efforts at locating them have been unsuccessful. In one of them, Ydígoras was said to have received six hundred fifty thousand dollars.

19. Samuel Stone, "Production and Politics," pp. 459–60.

20. Samuel Stone, *Dinastía,* chaps. 2, 3, 4.

Chapter 2

1. This story was adapted from German Arciniegas, "La familia que ya concebimos," in his *Nueva imágen del Caribe,* 1972, pp. 42–43. It was written toward the end of the 1950s.

2. *La República* (San José, Costa Rica), 6 August 1988, pp. 1, 4.

3. These ideas on dependency theory were outlined in an article I published in the Costa Rican press on the eve of Nelson Rockefeller's visit. See "La Visita de Rockefeller," *La Nación,* 16 May 1969, p. 15. In South America, similar sentiments were expressed as a result of the Mexican oil expropriations over half a century ago as well as in the novel *Doña Bárbara,* by Venezuelan President Rómulo Gallegos, where one of the principal protagonists is a North American named Mr. Danger. Some of the principal exponents of dependency theories are Fernando Henrique Cardozo and Enzo Faletto, *Dependencia y desarrollo en América Latina,* 1973; Aldo Solari, Rolando Franco, and Joel Jutkowitz, eds., *Teoría, acción social y desarrollo en América Latina,* 1976, pp. 440–41; and Pope Paul VI, *Popularum progressio,* 1968, pp. 77–78, note 29.

4. William H. Durham, *Scarcity and Survival in Central America: Ecological Origins of the Soccer War,* 1982, pp. vii, 1–3, 6–8, 21, 26.

5. Ibid., pp. 33–34.

6. Ibid., p. 43.

7. One of the principal Soviet agents, Agustín Farabundo Martí, sought support in Nicaragua from Augusto César Sandino, who turned him down because he found contradictions in Marxism. These had to do with his aversion to the concept of class struggle and his belief in the Catholic faith. See Christian, *Nicaragua*, p. 232. Farabundo Martí's mistake (and the Soviets') was to have confused a movement in Nicaragua for national liberation (from foreign capital and "oligarchic dominance") with what they took to be fertile grounds for communism. See Rodolfo Cerdas Cruz, "Stratégie et tactique de l'Internationale Communiste en Amérique Centrale, 1920–36" (Doctorat de Troisième Cycle, Université de Paris [Sorbonne], 1973): 273.

8. Durham, *Scarcity and Survival*, pp. 119, 123.

9. Ibid., p. 161.

10. Miami *Herald*, 28 November 1978, p. 3-AW.

11. J. Mark Ruhl, "Agrarian Structure and Political Stability in Honduras," *Journal of Interamerican Studies and World Affairs* 26, 1(1984): 36–38.

12. Ibid., p. 37.

13. Franklin D. Parker, *The Central American Republics*, 1968, p. 239.

14. Pedro Belli, "Prolegómeno para una historia económica de Nicaragua de 1905 a 1966," *Revista Conservadora del Pensamiento Centroamericano* 30, no. 146 (1975): 26–29.

15. Arturo Cruz, Jr., "One Hundred Years of Turpitude," *New Republic*, 16 November 1987, p. 30. For an account of how Somoza became head of the Nicaraguan National Guard, see Millett, *Guardianes*, chap. 7.

16. Francisco was a member of Spanish nobility. Information on the Somoza family was provided to me by Joaquín Alberto Fernández Alfaro, of San José, Costa Rica, in a letter dated 24 May 1987. Mr. Fernández was consul of Costa Rica in Managua, is a member of the Academia Costarricense de Ciencias Genealógicas, and has written extensively on Central American genealogy. Francisco's brother Gaspar, who also settled in Guatemala, is mentioned in Edgar Juan Aparicio y Aparicio, *Conquistadores de Guatemala y fundadores de familias guatemaltecas*, 1961, p. 28. Francisco married Catharina de Rivera y Guzmán (his second wife), and their progeny leading to Anastasio Somoza García are as follows: Juan Manuel de Somoza Rivera (married to Catharina Sánchez Valdés) had Casimiro Somoza Sánchez (wife unknown), father of Bernabé de Somoza (married to a Martínez). Their son Anastasio Somoza Martínez (married to Petronila Tejada) was father of Anastasio Somoza Tejada (as well as of the legendary bandit, Bernabé, described toward the midnineteenth century by United States consul, Ephraim G. Squier (see *Nicaragua, sus gentes y paisajes*, 1970, pp. 74–92; for Somoza García's relationship with Bernabé Somoza, also see Millett, *Guardianes*, pp. 28–29). Anastasio Somoza Tejada (killed in the campaign against United States filibuster William H. Walker) married Isabel Reyes and was father of Anastasio Somoza Reyes (wed to Julia García). Their son was Anastasio Somoza García, first of the dictators, who was followed by two sons, Luis and Anastasio Somoza Debayle. As descendants of Spanish nobility, numerous members of this family held political posts during the colonial period.

17. Cruz, "Turpitude," p. 26. Cruz also discusses the ancestors of Daniel and Humberto Ortega Saavedra.

18. Ibid., p. 30.

19. Ibid.

20. *La Nación Internacional*, 28 May–3 June 1982. The complete list presented in this source (with additional information concerning certain individuals) is as fol-

lows: Fernando Guzmán Cuadra (president of the National Development Bank and former minister of industry); a brother, Gilberto (general director of revenue); another brother, Alvaro (vice minister of foreign trade); these are nephews of Joaquín Cuadra Chamorro (minister of finance), whose son is Joaquín Cuadra Lacayo (chief of staff of the Sandinista army). A daughter of Joaquín Cuadra Chamorro is married to Carlos Núñez Telles (one of the nine Sandinista comandantes), and another to Hugo Torres (former head of the state security office).

The family of Jaime Wheelock Román, one of the nine comandantes and minister of agrarian reform, is related to some of Nicaragua's progenitors; in addition it illustrates the ongoing importance of family ties in politics. His wife, Vanessa Castro Cardenal, is a member of the important Sandinista assembly as well as of the state commission of the Frente Sandinista de Liberación Nacional (FSLN). Wheelock's mother is married to the Chilean Anastasio Sánchez, state representative on the nationalized radio corporation. Wheelock's brother, Ricardo, was ambassador to the Soviet Union. Ernesto Cardenal Martínez (minister of culture, and related to Wheelock's wife Vanessa) has a brother, Fernando (coordinator of the Sandinista Youth Organization), and another, Rodrigo (vice minister of transportation), who married a daughter of Rafael Córdoba Rivas of the National Reconstruction Junta. The Cardenal Martínez brothers are relatives of the Cuadra Chamorro and Guzmán Cuadra families.

Another of the nine comandantes, Luis Carrión Cruz, is director of the FSLN; a brother, Carlos, is secretary general of Sandinista youth; a sister, Gloria, is secretary general of the Sandinista Feminist Association; and their father, Luis Carrión Montoya, is coordinator of the state financial system. A cousin, Javier, is a guerrilla comandante. Sergio Ramírez Mercado, vice president of Nicaragua, has a brother, Rogelio, who is secretary of municipal affairs of the junta and manages the laborers' Christmas fund. He married the legal adviser of the Banco Nicaragüense. Filiberto Núñez Telles, brother of comandante Carlos (mentioned above), is vice minister of construction; another, René, is secretary of the national directory of the FSLN; and a sister, Milena, is president of the Sandinista Teachers' Organization. Roberto Lacayo Gabuardi is vice minister of housing; his brother, Oswaldo, is a guerrilla comandante; a sister, Patricia, is a director of the Sandinista Youth Association and married comandante Luis Carrión Cruz (mentioned above). Another sister, Tutú, married Horacio Argüello Hurtado, adviser to the Ministry of Finance.

In the Castillo Martínez family, Ernesto is former minister of justice (under the Sandinistas) and director of higher education; a brother, Mario, is purchaser for the FSLN in Nicaragua, and another, Miguel, holds the same position for purchases in the United States. A sister, Silvia, has an important job at the international airport. In the Coronel Kautz family, Ricardo is vice minister of agrarian reform; Manuel is manager of one of its branches; Blanca (married name Maturana) is in the Ministry of the Exterior; and Carlos, who directed the state fishing enterprise for the Sandinista regime, eventually joined the anti-Sandinista rebel forces of Eden Pastora (Comandante Zero). From the Argüello Hurtado family come Roberto, president of the Supreme Court; Alvaro, member of the Council of State; and Horacio (a cousin), adviser in the Ministry of Finance.

21. *La Nación,* 7 April 1988, p. 14A.

22. Cruz, "Turpitude," p. 26.

23. The bulk of the information concerning the Ortega brothers came from Cruz, "Turpitude," pp. 26, 30. Part of it came from Narciso Lacayo Pallais (in 1987), married to the sister of the late wife of Anastasio Somoza García, and additional data were obtained from Manuel Jirón, *¿Quién es quién en Nicaragua?,* 1986, p. 292.

24. Joaquín Alberto Fernández Alfaro (see note 16 above).

25. Cruz, "Turpitude," p. 26.

26. *La República*, 13 November 1987, p. 13. This source calls her a person from the upper class, which is undoubtedly true.

27. See Francisco Huezo (on Rubén Darío), "Sus últimos días," *Revista Conservadora del Pensamiento Centroamericano* 13, no. 65 (1966): 15–30. In the same issue, by an unnamed author (presumably someone on the staff), see "Rubén Darío: Breve biografía," pp. 3–14. Since his earliest childhood, Darío formed part of high society in both Nicaragua and El Salvador.

28. Jirón, *¿Quién es Quién?*, p. 272.

29. Arthur Schlesinger, Jr., "Reagan is Crying Wolf in Nicaragua," *Wall Street Journal*, 25 March 1988.

30. Jirón, *¿Quién es Quién?*, p. 321.

31. For a recent account of the way in which the Colombian guerrilla movement views this source of funding, see *La República*, 1 July 1988, pp. 16, 36.

32. Howard Banks, "Bankruptcy without Pain," *Forbes* 135 (1985):109–10.

33. *La República*, 13 January 1985, p. 3; *La República*, 1 August 1985, p. 4; *La Nación*, 1 August 1985, p. 1.

34. *La Nación*, 24 March 1985, pp. 1, 12A. "Wetbacks" is used figuratively.

35. *La Nación*, 17 March 1988, p. 22A.

36. Brinkmanship had been the policy of John Foster Dulles (secretary of state under President Dwight D. Eisenhower) of trying to satisfy United States interests in its relations with the Soviet Union, through pressures generated by creating tensions short of war. It was dubbed "brinkmanship," because it was the diplomatic art of knowing how far to go without "going over the brink."

37. *La República*, 3 August 1988, pp. 1, 4.

38. *Miami Herald*, 22 April 1988, p. 1.

39. *La Nación*, daily during the week of 3–10 March 1987. Statistics concerning distribution of income, GNP per capita, debt, and devaluations show Mexico to be one of the most socially and politically explosive countries on the continent.

40. This was revealed by Fernando Volio Jiménez, Costa Rican minister of foreign affairs, during a seminar at the Centro de Investigación y Adiestramiento Político-Administrativo (CIAPA), in San José, Costa Rica, held 10–12 July 1984.

41. Eusebio Mujal-León, "European Socialism and the Crisis in Central America," in *Rift and Revolution: The Central American Imbroglio*, ed. Howard J. Wiarda, 1984, pp. 253–302.

Chapter 3

1. This tale is a product of my own imagination (as are several others in this book), based in part on readings of the chronicler of the Conquest, Bernal Díaz del Castillo.

2. For information on the daughter of Pedrarias, who was named Isabel Arias de Peñalosa, married Balboa and then Contreras, and was said to have been named María, see Antonio de Herrera y Tordesillas, *Historia general de los hechos castellanos en las islas y tierrafirme del Mar Océano*, 1934–57, 12:45; see also Bernal Díaz del Castillo, *Historia verdadera de la conquista de la Nueva España*, 1961, pp. 15, 556, who first calls her "fulana," then Isabel. Kathleen Romoli, *Balboa of Darién: Discoverer of the Pacific*, 1953, p. 329, and Marqués de Lozoya (Juan de Contreras), *Vida del segoviano Rodrigo de Contreras, gobernador de Nicaragua, 1534–1544,* 1939, pp. 12–13,

call her María. For the mission entrusted to Gaspar Arias Dávila by Alvarado—to propose his marriage with the daughter of Pedrarias (probably seeking control of Central America)—see Claudio Urrutia, *Memorias sobre la cuestión de límites entre Guatemala y México, presentada al señor ministro de relaciones exteriores por el jefe de la delegación guatemalteca en 1900,* 1964, pp. 20–21; the same is suggested in Doris Stone, *Estampas de Honduras,* 1954, p. 70; also see Edgar Juan Aparicio y Aparicio, *Conquistadores,* p. 4. That Rodrigo de Contreras was governor of Nicaragua is shown in Carlos Molina Argüello, *El gobernador de Nicaragua en el siglo* XVII (1949), pp. 244–45. The cruelty and wickedness of Pedrarias are well known, and for similar traits in Alvarado, see Salvador de Madariaga, *El ocaso del imperio español en América,* 1959, p. 21; and Pablo Neruda, *Canto general,* 1976, p. 37. For Gaspar de Morales and Pedrarias el Mancebo, see Gonzálo Fernández de Oviedo, *Historia natural y general de las Indias,* 1944–45, 7:115.

3. Díaz del Castillo, *Historia verdadera,* p. 41.

4. Ibid., p. 12.

5. A holder of an encomienda. See chap. 1, note 5.

6. Webre, *Compañías,* p. 512. See also Pilar Sanchiz Ochoa, *Hidalgos de Guatemala.*

7. This stands out in Díaz del Castillo as well as in Ricardo Fernández Guardia, *Historia de Costa Rica: El descubrimiento y la conquista,* 1933.

8. Herrera y Tordesillas, *Historia general,* 3:401.

9. Ibid., p. 396.

10. Ibid., p. 401.

11. Ibid., 3:214; 6:387–90; 7:63–66, 79, 355–59.

12. Doris Stone, *Estampas,* pp. 67–68.

13. Herrera y Tordesillas, *Historia general,* 8:95; and Hubert Howe Bancroft, *The History of Central America,* vols. 6–8 of *The works of Hubert Howe Bancroft,* 1886–87, 7:102. This marriage apparently caused friction between Cortés and Alvarado, who was at the time said to have been betrothed to Cecilia Vázquez, a cousin of Cortés.

14. Doris Stone, *Estampas,* pp. 67–68.

15. For a discussion of the Central American area that came under the control of Pedrarias, see Pablo Alvarez Rubiano, *Pedrarias Dávila,* 1954, pp. 319–37, 356–58.

16. Herrera y Tordesillas, *Historia general,* 7:422.

17. For Honduras, see Robert S. Chamberlain, *The Conquest and Colonization of Honduras,* 1953, pp. 18–20.

18. Herrera y Tordesillas, *Historia general,* 7:467, 483; 8:45–51, 59–66, 149.

19. For a good account of this, see Chamberlain 1953, Part I.

20. Herrera y Tordesillas, *Historia general,* 11:288, 293–95; 12:50, 54.

21. Wendy Kramer, W. George Lovell, and Christopher H. Lutz, "Las tasaciones de tributos de Francisco Marroquín y Alonso Maldonado, 1536–41," *Mesoamérica* 7, no. 12 (1986): 357–65.

22. Herrera y Tordesillas, *Historia general,* 11:288.

23. Gonzalo Fernández de Oviedo, *Historia general y natural de las Indias,* 1944–45, 8:159–60.

24. Díaz del Castillo, *Historia verdadera,* pp. 41–44.

25. Macleod, *Spanish Central America,* pp. 41–42.

26. Ibid., pp. 40–45.

27. Ibid., p. 41.

28. Díaz del Castillo, *Historia verdadera,* p. 44. See also Hammond Innes, *The Conquistadores,* 1969, p. 22.

29. F. A. Kirkpatrick, *The Spanish Conquistadores,* 1962, pp. 104, 112; Alvaro Fer-

nández Peralta, "La familia de Alvarado," *Revista de la Academia Costarricense de Ciencias Genealógicas* 5 (1958): 3.
30. Herrera y Tordesillas, *Historia general*, 9:65.
31. This is an observation of Carlos Meléndez Chaverri, professor of history of the Universidad de Costa Rica. For the importance of blood ties among conquistadors, see Meléndez, *Conquistadores y pobladores*, 1982.
32. Bancroft, *Central America*, 7:79–80.
33. Ibid., p. 128.
34. Fernández Peralta, "Alvarado," p. 4.
35. Ibid.
36. Cleto González Víquez, "Orígenes de los costarricenses," in *Población de Costa Rica y orígenes de los costarricenses*, 1977, p. 77.
37. Fernández Peralta, "Alvarado," p. 4.
38. Herrera y Tordesillas, *Historia general*, 14:147.
39. Bancroft, *Central America*, 7:312.
40. Fernández Peralta, "Alvarado."
41. Herrera y Tordesillas, *Historia general*, 1:169; 2:183; 7:169.
42. *Colección Somoza: Documentos para la historia de Nicaragua*, 1954, 6:94–95.
43. Enrique Robert Luján, "Algunos datos sobre la descendencia de doña Andrea Vázquez de Coronado," *Revista de la Academia Costarricense de Ciencias Genealógicas* 2 (1955): 5.
44. *Diccionario enciclopédico hispano-americano* 1:429–30.
45. Díaz del Castillo, *Historia verdadera*, p. 645.
46. Madariaga, *Ocaso*, p. 19.
47. Alejandro Lipschütz, *El problema racial en la conquista de América*, 1975, pp. 219–25.
48. Norberto Castro Tosi, "La población de Cartago en los siglos XVII y XVIII," *Revista de los Archivos Nacionales de Costa Rica* 28, nos. 7–12 (1964): 153.
49. Lipschütz, *Problema racial*, p. 225.
50. Bancroft, *Central America*, 7:274–88.
51. William H. Prescott, *Histoire du règne de Ferdinand et d'Isabelle*, 1862, 4:195.
52. Ibid., pp. 195–96.
53. Ibid., p. 196. This had been done by their French contemporary Louis XI, who had been greatly mistreated at the hands of French nobility. See Albert León Guérard, *France*, 1959, pp. 116–17.
54. Prescott, *Ferdinand et d'Isabelle*, p. 196.
55. Magnus Mörner, *La mezcla de razas en la historia de América Latina*, 1969, p. 66, and Castro Tosi, "Cartago," pp. 153–54.
56. Norberto de Castro Tosi, *Colección Norberto de Castro*, 1975, p. 69.
57. Ibid., p. 68.
58. Ibid., pp. 69–70.
59. Herrera y Tordesillas, *Historia general*, 16:365.
60. Castro Tosi, *Colección*, p. 63.
61. Ibid., pp. 67–69, 88.
62. Ibid., pp. 82–83. For an idea of the importance attached to blood relationships with conquistadors, see also Miles L. Wortman, *Government and Society in Central America, 1680–1840*, 1982, pp. 65–66.
63. José María Pemán, "El hidalgo español," *Revista de la Academia Costarricense de Ciencias Genealógicas* 1 (1963): 37. This sonnet was taken from ABC (Madrid), 16 April 1953.

Chapter 4

1. Jacinto Benavente, *Más fuerte que el amor,* act 1, scene 3.
2. Lipschütz, *Problema racial,* p. 85.
3. Daisy Rípodas Ardanaz, *El matrimonio en Indias,* 1977. Quotation on p. 4; remainder on pp. 6–7, 13, 226.
4. Madariaga, *Ocaso,* p. 48.
5. Castro Tosi, "Colección," p. 88; and Rípodas Ardanaz, *Matrimonio,* pp. 6–7. The privileges of the Spanish noble led Indian women to "whiten" the skin of their children. This led to conflicts with men of their own race.
6. Alexander von Humboldt, *Ensayo político sobre el reino de la Nueva España,* 1973, pp. 36–37; and Sherman, *Forced Native Labor,* p. 4. Von Humboldt comments that nothing is more vague than initial judgments of newly discovered territories, citing the example of Captain James Cook, who estimated the population of Tahiti at one hundred thousand around 1769, while the Protestant London Missionary Society set it at some forty-nine thousand only a few years later.
7. Sherman, *Forced Native Labor,* Appendix A, pp. 347–48. Sherman's source is Angel Rosenblat, *La población indígena y el mestizaje en América, 1492–1950,* 1954, 1:303–6. The audiencia district refers to the Audiencia de los Confines, which had political jurisdiction over the area at the time. Some three-quarters of a century after the Conquest, appraisals of the number of inhabitants of Guatemala (which at the time included El Salvador) range from thirty-seven to fifty-six thousand (Sherman, *Forced Native Labor,* p. 348, uses as sources Juan López de Velasco, *Geografía y descripción universal de las Indias . . . desde el año de 1571 al de 1574,* 1894, pp. 286–97, and a letter from Dr. Pedro de Villalobos, president of the Audiencia de Guatemala, to the crown, dated 15 March 1575, from Santiago de Guatemala [Archivo General de Indias, Guatemala 39], respectively). Corresponding figures presented by Sherman for Honduras go from thirty-two to thirty-six thousand, and for Nicaragua, from forty-eight to fifty thousand; these are also based on López de Velasco, *Geografía,* pp. 306–13, 318–31. The figures for Nicaragua are deemed by Sherman to be low. See also Linda Newson, "La población indígena de Honduras bajo el régimen colonial," *Mesoamerica* 6, no. 9 (1985): 1–3, and "The Depopulation of Nicaragua," *Journal of Latin American Studies,* 1982.
8. MacLeod, *Spanish Central America,* pp. 53, 59, 93.
9. Manuel de María Peralta, *Journal de la Société d'Américanistes de Paris,* 1896, in Luis Demetrio Tinoco, *Población de Costa Rica y orígenes de los costarricenses,* no. 5, 1977, p. 8n. Costa Rica was not conquered until half a century after the rest of Central America, and early population figures are difficult to find. The generally accepted ones have been those presented by Bishop Bernardo Augusto Thiel (see "Monografía de la población de la República de Costa Rica en el siglo XIX," in *Población de Costa Rica,* ed. Tinoco, p. 71. Thiel states that there were 27,200 Indians in 1522. This is low by all reckonings, however, and many feel that he counted only those in baptismal records (see Eugenio Rodríguez Vega, *Biografía de Costa Rica,* 1980, p. 8). I have chosen the estimate of one hundred thousand Indians for 1564 (the year of the founding of Cartago), because that figure appears to be more in keeping with those corresponding to Nicaragua (see Tinoco, *Población de Costa Rica,* pp. 7–8, 8n). Furthermore, in examining the literature on the Costa Rican population, I am inclined to accept the observations of Monsignor Victor Sanabria Martínez in the introduction to his work, *Genealogías de Cartago hasta 1850,* 1957. Sanabria comments on remarks made by Thiel concerning the status of baptismal records, and concludes that the first one was already lost by the beginning of the

seventeenth century (Thiel wrote during the nineteenth), that the second record (of 1594) is incomplete, and that from 1595 to 1600 there are no entries whatsoever. From 1637 to 1640, few if any Spaniards were baptized; the book that has been conserved contains only the names of "Indians and others." For this reason, I have used Thiel's Indian population figure of 14,908, corresponding to 1611 (see Tinoco, *Población de Costa Rica*, p. 225).

10. Lipschütz, *Problema racial*, pp. 211, 213.

11. Ibid., pp. 92–94. Quoted from Heinrich Heine, *Romanzero von Heinrich Heine*, n.d.

12. Lipschütz, *Problema racial*, p. 101. Values such as the ones reflected in verses and quotations from the colonial period, but with other nuances, are quite common even in the present. That is why Peruvian historian Luis E. Valcárcel presents the following pathetic image: "The Indian, in his relations with his oppressors, cannot be any different from what he is; his only defense is not telling the truth to the white man, or working for him, or respecting his property. . . . In this way he avenges himself and makes up for all he has suffered." Quoted by Lipschütz, *Problema racial*, p. 87.

13. Neruda, *Canto general*, p. 37.

14. Lipschütz, *Problema racial*, p. 86. This is an outstanding work on the subject. The pages that follow are based fundamentally on it.

15. Ibid., p. 90. Taken from Fray Bernardino de Sahagún, *Historia general de las cosas de Nueva España*, 1956, 1:29.

16. Ibid., pp. 91–92, taken from *Cantares Mexicanos* (1523), in *Visión de los vencidos: Relaciones indígenas de la Conquista*, ed. Miguel León-Portilla, 1976, p. xii.

17. Rípodas Ardanaz, *Matrimonio*, p. 12. The actual word is *barraganería*, a more or less stable union between a Spaniard and an Indian woman while the man looked for a Spanish wife.

18. Richard Konetzke, *America Latina*, vol. 2: *La época colonial*, 1972, p. 78.

19. Rípodas Ardanaz, *Matrimonio*, p. 12n.37.

20. Sherman, *Forced Native Labor*, pp. 317–19. The author mentions the offspring of Cortés, Alvarado, and Pizarro as good examples.

21. Rípodas Ardanaz, *Matrimonio*, pp. 3, 12. Several sources are cited: Carlos Pereyra, *Las huellas de los conquistadores*, 1942, pp. 189–96; Rodolfo Barón Castro, *La población de El Salvador*, 1942, p. 17.

22. Sherman, *Forced Native Labor*, pp. 217, 306.

23. Bancroft, *Central America*, 7:201.

24. Magnus Mörner, "La política de segregación y el mestizaje en la Audiencia de Guatemala," *Revista de Indias* 24 (1964): 137.

25. Bancroft, *Central America*, 7:202, and Carlos Cuadra Pasos, "Los Cuadra: Una hebra en el tejido de la historia de Nicaragua," *Revista Conservadora del Pensamiento Centroamericano* 17, no. 83 (1967): 13.

26. In terms of discrimination, Venezuela was an extreme case in Latin America. In Caracas, in 1803 the son of a pardo (a mixture of black and white) was not admitted to the university due to a protest from that institution to the crown. The complaint was that "the presence of pardos would extinguish the splendor of letters and would shock those who justly glorified their Castilian blood, with no mixtures circulating through their veins." In the same city aristocrats spoke with indignation of the "immense distance that separates whites from pardos and of the superiority of whites and lowliness of the latter." People also mentioned mulattos (also a mixture of black and white) "who [were] uglier for being bastards and for their wrongdoings." A son of a Columbian creole landowner, after nine years of

NOTES TO PAGES 64–78 · 215

living with a *mulata*, married her and was disinherited (Mörner, *La mezcla de razas*, p. 69).

27. Tierno Galván, *Actas*, pp. 93, 161.

28. Luis Alberto Sánchez, *Historia general de América*, 1963, p. 349.

29. Mörner, *La mezcla de razas*, p. 64.

30. Rípodas Ardanaz, *Matrimonio*, pp. 6–7, 9–11, 21. See also Sherman, *Forced Native Labor*, p. 317.

31. Norberto de Castro Tosi, "La población de Cartago en los siglos XVII y XVII," *Revista de los Archivos Nacionales*, 1964, pp. 154–56; Rípodas Ardanaz, *Matrimonio*, chap. 1.

32. Rípodas Ardanaz, *Matrimonio*, pp. 20–23.

33. Sherman, *Forced Native Labor*, p. 315.

34. Bancroft, *Central America*, 7:134–35, 139, 298, 298n.15, 300, 373.

35. Ibid., pp. 303, 347.

36. Samuel Stone, *Dinastía*. This information is based on Bishop Bernardo Augusto Thiel, *Revista de Costa Rica en el siglo XIX*, 1902, p. 303.

37. Ricardo Blanco Segura, *Historia eclesiástica de Costa Rica*, 1967, and Rafael Obregón Loría, *El presbítero doctor Francisco Calvo*, 1963.

38. Víctor Sanabria Martínez, *Genealogías*, 1:xix. This is a mimeographed set of books that does not mention a publishing house. On the role of priests, see also Castro Tosi, "Cartago," p. 154.

39. Rípodas Ardanaz, *Matrimonio*, p. 31.

40. This is when the first important conquistadors had died and when patterns of colonization had become consolidated.

41. Tomás Soley Güell, *Historia económica y hacendaria de Costa Rica* (1947), 1:94–102.

Chapter 5

1. This chapter was adapted for this book from an article prepared under the auspices of the School of American Research, Santa Fé, New Mexico (*Central America: The Myth of Unity*, ed. Doris Stone [forthcoming]). "Patterns of Power in the South" was adapted from Adolfo Calero Orozco, "El Gatillo," in his *Cuentos pinoleros*, 1944, pp. 106–19.

2. Abridged from Carlos Wyld Ospina, "De dura cerviz," in *Antología del cuento centroamericano*, ed. Sergio Ramírez Mercado, 1977, pp. 164–65.

3. Abridged from Arturo Ambrogi, "El jetón," in *Antología del cuento centroamericano*, pp. 103–26.

4. Abridged from Arturo Mejía Nieto, "El Chele Amaya," in *El Chele Amaya y otros cuentos*, 1936, pp. 19–26.

5. Abridged from Pablo Antonio Cuadra, "Agosto," in his *Obra poética completa*, 1986, pp. 155–80.

6. Abridged from Manuel González Zeledón, "Episodios nacionales," in *Cuentos de Magón*, ed. José María Arce, 1968, pp. 101–6.

7. Abridged from Manuel González Zeledón, "Un almuerzo campestre," ibid., pp. 19–25.

8. Two outstanding examples are Sergio Ramírez Mercado (vice president) and Miguel D'Escoto Brockman (minister of foreign affairs). See Jirón, *¿Quién es Quién?*, pp. 161, 381.

9. Samuel Stone, "Convulsiones."

10. Kalman Silvert, "Caudillismo," in *Enciclopedia internacional de las ciencias sociales* 2 (1974): 223–35.

11. *Progreso* magazine, January–February 1987. These figures correspond to the years 1980–85.

12. The use of GNP or national income per capita has long been a moot question—even among economists—for measuring the relative welfare of populations. When former Costa Rican President José Figueres was queried on the subject by a group of economists at the University of Costa Rica, his explanation in his characteristic facetious style was that if he put an oven over the head of a person standing on a block of ice, a thermometer placed in the person's navel would provide him with the body's mean temperature. This, however, would give no indication of how things were on the extremes.

13. Antonio Jiménez, ed., *Picardía mexicana*, 1961.

14. Santiago Ramírez, "Sicoanalítico," ibid., pp. 219–23.

15. This is brought out quite clearly by Oscar Lewis in *Los hijos de Sánchez*, 1965. See also Roderic A. Camp, *Mexico's Leaders: Their Education and Recruitment*, 1980, pp. 15–38.

16. See *La República*, 3 March 1988, p. 4, where President Oscar Arias must decide the color of uniforms school children will wear.

17. Samuel Stone, *Dinastía*, chapter 3.

18. *Euromoney*, October 1984, p. 283. The indexes for measuring this ranking were real Gross Domestic Product (GDP), consumer price inflation rate, currency rate in terms of special drawing rights, current account balance relative to GDP, and strength of exports.

19. See table 6.

20. Ephraim G. Squier, *The States of Central America*, 1968, p. 462.

21. Warren Dean, "The Planter as Entrepreneur: The Case of São Paulo," in *Hispanic American Historical Review* 46 (1966): 138–52.

22. Squier, 1968, p. 462.

23. See Pablo Antonio Cuadra "Los cuentos de Tío Coyote y Tío Conejo," *Revista Conservadora del Pensamiento Centroamericano* 15, no. 74 (1966): 51–56 and compare with Carmen Lyra, *Los cuentos de mi Tía Panchita*, 1966.

24. Alfredo Balsells Rivera, "El tamagás," *Revista Conservadora del Pensamiento Centroamericano* 9, no. 47 (1964): 54–56.

25. Arturo Mejía Nieto, "La culebra," *Revista Conservadora del Pensamiento Centroamericano* 9, no. 47 (1964): 57–59.

26. Carlos Salazar Herrera, "La bocaracá," in his *Cuentos de angustias y paisajes*, 1977, pp. 7–10.

27. Félix Belly, *Amerique Centrale*, 1:155.

28. Ibid., 39n.

29. I recall several comments on this situation made to my father at the time by United States embassy officials. The site was located at the southwest corner of the intersection of Avenida Central and Calle Primera, the current location of Hardee's restaurant.

30. Patricia Antell Andrews, "Tomás Regalado and El Salvador, 1895–1906" (M.A. thesis, Lousiana State University in New Orleans, 1971), chap. 3.

Chapter 6

1. *Central America Report,* 15 January 1988, 15(2):9; 22 January 1988, 15(3):17, 21; 5 February 1988, 15(5):33; 25 March 1988, 15(12):89, 90; 27 May 1988, 15(20):159; 15 July 1988, 15(27):209.

2. Ibid., 15 January 1988, 15(2):13; 4 March 1988, 15(9):71; 3 June 1988, 15(22):171; 17 June 1988, 15(23):177; 24 June 1988, 15(24):185; 29 July 1988, 15(29):227; 16 September 1988, 15(36):281.

3. Ibid., 19 February 1988, 15(7):52; and 16 September 1988, 15(36):283.

4. Ibid., Special Document, 10 October 1986, 13(39):317; and 5 December 1986, 13(47):374–75; 15 January 1988, 15(2):12; 16 December 1988, 15(49):385.

5. Ibid., 17 October 1986, 13(40); 20 March 1987, 14(11):81 and Special Document. Foreign debt increased from $1.7 billion U.S. in 1982 to $2 billion in 1985.

6. Ibid., Special Document, 22 August 1986, 13(32); 17 October 1986, 13(40):317; 12 February 1988, 15(6):47; 11 March 1988, 15(10):87; and 3 June 1988, 15(21):166.

7. Ibid., 8 May 1987, 14(17):130–31; and 25 March 1988, 15(12):94.

8. An automobile that could be purchased in two and a half years can now be acquired over a five-year period with a 28 percent annual financing charge.

9. *Central America Report,* 12 February 1988, 15(6):45; 4 March 1988, 15(9):72; 18 April 1986, 13(14):108–9; 18 November 1988, 15(45):356. One justification for these small countries owing so much is the example set by the United States with its excessive deficit that attracts foreign investment at high interest rates. The International Monetary Fund has taken the position that it makes little sense to attempt to straighten out any economy until the United States puts its own house in order.

10. *La Nación,* 17 May 1987, p. 4A.

11. *La República,* 3 June 1986, p. 2.

12. *Central America Report,* 21 August 1987, 14(32):255–56.

13. Ibid., 8 May 1987, 14(17):131.

14. *La República,* 9 June 1987, p. 2.

15. *Central America Report,* Special Document, 22 August 1986, 13(32); 22 January 1988, 15(3):19; and 1 July 1988, 15(25):198.

16. Ibid., 7 November 1986, 13(43):342–43. This source applies this concept to Guatemala, but it is valid for all of Central America.

17. Ibid., 11 July 1986, 15(26):203; 12 February 1988, 15(6):44; 29 July 1988, 13(29):228; 11 March 1988, 15(10):85; 1 July 1988, 15(25):193.

18. *La República,* 6 August 1988, p. 6.

19. Inforpress Centroamericana, *Los empresarios centroamericanos ante la crisis,* 1988, pp. 1–8.

20. *Central America Report,* 1 August 1986, 13(29):229.

21. Carlos Alberto Montaner, "Los soviéticos saben mejor con azúcar," *La Nación,* 31 May 1987, p. 15A.

22. The economically active population, shown in table 9, represented almost 17 percent of total population in 1985. The Arenal hydroelectric plant, although state owned, required many laborers from the private sector who had been working on similar projects since 1953. Firms that win in biddings for public works construction depend on public funds; for this reason their employees should be considered on state payrolls. They make up a floating labor force whose members hold jobs thanks to the state and who could find employment only with difficulty without it. This is the reason why I feel, after making estimates, that Costa Rica has a public sector of close to one-third of total population.

23. *Central America Report,* 1 May 1987, 14(16):127.

24. *Central America Report,* May 1986, 13(17):134; 5 December 1986, 13(47):372.

25. Ibid., 3 October 1986, 13(38):302–3. El Salvador and Honduras have supersonic jet fighters, advanced bombers, and support systems to back them up effectively. Their aircraft include the Dassault Super-Mystère B-2, a fighter bomber built in France and perfected in Israel. El Salvador's armed forces have concentrated their attention on air mobility and fire power. The Honduran air force hopes to continue being the best in Central America and is developing its infrastructure. Experts agree that the MI-24 helicopters currently being used by Nicaragua would be relatively useless in an air fight with Honduran or Salvadoran jets. Furthermore, most of Nicaragua's force is made up of out-dated equipment.

26. For many of the ideas presented concerning the armed forces, see Constantino Urcuyo Fournier, "Strategic Central America," in *Central America: The Myth of Unity,* ed. Doris Stone, forthcoming.

27. See Guillermo Villegas Hoffmeister, *El cardonazo,* 1987, for an account of this attempted military coup against Figueres.

28. Information concerning the circumstances leading to the abolition of the Costa Rican army in 1949 was obtained from Constantino Urcuyo Fournier, of the CIAPA staff, in San José, Costa Rica. Urcuyo has done research and published material on Central American armies, and is considered an authority on the subject. See "Strategic Central America," in Doris Stone, ed., *Central America: The Myth of Unity,* forthcoming.

29. *Central America Report,* Special Report, 11 July 1986, 13(26):205; 3 October 1986, 13(38):300; 28 November 1986, 13(46):366; 25 March 1988, 15(12):92–93.

30. Ibid., 18 March 1988, 15(11):81–86; 15 July 1988, 15(27):213; 12 August 1988, 15(31):242–43; and 26 August 1988, 15(33):259.

31. Ibid., 23 May 1986, 13(19):148; 13 June 1986, 13(22):169; 7 November 1986, 13(43):343; 21 November 1986, 13(45):353; and 28 November 1986, 13(46):366.

32. This was announced over National Public Radio in English, over short wave on 12 May 1987.

33. *Central America Report,* 8 July 1988, 15(26):206.

34. Ibid., 22 January 1988, 15(3):22; 26 February 1988, 15(8):57; 11 March 1988, 15(10):86; 13 May 1988, 15(18):144; 26 August 1988, 15(33):262; 9 September 1988, 15(35):279; 23 September 1988, 15(37):293; 2 December 1988, 15(47):369.

35. Rodolfo Cerdas Cruz, "Crisis and Conflict in Central America: The Changing Nature of Power since Somoza," in Doris Stone, ed., *Central America: The Myth of Unity,* forthcoming. This included preparations for the Bay of Pigs invasion against Fidel Castro.

36. *Central America Report,* 25 July 1986, 13(28):222–23.

37. Ibid., 19 February 1988, 15(7):56; 22 April 1988, 15(15):118; and 23 September 1988, 15(37):291.

38. Ibid., 25 July 1986, 13(28):222–23; and 13 May 1988, 15(18):142.

39. Ibid., 11 April 1986, 13(13):97; 20 June 1986, 13(23):183; 11 July 1986, 13(26):203; 1 August 1986, 13(29):229; 15 August 1986, 13(31):241; 29 August 1986, 13(33):262; 14 November 1986, 13(44):351; 12 December 1986, 13(48):380.

Chapter 7

1. These tales were adapted from my "Costa Rica: Sobre la clase dirigente y la sociedad nacional," *Revista de ciencias sociales* 11 (1976): 41–43.

2. This actually occurred. See *La República,* 10 July 1975, p. 3.

3. Samuel Stone, *Dinastía*, pp. 57–58.

4. Ibid., p. 59.

5. Ibid., p. 149, table V-1.

6. Ibid., p. 118. See pp. 108, 118–19 for a more detailed discussion of this financing process and changes.

7. Samuel Stone, "La herencia de una dinastía," 1976, part 2, appendix. Mimeographed and available in the national library.

8. Samuel Stone, *Dinastía*, pp. 190–94.

9. *Estudio del sector público*, San José: Instituto de Investigaciones Económicas, University of Costa Rica, 1962, p. 9.

10. See chap. 6, section on public sectors.

11. Abridged from Lester C. Thurow, *The Zero-Sum Society: Distribution and the Possibilities for Economic Change*, 1981, pp. 3–25.

12. Interview with Rafael Villegas Antillón, magistrate of the Supreme Electoral Tribunal and member of CIAPA's staff, in December 1986.

13. Samuel Stone, *Dinastía*. For a discussion of this idea see Joseph A. Schumpeter, *Imperialism and Social Classes*, 1966, especially his essay on social classes.

14. Geraint Parry, *Political Elites*, 1969, p. 32. This concept is taken from Gaetano Mosca, *The Ruling Class*, 1939.

15. Samuel Stone, *Dinastía*, chap. 11. Sources of information regarding "paid in capital" were confidential.

16. This was confirmed during insistent inquiries in both institutions.

17. This strong statement is commonly expressed by many Costa Ricans. However, few have wanted to come to grips with the question. For examples of people who have had the courage to openly discuss ethical problems, see Fernando Trejos Escalante, "Costa Rica está enferma" (Costa Rica is sick), *La Nación*, 13 December 1986, p. 15A. Trejos Escalante ran for the presidency (and lost) in 1974. See also Manuel Felipe Calvo, "Confianza y credibilidad" (Confidence and credibility), *La Nación*, 18 December 1986, p. 15A.

18. This amounted to some U.S.$4.4 billion in 1985; $3.9 billion in the public sector and $0.5 billion in the private sector. On a per capita basis, this is one of the highest debts in the world (U.S.$1,744).

19. Around 1960, the United Fruit Company was the biggest employer in the country, with more than eleven thousand employees. This point is also made by Howard Banks in "Bankruptcy without Pain," *Forbes* magazine 135 (1985): 112.

20. By proletariat I mean that sector of a population whose only assets are its hands to work with. In that sense, El Salvador is the only country in Central America with a proletariat.

21. *Central America Report*, 25 July 1986, 13(28):223.

22. For the role of the Mexican Universidad Nacional Autónoma de México (UNAM) in the recruitment of youth (very similar to that of the universities in Costa Rica), see Peter H. Smith, *Labyrinths of Power: Political Recruitment in Twentieth-Century Mexico*, 1979, pp. 115–16.

23. For the role of labor unions in the Mexican system, see Roderic A. Camp, *Mexico's Leaders: Their Education and Recruitment*, 1980, pp. 4–6.

24. This information was obtained from Constantino Urcuyo Fournier, director of the 1986 presidential campaign of the second largest party in the country, the Partido Unidad Social Cristiana (PUSC), which obtained just under half the votes.

25. See chap. 6, section on public sectors.

26. There have been political clienteles since the nineteenth century, but in other forms. See Samuel Stone, *Dinastía*, chaps. 7, 8.

27. *La Nación,* 9 July 1987, p. 4A.

28. Seymour Martin Lipset, *El hombre político,* 1987, p. 288, makes a similar observation concerning members of the Social Democratic party in Germany.

29. Rafael Obregón Loría, *El poder legislativo en Costa Rica,* 1963.

30. The following thoughts are taken fundamentally from *The New Authoritarianism in Latin America,* ed. David Collier, 1979. Two chapters are of particular relevance: David Collier, "Overview of the Bureaucratic-Authoritarian Model," pp. 19–32, and Guillermo O'Donnell, "Tensions in the Bureaucratic-Authoritarian State and the Question of Democracy," pp. 285–319.

31. *La República,* 14 July 1988, pp. 1, 4; 16 July 1988, pp. 1, 4; 24 July 1988, pp. 1, 4; 6 August 1988, pp. 1, 4; *La Nación,* 22 August 1988.

32. The only president since World War II who has tackled the debt problem has been José Joaquín Trejos Fernández, who held office from 1966 to 1970. Public spending under all the others has been far beyond the means of production.

33. Samuel Stone, "The Cubans Are Not Little Costa Rica's First Refugees," *Los Angeles Times,* 27 April 1980, pp. 2–3, Part V. One example was the establishment in Costa Rica of the Aprista movement of Victor Raúl Haya de la Torre.

34. During the second world war, the city of Casablanca, Morocco, became a center for intrigue and espionage among the nations engaged in that conflict.

35. I based this story on an actual incident that took place in Aspen, Colorado, and heard similar remarks about emigrant Iranian families in Paris in 1980.

36. Samuel Stone, *Dinastía,* chaps. 7 and 8, p. 120.

37. Ibid., p. 120.

38. *Central America Report,* 14 November 1986, 13(44):350.

39. *La República,* 8 September 1987, pp. 1, 10–11.

40. *Central America Report,* 11 July 1986, 13(26).

41. Rodolfo Cerdas Cruz, "La educación nacional: Entre el zapallo y lo medular," *La Nación,* 17 January 1980, p. 15A.

42. *La Nación,* 17 January 1987. The minister was Antonio Pacheco.

43. Ibid., 29 May 1987, p. 1. See also *La República,* 2 March 1988, main editorial on p. 14.

44. I prefer the term radicalism (rather than liberalism) as a concept opposed to conservatism, for it seems to describe better certain parties that have become important, such as the Partido Liberación Nacional and much of the traditional clientele of the Partido Unidad Social Cristiana. Radicalism implies an ideology with social programs that require state intervention to carry them out, as well as a rejection of traditional structures. Furthermore, it can be a movement of the right, center, or left. Conservatism also undoubtedly opposes liberalism but is more precisely an antonym of radicalism, for many conservatives today would accept certain liberal tenets. See Samuel Stone, *Dinastía,* pp. 271–72. Definitions were taken from Geoffrey K. Roberts, *A Dictionary of Political Analysis,* 1971, pp. 43, 183.

45. Jiménez Oreamuno withdrew his fourth candidacy before the end of the campaign.

46. Former President José Figueres Ferrer, who was one of the principal people responsible for the development of the welfare state, called it an "estado cocinero" (a mess-hall manager) when his own party member, President Daniel Oduber Quirós, involved the state in so many activities.

47. *La República,* 6 December 1986, p. 14. Some of my concepts are quoted in the main editorial.

48. Some of the ideas expressed in this paragraph are taken from E. Digby Baltzell, *Puritan Boston and Quaker Philadelphia,* 1982.

Chapter 8

1. Silvia Padilla Altamirano, "Guatemala y las provincias centroamericanas," in *Historia general de España y América*, 1983, vol. XI-1, pp. 547–74.
2. Jan Knippers Black and Martin C. Needler, "Historical Setting of Guatemala," in *Guatemala: A Country Study*, ed. Richard F. Nyrop, 1984, p. 13.
3. Padilla Altamirano, p. 560.
4. Félix Belly, *A travers l'Amérique Centrale*, 1867, 1:154.
5. Luis Mariñas Otero, *Las constituciones de Guatemala*, 1958, pp. 18–20.
6. Padilla Altamirano, pp. 561–62.
7. H. D. Lasswell, "Elites," *A Dictionary of the Social Sciences*, ed. Julius Gold and William L. Kolb, 1964, p. 234.
8. *Central America Report*, 19 June 1987, 14(32):182. In this example, Milton Cerezo Arévalo, the president's brother and assistant director of immigration, was forced to resign for illegally issuing blank passports to foreigners excluded from citizenship.
9. Samuel Stone, *Dinastía*, pp. 54–57.
10. Mariñas Otero, pp. 6–8.
11. William J. Griffith, "Guatemala," *Encyclopaedia Britannica*, 1986, 15:710.
12. Mariñas Otero, pp. 8–14.
13. Ibid., pp. 16–18.
14. Black and Needler, p. 17.
15. Ralph Lee Woodward, Jr., *Central America: A Nation Divided*, 1976, pp. 98–105.
16. Mariñas Otero, p. 109.
17. Richard F. Nyrop, p. xxv.
18. Severo Martínez Peláez, *La patria del criollo*, 1976.
19. Black and Needler, p. 19.
20. *Central America Report*, 14 November 1986, 13(44):351; 12 December 1986, 13(48):380; 19 December 1986, Special Report, 13(49).
21. An example of this is a farm called La Perla in the Quiché region of Guatemala, property of the Arena family. The family transferred 40 percent of the value of the farm to its employees. The results have been impressive: as the workers have come to be proprietors in a cooperative effort, they have taken greater interest in the business and have increased productivity by 400 percent. This was discussed on National Public Radio on 9 August 1987 during the morning news report. My personal feeling is that not many other landowners would want to do something similar with their property. It would be important to know how the Arena family has gone about this, because cooperative efforts in El Salvador, Nicaragua, and Costa Rica have been generally unsatisfactory.
22. *Central America Report*, 17 July 1987, 14(27):214; 27 November 1987, 14(46):365–66; 18 December 1987, 14(49); 28 January 1987, 15(4):1; 26 February 1988, 15(8):63; 18 March 1988, 15(11):88.
23. Robert Bierstedt. "Oligarchy," in *A Dictionary of the Social Sciences*, ed. Julius Gould and William L. Kolb, 1967, p. 475.
24. This is my opinion. For a background against which this can be better understood, see Howard I. Blutstein, *El Salvador: A Country Study*, 1979, pp. 96–104.
25. René Santamaría Varela, "El Salvador," *Encyclopaedia Britannica*, 1986, 15:704–5.
26. *Central America Report*, 11 July 1986, 13(26):206–7, 201–3; 10 October 1986, 13(39):305–6; 28 November 1986, 13(46):366–67; 12 December 1986, 13(48):383–84; 27 November 1987, 14(46):361; Special Document, 11 December 1987, 14(48).

27. Wayne M. Clegern, "Honduras," *Encyclopaedia Britannica*, 1986, 15:716.
28. *La Nación*, 7 April 1988, p. 1.
29. *Central America Report*, 1 May 1987, 14(16):121.
30. Ibid., 1 May 1987, 14(16):121; 29 May 1987, 14(20):154; 5 June 1987.
31. *La Nación*, 25 April 1988, p. 1.
32. *Newsweek*, 4 April 1988, pp. 7–8.
33. *Central America Report*, 24 April 1987, 14(15):118; 12 June 1987, 14(22):171; 26 June 1987, 14(24):189; 17 July 1987, 14(27):214; 31 July 1987, 14(13):227; 26 February 1988, 15(8):57; 10 April 1987, 14(14):107–8; 10 July 1987, 14(26):206; 14 August 1987, 14(31):243; 4 September 1987, 14(34):270; 11 September 1987, 14(35):276; 2 October 1987, 14(38):303; 6 November 1987, 14(43):341; 27 November 1987, 14(46):365; 18 December 1987, Special Report, 14(49); 19 February 1988, 15(7):54.

Bibliography

Books, articles, and dissertations

Adams, Richard N. "Rural Labor." In *Continuity and Change in Latin America*, ed. John J. Johnson, pp. 49–78. Stanford, Calif.: Stanford University Press, 1964.

Alvarez Rubiano, Pablo. *Pedrarias Dávila*. Madrid: Consejo Superior de Investigaciones Científicas, Instituto Gonzalo Fernández de Oviedo, 1954.

Ambrogi, Arturo. "El jetón." In *Antología del cuento centroamericano*, ed. Sergio Ramírez, pp. 103–26. 2d ed. San José, Costa Rica: Editorial Universitaria Centroamericana (EDUCA), 1977.

Andrews, Patricia Antell. "Tomás Regalado and El Salvador." M. A. thesis. Louisiana State University in New Orleans, 1971.

Aparicio y Aparicio, Edgar Juan, Marqués de Vistabella. *Conquistadores de Guatemala y fundadores de familias guatemaltecas*. Mexico City: Tip. Guadalajara, 1961.

———. "La familia Cabarrús." *Revista de la Academia Guatemalteca de Estudios Genealógicos, Heráldicos e Históricos* 3–4 (1969–70): 321–45.

———. "La familia de Arzú." *Revista de la Academia Guatemalteca de Estudios Genealógicos, Heráldicos e Históricos* 3–5 (1969–70): 69–113.

———. "La familia Lacayo de Briones." *Revista de la Academia Guatemalteca de Estudios Genealógicos, Heráldicos e Históricos* 5–6 (1971–72): 463–76.

———. "La familia Maestre." *Revista de la Academia Guatemalteca de Estudios Genealógicos, Heráldicos e Históricos* 5–6 (1971–72): 335–82.

Aparicio y Aparicio, Edgar Juan, and Juan José Falla Sánchez. "La familia Sánchez de Perales." *Revista de la Academia Guatemalteca de Estudios Genealógicos, Heráldicos e Históricos* 2 (1968): 41–166.

———. "El Licenciado don Simón Vasconcelos." *Revista de la Academia Guatemalteca de Estudios Genealógicos, Heráldicos e Históricos* 2 (1969): 21–28.

Aparicio y Aparicio, Edgar Juan, Juan José Falla Sánchez, and Ramiro Ordóñez y Jonama. "Datos genealógicos de los trece próceres que firmaron el Acta de la Independencia de Centro América en 1821." *Revista de la Academia Guatemalteca de Estudios Genealógicos, Heráldicos e Históricos* 5–6 (1971–72): 11–38.

Arciniegas, Germán. "La familia que ya conocemos." In his *Nueva imagen del Caribe*. Buenos Aires: Editorial Sudamericana, 1970.

Balsells Rivera, Alfredo. "El tamagás." *Revista Conservadora del Pensamiento Centroamericano* 9, no. 47 (1964): 54–56.

Baltzell, E. Digby. *Puritan Boston and Quaker Philadelphia*. Boston, Massachusetts: Beacon Press, 1982.

Bancroft, Hubert Howe. *The History of Central America*, vols. 6–8 of *The Works of Hubert Howe Bancroft*. San Francisco: The History Company, 1886–87.

Banks, Howard. "Bankruptcy without Pain," *Forbes* 135 (1985): 109–10.

Baron Castro, Rodolfo. *La población de El Salvador*. Madrid: Consejo Superior de Investigaciones Científicas, 1942.

Bell, John Patrick. *Crisis in Costa Rica: The 1948 Revolution*. Austin: University of Texas Press, 1971.

Belli, Pedro. "Prolegómeno para una historia económica de Nicaragua de 1905 a 1966." *Revista Conservadora del Pensamiento Centroamericano* 30, no. 146 (1975): 2–30.

Belly, Félix. *A travers l'Amerique Centrale*. Paris: Librairie de la Suisse Romande, 1867.

Bierstedt, Robert. "Oligarchy." In *A Dictionary of the Social Sciences*, ed. Julius Gould and William L. Kolb, p. 475. 4th printing. New York: Free Press, 1967.

Blachman, Morris, William LeoGrande, and Kenneth Sharpe, eds. *Confronting Revolution: Security through Diplomacy in Central America*. New York: Pantheon Books, 1986.

Black, Jan Knippers, and Martin C. Needler. "Historical Setting of Guatemala." In *Guatemala: A Country Study*. ed. Richard F. Nyrop, pp. 1–39. Washington, D.C.: American University, 1984.

Blanco Segura, Ricardo. *Historia eclesiástica de Costa Rica*. San José: Editorial Costa Rica, 1967.

Blutstein, Howard I. *El Salvador: A Country Study*. Washington, D.C.: American University, 1979.

Bolton, Herbert E. *Coronado: Knight of Pueblos and Plains*. New York: Whittlesey House, 1949.

Bullock, Alan, and Oliver Stallybrass. *Dictionary of Modern Thought*. 6th ed. London: Fontana Press, 1980.

Burton, Michael G., and John Higley. *Elite Settlements*. Austin: University of Texas Press, Texas Papers on Latin America, 1986.

Calero Orozco, Adolfo. "El Gatillo." In his *Cuentos pinoleros*, pp. 106–9. Managua: Editorial Nuevos Horizontes, 1944.

Calvo, Manuel Felipe. "Confianza y credibilidad." *La Nación* (San José, Costa Rica), 18 December 1986, p. 15A.

Camp, Roderic A. *Mexico's Leaders: Their Education and Recruitment*. Tucson: University of Arizona Press, 1980.

Cardoso, Ciro F. S., and Héctor Pérez Brignoli. *Centroamérica y la economía occidental, 1520–1930*. San José: Editorial Universidad de Costa Rica, 1977.

———. *Historia económica de América Latina*, vol. 2. Barcelona: Editorial Crítica, 1979.

Cardoso, Fernando Henrique, and Enzo Faletto. *Dependencia y desarrollo en América Latina*. 7th ed. Mexico City: Siglo Veintiuno, 1973.

Castro Tosi, Norberto de. "Colección Norberto de Castro." *Revista de la Academia Costarricense de Ciencias Genealógicas* 22 (1975).

———. "Los Oriamuno en Panamá." *Revista de la Academia Costarricense de Ciencias Genealógicas* 11–12 (1963–64).

———. "La población de Cartago en los siglos XVII y XVIII." *Revista de los Archivos Nacionales de Costa Rica* 28, nos. 7–12 (1964).

Cerdas Cruz, Rodolfo. "Crisis and Conflict in Central America: The Changing Nature of Power since Somoza." 1987. On file in the Centro de Investigación y Adiestramiento Político–Administrativo, San José.

———. "La educación nacional: Entre el zapallo y lo medular." *La Nación* (San José, Costa Rica), 17 January 1980, p. 15A.

———. "Strategie et tactique de l'Internationale Communiste en Amérique Centrale, 1920–1936." Doctorat de troisième cycle, Université de Paris, Sorbonne, 1973.

Chamberlain, Robert S. *The Conquest and Colonization of Honduras, 1502–1550*. Washington, D.C.: Carnegie Institution of Washington, 1953.

Christian, Shirley. *Nicaragua: Revolution in the Family*. New York: Random House, 1985.

Clawson, Marion. "Aspectos económicos de la tierra." *Enciclopedia de las ciencias sociales*. Madrid: Aguilar, 1977.

Clegern, Wayne M. "Honduras." *Encyclopaedia Britannica* 15 (1986): 712–16.

Cohen, Percy S. *Modern Social Theory*. London: Heinemann, 1968.

Colección Somoza: Documentos para la historia de Nicaragua, ed. Andrés Vega Bolaños. Madrid: Imprenta Viuda de Galo Sáez, 1954.

Collier, David. "Overview of the Bureaucratic-Authoritarian Model." In his *The New Authoritarianism in Latin America*. pp. 19–32. Princeton: Princeton University Press, 1979.

Coste, René. *Les caféiers et les cafés dans le monde*. Paris: Maisonneuve et Larose, 1955–61.

Cruz, Arturo, Jr. "One Hundred Years of Turpitude." *New Republic*, 16 November 1987.

Cuadra, Pablo Antonio. "Los cuentos de Tío Coyote y Tío Conejo." *Revista Conservadora del Pensamiento Centroamericano* 15, no. 74 (1966): 51–61.

———. "Agosto." In his *Obra poética completa*, pp. 155–80. San José: Libro Libre, 1986.

Cuadra Pasos, Carlos. "Los Cuadra: Una hebra en el tejido de la historia de Nicaragua." *Revista Conservadora del Pensamiento Centroamericano* 17, no. 83 (1967): 1–26 (supplement).

Dean, Warren. "The Planter as Entrepreneur: The Case of São Paulo." *Hispanic American Historical Review* 46 (1966): 138–52.

Díaz del Castillo, Bernal. *Historia verdadera de la conquista de la Nueva España*. Mexico City: Fernández Editores, 1961.

Diccionario enciclopédico hispano-americano. Barcelona: Montaner y Simón, 1987–88.

Drekonja, Gerhard, and Fernando Zepeda Ulloa. "La política exterior de Colombia." In *América Latina: Políticas exteriores comparadas*, ed. Juan Puig, pp. 313–42. Buenos Aires: Grupo Editor Latinoamericano, 1984.

Durham, William H. *Scarcity and Survival in Central America: Ecological Origins of the Soccer War*. Stanford, Calif.: Stanford University Press, 1979.

Erlich, Paul R., Anne H. Erlich, and John P. Holdren. *Ecoscience: Population, Resources, and Environment*. San Francisco: W. H. Freeman, 1977.

Estudio del sector público. San José: Instituto de Investigaciones Económicas, Universidad de Costa Rica, 1981.

Facio Brenes, Rodrigo. *Estudio sobre economía costarricense*. San José: Editorial Soley y Valverde, 1942.

Falla Sánchez, Juan José. "La familia Martín del Cerro." *Revista de la Academia Guatemalteca de Estudios Genealógicos, Heráldicos e Históricos* 3–4 (1969–70): 157–260.

Fernández Alfaro, Joaquín Alberto. *Los adelantados de Costa Rica*. Managua, Nicaragua: Editorial Unión, 1976.

———. "Cuarenta y cinco presidentes y cuatro obispos de la casa encomendera Alfaro." On file in National Library, San José, Costa Rica, 1979.

Fernández de Oviedo, Gonzalo. *Historia general y natural de las Indias*. Asunción, Paraguay: Editorial Guaranía, 1944–45.

Fernández Guardia, Ricardo. *Historia de Costa Rica: El descubrimiento y la conquista*. San José, Costa Rica: Alsina, Josef Sauter, 1933.

———. *History of the Discovery and Conquest of Costa Rica*. New York: Thomas Y. Crowell Company, 1913.

Fernández Peralta, Alvaro. "La familia de Alvarado." *Revista de la Academia Costarricense de Ciencias Genealógicas* 5 (1958): 2–6.

Fernández Piza, Mario, ed., "Colección Norberto de Castro." *Revista de la Academia Costarricense de Ciencias Genealógicas* 22 (1975).

———. "Genealogía de la noble casa Rohrmoser von Chamier." *Revista de la Academia Costarricense de Ciencias Genealógicas* 21 (1974): 83–102.

Figueroa, Rethelny, and Juan Francisco Pinto. "Centro América: Número de puestos del sector público." *Revista Centroamericana de Administración Pública* (Sección Estadística, 1985): 92.

Galeano, Eduardo. "Con las guerrillas en Guatemala." In *América Latina: ¿Reforma o revolución?*, ed. James F. Petras and Maurice Zeitlin, pp. 319–28. Trans. Floreal Mazia. Buenos Aires: Tiempo Contemporáneo, 1973.

Gerbi, Antonello. *La naturaleza de las Indias nuevas*. Mexico City: Fondo de Cultura Económica, 1978.

González Viquez, Cleto. "Orígenes de los costarricenses." In *Población de*

Costa Rica y orígenes de los costarricenses, ed. Luis Demetrio Tinoco, pp. 73–133. San José: Editorial Costa Rica, 1977. (Reprint of 1921 article.)

González Zeledón, Manuel. "Un almuerzo campestre." In *Cuentos de Magón,* ed. José M. Arce, pp. 9–25. San José, Costa Rica: Lehmann, 1977.

———. "Episodios nacionales, 1885." In *Cuentos de Magón,* ed. José M. Arce, pp. 101–6. San José, Costa Rica: Lehmann, 1968.

———. "Yo y Pedro." In *Cuentos de Magón,* ed. José M. Arce, pp. 184–96. San José, Costa Rica: Lehmann, 1968.

Gould, Julius, and William L. Kolb. *A Dictionary of the Social Sciences.* 4th printing. New York: Free Press, 1967.

Grabendorff, Wolf. "El papel de las potencias regionales en la crisis centroamericana: Comparación entre México, Venezuela, Cuba, y Colombia." *Revista Occidental* 4 (1984): 437–60.

Griffith, William J. "Guatemala." *Encyclopaedia Britannica* 15 (1986): 705–12.

Guerard, Albert León. *France.* Ann Arbor: University of Michigan Press, 1959.

Guier Esquivel, Fernando. "El gran colegio." *La Nación* (San José, Costa Rica) 26 October 1988, p. 15A.

Guirola Leal de Acuña Durán, Mercedes. "La familia Durán." *Revista de la Academia Guatemalteca de Estudios Genealógicos, Heráldicos e Históricos* 5–6 (1971–72): 199–334.

Heine, Heinrich. *Romanzero von Heinrich Heine.* Leipzig: Druck und Verlag Bon Philipp Reclam, n.d. (first published in 1851).

Herrera y Tordesillas, Antonio de. *Historia general de los hechos castellanos en las islas y tierrafirme del Mar Océano.* Madrid: Tipografía de Archivos, 1934–57.

Huezo, Francisco. "Sus últimos días." *Revista Conservadora del Pensamiento Centroamericano* 13, no. 65 (1966): 15–30.

Humboldt, Alexander von. *Ensayo político sobre el reino de la Nueva España.* Mexico City: Editorial Porrúa, 1973.

Inforpress Centroamericana, *Los empresarios centroamericanos ante la crisis.* 1988.

Innes, Hammond. *The Conquistadores.* London: Collins, 1969.

Jiménez, Antonio. *Picardía mexicana.* Mexico City: B. Costa-Amie, 1961.

Jirón, Manuel. *¿Quién es quién en Nicaragua?* San José, Costa Rica: Ediciones Radio Amor, 1986.

Johnson, John J., ed. *Continuity and Change in Latin America.* Stanford, Calif.: Stanford University Press, 1964.

Kirkpatrick, F. A. *The Spanish Conquistadores.* New York: World Publishing Co., 1962.

Konetzke, Richard. *América Latina,* vol. 2: *La época colonial.* Mexico City: Siglo Veintiuno, 1976.

Kramer, Wendy, W. George Lovell, and Christopher H. Lutz. "Las tasaciones de tributos de Francisco Marroquín and Alonso Maldonado, 1536–1541." *Mesoamérica* 12 (1986): 357–94.

Leon-Portilla, Miguel, ed. *Visión de los vencidos: Relaciones indígenas de la*

Conquista. 7th ed. Mexico City: Universidad Nacional Autónoma de México (UNAM), 1976.

Lewis, Oscar. *Los hijos de Sánchez.* Mexico City: Editorial Joaquín Mortiz, 1968.

Lipschütz, Alejandro. *El problema racial en la conquista de América.* 3d ed. Mexico City: Siglo Veintiuno, 1975.

Lipset, Seymour Martin. *El hombre político: Las bases sociales de la política.* Madrid: Editorial Tecnos, 1987.

————. "Values, Education and Entrepreneurship." In *Elites in Latin America,* ed. Seymour Martin Lipset and Aldo Solari, pp. 3–60. New York: Oxford University Press, 1967.

López, Roberto. "The Nationalization of Foreign Commerce in El Salvador: Myths and Reality about Coffee." *Central America Report* 13, no. 26 (1986): 206–7.

López de Velasco, Juan. *Geografía y descripción universal de las Indias . . . desde el año 1571 al de 1574.* Madrid: Fortanet, 1894.

Lozoya, Juan Contreras, Marqués de. *Los orígenes del imperio: La España de Fernando e Isabel.* Madrid: Biblioteca Nueva, 1939.

————. *Vida del segoviano Rodrigo de Contreras, gobernador de Nicaragua, 1534–1544.* Madrid: Biblioteca Nueva, 1939.

Lyra, Carmen. *Los cuentos de mi tía Panchita.* San José: Litografía e Imprenta Costa Rica, 1966.

McBryde, F. Webster. "The United Provinces of Central America," *Encyclopaedia Britannica* 5 (1986): 693–94.

MacLeod, Murdo J. *Spanish Central America.* Berkeley: University of California Press, 1973.

Madariaga, Salvador de. *El ocaso del imperio español en América.* 2d. ed. Buenos Aires: Editorial Sudamericana, 1959.

Mariñas Otero, Luis. *Las constituciones de Guatemala.* Madrid: Instituto de Estudios Políticos, 1958.

Marletti, Carlo. "Clases y élites políticas: Teorías y análisis." In *Cuestiones de sociología,* ed. Francesco Alberoni, p. 345. Barcelona: Herder, 1971.

Martínez Peláez, Severo. *La patria del criollo.* San José, Costa Rica: Editorial Universitaria Centroamericana (EDUCA), 1976.

Mejía Nieto, Arturo. *El Chele Amaya y otros cuentos.* Santiago, Chile: Ediciones Ercilla, Biblioteca América, 1936.

————. "La Culebra." *Revista Conservadora del Pensamiento Centroamericano* 9, no. 47 (1964): 57–59.

Melendez Chaverri, Carlos. *Conquistadores y pobladores.* San José, Costa Rica: Editorial Universidad Estatal a Distancia, 1982.

————. *Costa Rica: Evolución histórica de sus problemas más destacados.* San José, Costa Rica: Imprenta Atenea, 1953.

————. *Costa Rica: Tierra y poblamiento en la colonia.* San José: Editorial Costa Rica, 1977.

————. Ed., *Documentos fundamentales del siglo XIX.* San José: Editorial Costa Rica, 1978.

Millett, Richard. *Guardianes de la dinastía.* San José, Costa Rica: Editorial Universitaria Centroamericana (EDUCA), 1979.

Molina Argüello, Carlos. *El gobernador de Nicaragua en el siglo XVI: Contribución al estudio del derecho nicaragüense.* Seville: Publicaciones de la Escuela de Estudios Hispano-Americanos, 1949.

Montaner, Carlos Alberto. "Contadora, la hipocresía y la historia." *La Nación* (San José, Costa Rica) 9 June 1984, p. 15A.

———. "Los soviéticos saben mejor con azúcar." *La Nación* (San José, Costa Rica) 31 May 1987, p. 15A.

Monteforte Toledo, Mario. *Centro América.* Mexico City: Universidad Nacional Autónoma de México (UNAM), 1972.

Montúfar, Lorenzo. *Reseña histórica de Centro América,* vol. 1. Guatemala City: Tipografía de "El Progreso," 1878.

Mörner, Magnus. *La mezcla de razas en la historia de América Latina.* Buenos Aires: Paidós, 1969.

———. "La política de segregación y el mestizaje en la Audiencia de Guatemala." *Revista de Indias* 24, nos. 95–96 (1964): 137–52.

Mosca, Gaetano. *The Ruling Class.* Trans. Hannah D. Kahn. Ed. Arthur Livingston. New York: McGraw-Hill, 1939.

Mujal-León, Eusebio. "European Socialism and the Crisis in Central America." In *Rift and Revolution: The Central American Imbroglio,* ed. Howard J. Wiarda, pp. 253–302. Washington: American Enterprise Institute for Public Policy Research, 1984.

Munro, Dana Gardner. *The Latin American Republics: A History.* New York: Appleton-Century-Crofts, 1942.

Neruda, Pablo. *Canto general.* Caracas, Venezuela: Biblioteca Ayacucho, 1976.

Newson, Linda. "The Depopulation of Nicaragua in the Sixteenth Century." *Journal of Latin American Studies* 14, pt. 2 (1982): 253–86.

———. "La población indígena de Honduras bajo el régimen colonial." *Mesoamérica* 6, no. 9 (1985): 1–44.

Nietschmann, Bernard. "Scarcity and Survival in Central America: Ecological Origins of the Soccer War." *Geographical Review* (1979).

Nyrop, Richard F., ed. *Guatemala: A Country Study.* Washington, D.C.: American University, 1984.

Obregón Loría, Rafael. *Conflictos militares y políticos de Costa Rica: Hechos militares y políticos.* San José, Costa Rica: Imprenta La Nación, 1951.

———. *El poder legislativo en Costa Rica.* San José: Imprenta Nacional, 1966.

———. *El presbítero doctor Francisco Calvo (Ganganelli).* San José, Costa Rica: Borrasé, 1963.

O'Donnell, Guillermo. "Tensions in the Bureaucratic-Authoritarian State and the Question of Democracy." In *The New Authoritarianism in Latin America,* ed. David Collier, pp. 285–318. Princeton: Princeton University Press, 1979.

Ordóñez y Jonama, Ramiro. "La familia Buonafede." *Revista de la Aca-*

demia Guatemalteca de Estudios Genealógicos, Heráldicos e Históricos 5–6 (1971–72): 98–198.

Padilla Altamirano, Silvia. "Guatemala y las provincias centroamericanas." In *Historia general de España y América*, ed. Luis Navarro García, 11-1: 547–74. Madrid: Ediciones Rialp, 1983.

Paige, Jeffrey M. "Coffee and Politics in Central America." In *Crises in the Caribbean Basin*, ed. Richard Tardanico, pp. 141–90. Political Economy of the World-System Series, no. 9. Newbury Park, Calif.: Sage Publications, 1987.

PanAmerican Coffee Bureau. *Annual Coffee Statistics*. New York.

Parker, Franklin D. *The Central American Republics*. London: Oxford University Press, 1968.

Parry, Geraint. *Political Elites*. London: George Allen and Unwin, Ltd., 1969.

Paul VI, Pope. *Popularum progressio*. Barcelona: Herder, 1968.

Pemán, José María. "El hidalgo español." *Revista de la Academia Costarricense de Ciencias Genealógicas* 1 (1963): 37.

Peralta, Manuel de María. *Journal de la Société d'Americanistes de Paris*, 1886, in *Población de Costa Rica y orígenes de los costarricenses*, ed. Luis Demetrio Tinoco, San José: Editorial Costa Rica, 1977.

Pereyra, Carlos. *Las huellas de los conquistadores*. Madrid: Consejo de la Hispanidad, 1942.

Pérez Brignoli, Héctor. *Breve historia de Centro América*. Madrid: Alianza Editorial, 1985.

Prescott, William H. *Histoire du règne de Ferdinand et d'Isabelle*, vol. 4. Trans. G. Renson. Bruxelles: A. Lacroix, Verboeckhoven, 1862.

Ramírez, Santiago. "Sicoanalítico." *Picardía mexicana*, ed. Antonio Jiménez, pp. 219–23. Mexico City: B. Costa-Amie, 1961.

Ripodas Ardenaz, Daisy. *El matrimonio en Indias*. Buenos Aires: Fundación para la Educación, la Ciencia y la Cultura, 1977.

Robert Luján, Enrique. "Algunos datos sobre la descendencia de doña Andrea Vázquez de Coronado." *Revista de la Academia Costarricense de Ciencias Genealógicas* 2 (1955): 4–21.

Roberts, Geoffrey. *A Dictionary of Political Analysis*. London: Longman, 1971.

Rodríguez, Mario. *Central America*. Englewood Cliffs, N.J.: Prentice-Hall, 1965.

Rodríguez Becerra, Salvador. *Encomienda y conquista: Los inicios de la colonización en Guatemala*. Seville: Publicaciones del Seminario de Antropología Americana, Universidad de Sevilla, 1977.

Rodríguez Vega, Eugenio. *Biografía de Costa Rica*. San José: Editorial Costa Rica, 1980.

Romoli, Kathleen. *Balboa of Darién: Discoverer of the Pacific*. Garden City, N.Y.: Doubleday, 1953.

Rosenblat, Angel. *La población indígena y el mestizaje en América, 1492–1950*. Buenos Aires: Editorial Nova, 1954.

Rubio Sánchez, Manuel. *Comercio de y entre las provincias de Centro América.* Guatemala City: Editorial del Ejército, 1973.

Rudolph, James D., ed. *Honduras: A Country Study.* Washington, D.C.: American University, 1984.

Ruhl, J. Mark. "The Economy." In *Honduras: A Country Study,* ed. James D. Rudolph, pp. 103–45. Washington, D.C.: American University, 1984.

————. "Agrarian Structure and Political Stability in Honduras." *Journal of Interamerican Studies and World Affairs* 26, no. 1 (1984): 33–68.

Sahagún, Fray Bernardino de. *Historia general de las cosas de Nueva España.* 4 vols. Mexico City: Editorial Porrúa, 1956.

Salazar Herrera, Carlos. "La bocaracá." In his *Cuentos de angustias y paisajes,* pp. 7–10. San José: Editorial Costa Rica, 1977.

Sanabria Martínez, Víctor. *Genealogías de Cartago hasta 1850.* 6 vols. San José, Costa Rica: Servicios Secretariales, 1957.

Sánchez, Luis Alberto. *Historia general de América,* vol. 1. 7th ed. Santiago, Chile: Ediciones Ercilla, 1963.

Sanchiz Ochoa, Pilar. *Los hidalgos de Guatemala: Realidad y apariencia en un sistema de valores.* Seville: Publicaciones del Seminario de Antropología Americana, Universidad de Sevilla, 1976.

Santamaría Varela, René. "El Salvador." *Encyclopaedia Britannica* 15 (1986): 701–5.

Schlesinger, Arthur, Jr. "Reagan is Crying Wolf on Nicaragua." *Wall Street Journal,* 1988.

Schumpeter, Joseph A. *Imperialism and Social Classes.* Trans. Heinz Norden. New York: World Publishing Company, 1966.

Sherman, William L. *Forced Native Labor in Sixteenth-Century Central America.* Lincoln: University of Nebraska Press, 1979.

Silvert, Kalman. "Caudillismo." In *Enciclopedia internacional de las ciencias sociales,* pp. 223–35. Madrid: Aguilar, 1974.

Smith, Peter H. *Labyrinths of Power: Political Recruitment in Twentieth-Century Mexico.* Princeton: Princeton University Press, 1979.

Solari, Aldo E. *El tercerismo en el Uruguay.* Montevideo, Uruguay: Editorial Alfa, 1965.

Solari, Aldo E., Rolando Franco, and Joel Jutkowitz, eds. *Teoría, acción social y desarrollo en América Latina.* Mexico City: Siglo Veintiuno, 1976.

Soley Güell, Tomás. *Historia económica y hacendaria de Costa Rica,* vol. 1. San José, Costa Rica: Editorial Universitaria, 1947.

Squier, Ephraim G. *Nicaragua: Sus gentes y paisajes.* Trans. Luciano Cuadro. San José, Costa Rica: Editorial Universitaria Centroamericana, 1970.

————. *The States of Central America.* New York (reprint of 1858 ed.), 1968.

Stabler, Charles N. "The Outlook: What Is Culture's Role in Economic Policy?" *Wall Street Journal,* 22 December 1986, p. 1.

Stanislawski, Dan. *The Transformation of Nicaragua: 1519–1548.* Berkeley: University of California Press, 1983.

Stone, Doris. *Estampas de Honduras.* Mexico City: Impresora Galve, 1954.

————. Ed., *Central America: The Myth of Unity,* forthcoming.

Stone, Samuel. "Algunos de los aspectos de la distribución del poder político en Costa Rica." *Revista de ciencias jurídicas* 17 (1971). San José: Universidad de Costa Rica, Facultad de Derecho.

———. "Los cafetaleros: Un estudio de la clase de grandes caficultores de Costa Rica." *Revista de ciencias jurídicas* 13 (1969): 167–75. San José: Universidad de Costa Rica, Facultad de Derecho.

———. "*Los cafetaleros:* Une étude de la classe des grands planteurs de café au Costa Rica." Doctorat de troisième cycle, Université de Paris, Sorbonne, 1968.

———. "Las convulsiones del Istmo Centroamericano: Raíces de un conflicto entre élites." *Estudios,* no. 1. San José, Costa Rica: Centro de Investigación y Adiestramiento Político-Administrativo (CIAPA), 1979.

———. "Costa Rica: Sobre la clase dirigente y la sociedad nacional." *Revista de Ciencias Sociales* 11 (1976): 41–69. San José: Universidad de Costa Rica.

———. "The Cubans Are Not Little Costa Rica's First Refugees." Los Angeles *Times.* 27 April 1980, pp. 2–3, part 5.

———. *La dinastía de los conquistadores: La crisis del poder en la Costa Rica contemporánea.* San José, Costa Rica: Editorial Universitaria Centroamericana (EDUCA), 1975.

———. "La herencia de una dinastía." Mimeographed. San José, Costa Rica: Centro de Investigación y Adiestramiento Político-Administrativo (CIAPA), 1976.

———. "Patterns of power in the north." 1987. On file in CIAPA, San José.

———. "Production and Politics in Central America's Convulsions." *Journal of Latin American Studies* 15, part 2 (1983): 453–69.

———. "El surgimiento de los que mandan: Tierra, capital y trabajo en la forja de las sociedades centroamericanas." *Estudios,* no. 5. San José, Costa Rica: Centro de Investigación y Adiestramiento Político-Administrativo (CIAPA), 1980.

Tardanico, Richard, ed. *Crises in the Caribbean Basin.* Political Economy of the World-System Series, no. 9. Newbury Park, Calif.: Sage Publications, 1987.

Thiel, Bernardo Augusto. "Monografía de la población de la República de Costa Rica en el siglo XIX." In *Población de Costa Rica y orígenes de los costarricenses,* ed. Luis Demetrio Tinoco, pp. 15–72. San José: Editorial Costa Rica, 1977.

———. *Revista de Costa Rica en el siglo XIX.* San José, Costa Rica: Imprenta Nacional, 1902.

Thurow, Lester C. *The Zero-Sum Society: Distribution and the Possibilities for Economic Change.* New York: Penguin Books, 1981.

Tierno Galván, Enrique. *Actas de las cortes de Cádiz.* Madrid: Taurus, 1964.

Tinoco, Luis Demetrio, ed. *Población de Costa Rica y orígenes de los Costarricenses.* Biblioteca Patria, no. 5. San José: Editorial Costa Rica, 1977.

Travis, Martin B. "Elites." In *A Dictionary of the Social Sciences,* ed. Julius Gould and William L. Kolb, p. 234. New York: Free Press, 1964.

Trejos Escalante, Fernando. "Costa Rica está enferma." *La Nación* (San José, Costa Rica), 13 December 1986.

Tylor, Edward Burnett. "Primitive Culture." *Encyclopaedia Britannica* 3 (1986): 782.

Urcuyo Fournier, Constantino. "Soy agradecido." *La Nación* (San José, Costa Rica), 30 January 1987, p. 15A.

———. "Strategic Central America: Superpowers and the Security of Five Individual Nations." 1987. On file in the Centro de Investigación y Adiestramiento Político-Administrativo, San José.

Urrutia, Claudio. *Memoria sobre la cuestión de límites entre Guatemala y México, presentada al señor ministro de relaciones exteriores por el jefe de la delegación guatemalteca en 1900.* Guatemala City: Centro Editorial "José de Pineda Ibarra," 1964.

Valcarcel, Luis E. *Ruta cultural del Perú.* Mexico City: Fondo de Cultura Económica, 1945.

Valle, Rafael Heliodoro, ed. *Pensamiento vivo de José Cecilio del Valle.* San José, Costa Rica: Editorial Universitaria Centroamericana, 1971.

Villegas Hoffmeister, Guillermo. *El cardonazo.* San José, Costa Rica: Borrasé, 1987.

Vivas Benard, Pedro Pablo. "La familia Cuadra en Nicaragua." *Revista Conservadora del Pensamiento Centroamericano* 17, no. 83 (1967): 1–36 (supplement).

Webre, Stephen. "Las compañías de milicia y la defensa del Istmo Centroamericano en el siglo XVII: El alistamiento general de 1673." *Mesoamérica* 8, no. 14 (1987): 511–24.

Wilkie, James W., and Adam Terkal, eds. *Statistical Abstract of Latin America,* vol. 24. Los Angeles: UCLA Latin American Center Publications, 1985.

Wittfogel, Karl August. *El despotismo oriental.* Trans. Francisco Presedo. Madrid: Guadarrama, 1966.

Woodward, Ralph Lee, Jr. *Central America: A Nation Divided.* New York: Oxford University Press, 1976.

Wortman, Miles L. *Government and Society in Central America, 1680–1840.* New York: Columbia University Press, 1982.

Wyld Ospina, Carlos. "De dura cerviz." In *Antología del cuento centroamericano,* ed. Sergio Ramírez, pp. 159–66. San José, Costa Rica: Editorial Universitaria Centroamericana (EDUCA), 1977.

Zavala, Silvio. *El mundo americano en la época colonial.* 2 vols. Mexico City: Editorial Porrúa, 1967.

Zavala Urtecho, Joaquín. "Huellas de una familia vasco-centroamericana en cinco siglos de historia." *Revista Conservadora del Pensamiento Centroamericano* 23, no. 112 (1970).

Interviews

Richard N. Adams
François Bourricaud
Narciso Carmona Binayan
Rodolfo Cerdas Cruz
Jaime Daremblum Rosenstein
Joaquín Alberto Fernández Alfaro
Mario Fernández Piza
Richard E. Greenleaf
Joaquín Jiménez Rodríguez
Narciso Lacayao Pallais
Aminta Lacayo de Quirce
Enrique Robert Luján
Luis Guillermo Solís Rivera
Constantino Urcuyo Fournier
Enrique Valverde Runnebaum
Rafael Villegas Antillón

Periodicals

Central America Report (Guatemala City)
Euromoney
Forbes
Miami Herald
La Nación (San José, Costa Rica)
La Nación Internacional (San José, Costa Rica)
Newsweek
Progreso (New York, N.Y.)
La República (San José, Costa Rica)
Time

Index